THE BEDFORD SERIES IN HISTORY AND CULTURE

The Jesuit Relations

Natives and Missionaries in Seventeenth-Century North America

Edited with an Introduction by

Allan Greer

University of Toronto

BEDFORD/ST. MARTIN'S   Boston • New York

To Eleanor

For Bedford/St. Martin's
Executive Editor for History and Political Science: Katherine E. Kurzman
Developmental Editor: Molly E. Kalkstein
Production Supervisor: Cheryl Mamaril
Marketing Manager: Charles Cavaliere
Project Management: Books By Design, Inc.
Text Design: Claire Seng-Niemoeller
Indexer: Books By Design, Inc.
Cover Design: Richard Emery Design, Inc.
Cover Art: Inset from a 1657 illustrated map of New France, *Novae Franciae Accurata Delineatio,* attributed to Francesco-Giuseppe Bressani. Courtesy of the University of Western Ontario.
Composition: G & S Typesetters, Inc.
Printing and Binding: Haddon Craftsmen, an R. R. Donnelley & Sons Company

President: Charles H. Christensen
Editorial Director: Joan E. Feinberg
Director of Marketing: Karen R. Melton
Director of Editing, Design, and Production: Marcia Cohen
Manager, Publishing Services: Emily Berleth

Library of Congress Catalog Card Number: 99-62389

5 4 3 2 1 0
f e d c b a

For information, write: Bedford/St. Martin's, 75 Arlington Street, Boston, MA 02116
(617-399-4000)

ISBN: 0-312-16707-5 (paperback)
   0-312-22744-2 (hardcover)

Foreword

The Bedford Series in History and Culture is designed so that readers can study the past as historians do.

The historian's first task is finding the evidence. Documents, letters, memoirs, interviews, pictures, movies, novels, or poems can provide facts and clues. Then the historian questions and compares the sources. There is more to do than in a courtroom, for hearsay evidence is welcome, and the historian is usually looking for answers beyond act and motive. Different views of an event may be as important as a single verdict. How a story is told may yield as much information as what it says.

Along the way the historian seeks help from other historians and perhaps from specialists in other disciplines. Finally, it is time to write, to decide on an interpretation and how to arrange the evidence for readers.

Each book in this series contains an important historical document or group of documents, each document a witness from the past and open to interpretation in different ways. The documents are combined with some element of historical narrative — an introduction or a biographical essay, for example — that provides students with an analysis of the primary source material and important background information about the world in which it was produced.

Each book in the series focuses on a specific topic within a specific historical period. Each provides a basis for lively thought and discussion about several aspects of the topic and the historian's role. Each is short enough (and inexpensive enough) to be a reasonable one-week assignment in a college course. Whether as classroom or personal reading, each book in the series provides firsthand experience of the challenge — and fun — of discovering, recreating, and interpreting the past.

Natalie Zemon Davis
Ernest R. May

Preface

Over the last hundred years, the *Jesuit Relations* have provided source material for countless studies in history, anthropology, religious studies, geography, and other fields. These missionary reports, first published in French in the seventeenth century, became more widely available to researchers in the 1890s thanks to the monumental seventy-three-volume compilation, *The Jesuit Relations and Allied Documents*, published under the editorship of Reuben Gold Thwaites. Thwaites and his team of editors and translators assembled all the *Relations*, together with other Jesuit materials from the period, and presented them in bilingual format, with original French and English translation facing each other on alternating pages. The impact of this editorial project on the world of scholarship was immense, and its influence in stimulating historical studies of Europeans and North American Indians has by no means been exhausted. And yet the *Relations* themselves, highly readable and intrinsically interesting though they may be, are available only in major research libraries, and even there they are too bulky to be of much use to students and nonspecialist readers. This book of selections from the *Jesuit Relations* is meant to open up that textual treasure chest to a wider audience.

It was not easy to make a choice from among the more than twenty-one thousand pages of material that the Thwaites collection comprises. I ended up focusing on the native nations that the Jesuits knew best: the Montagnais, the Hurons, and the Mohawks. I also assembled writings on certain themes — war, medicine, and nature — that preoccupied those missionaries. To give readers a real feel for the *Relations*, I favored comparatively long texts and tried to avoid the pastiche approach.

The Thwaites edition is not the only modern edition of the *Jesuit Relations*. Since 1967 the Jesuit historian Lucien Campeau has produced eight volumes of Jesuit documents, including the *Relations* and much more. This collection sets a new standard for completeness and rigorous editing. It reproduces texts only in their original language (mostly

French, though there are some Latin and Italian documents), however, and so far it covers only the early decades of the Jesuit missions. I consulted Campeau's edition extensively, both to verify the accuracy of the Thwaites texts and to benefit from the editor's learned annotations.

Though basically sound, Thwaites's hundred-year-old translation is frequently awkward and occasionally incomprehensible. In revising the English text, I did my best to untangle convoluted sentences, update archaic vocabulary (for example, translating the French *tu* as "you" rather than "thou"), and correct the occasional error. The most problematic term proved to be *sauvage,* which the Thwaites team rendered as "savage." I decided that the English term *Indian* gives a better sense of the connotations of *sauvage,* except in a few cases where the Jesuits wanted to emphasize savagery.

Readers should be aware of thorny issues connected to another term, *demon.* Quoting or paraphrasing Indians, the Jesuits often referred to a person, object, or unseen force as a demon. This was their way of conveying what the Hurons would have called *oki* and the Algonquins *manitou,* by which they meant the soul or spirit that gave a thing or a feature of the landscape, such as a rock or a waterfall, the power to influence human affairs. Some exceptional people also possessed such supernatural abilities. The Jesuits took such claims to supernatural power seriously, but since they knew that this power had nothing to do with Christianity, they assumed that these were diabolical forces, thus the use of the word *demon.* Rather than translate this word as "spirit," which might give a better sense of what the natives were talking about, I opted to leave it as *demon* to remain true to the historical text, with its characteristic blend of ethnographic reporting and religious judgment.

Finally, there is the vexed problem of what to call the original inhabitants of North America. The terms *Indians* and *Native Americans,* commonly used in the United States, sometimes raise objections in Canada, whereas the favored Canadian terms, *natives, aboriginal people,* and *First Nations Peoples,* seem awkward and unfamiliar to most Americans. In my introductory sections, I decided to compromise (by definition, a compromise is less than a perfect solution) by alternating between *natives* and *Indians.*

ACKNOWLEDGMENTS

In addition to acknowledging the work of Thwaites and Campeau, I would like to take this opportunity to thank some people who made more immediate contributions to this book. Over the years, my students at the

University of Toronto have read and discussed selections from the *Jesuit Relations* with passion and insight, and their reactions have done much to shape this collection. One student, Jeff d'Hondt, acted as an able and resourceful research assistant on this project. Jeff's forbearance was put to the test by the tone of some of the missionaries' comments about his native ancestors, but his good humor and dedication to history always carried the day. Recognition also is due to Naida Harris-Morgan for her anthropologically informed word processing services. And to Gary W. Kronk, my thanks for helping me understand Jesuit astronomical observations.

The Newberry Library, Chicago, provided the ideal setting in which to annotate the chapter on Father Marquette's explorations. I am grateful to the Newberry staff and to library fellow Helen Tanner.

It has been a great pleasure working with the staff at Bedford/St. Martin's. I particularly appreciated development editor Molly Kalkstein's ability to combine editorial rigor with warm enthusiasm. I also want to thank Katherine Kurzman for getting the project off on the right foot and Melissa Lotfy and Emily Berleth for guiding it to completion. I am indebted to the following readers for their thoughtful criticism of the draft manuscript: Colin G. Calloway, Catherine Desbarats, James D. Rice, Gordon Sayre, Timothy J. Shannon, and Laurier Turgeon. Finally, my thanks go to series editor Natalie Zemon Davis for her encouragement and her helpful editorial suggestions.

Allan Greer
University of Toronto

Contents

Maps and Illustrations

Introduction:
Native North America and the French Jesuits

The *Jesuit Relations* constitute the most important set of documentary materials on the seventeenth-century encounter of Europeans and native North Americans. The *Relations* are, in essence, annual reports of French missionaries of the Society of Jesus on their efforts to convert the "pagan savages" to Catholic Christianity. Published in Paris between 1632 and 1673, these yearly chronicles always included much more than a simple account of the business of evangelizing. Each fat volume was crammed with news about the progress of colonization, the devastation of epidemics, the outbreak of war, and other important events affecting the Indians of the Northeast. There were also narratives of voyages to distant lands. The key to the popularity of the *Relations* then and now, however, is the detailed description of the customs, habits, and cultures of various native nations. The unparalleled richness of this ethnographic detail has made the *Relations* a precious resource for modern scholars interested in culture contact and the experience of Amerindian peoples in the early phases of colonization.

There are two main reasons why the *Jesuit Relations* are so illuminating in this connection. First, the Jesuits knew what they were talking about. Admittedly, there were many aspects of aboriginal culture they did not understand and did not wish to understand, but even when these missionaries disapproved of "diabolical pagan ceremonies" and misconstrued their purpose, they were still capable of describing them accurately. Because they lived in native villages for years on end, learned the local languages, got to know the people, and took their place on the margins of Amerindian society, they came to know native peoples as few other Europeans did. Also, they were inveterate writers. Unlike most of the French Canadian fur traders and *coureurs de bois,*[1] who also knew ab-

---

[1] Men of French origin who traded with and lived among the Indians of the interior, adopting a way of life shaped by native culture.

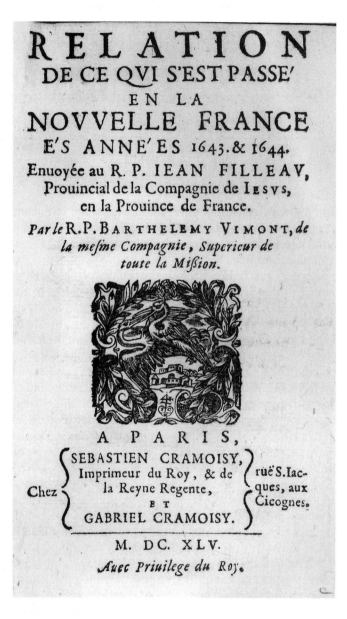

RELATION

DE CE QVI S'EST PASSE'

EN LA

NOVVELLE FRANCE

E'S ANNE'ES 1643. & 1644.

Enuoyée au R. P. IEAN FILLEAV,
Prouincial de la Compagnie de IESVS,
en la Prouince de France.

Par le R. P. BARTHELEMY VIMONT, *de*
la mesme Compagnie, Superieur de
toute la Mißion.

A PARIS,

Chez {
SEBASTIEN CRAMOISY,
Imprimeur du Roy, & de
la Reyne Regente,
ET
GABRIEL CRAMOISY.
} rüe S. Iac-
ques, aux
Cicognes.

M. DC. XLV.

Auec Priuilege du Roy.

Title page for the Jesuit Relation of 1644

Written in New France, the *Relations* were shipped to France annually and published in Paris the following year.

Courtesy of the Newberry Library, Chicago.

original America intimately, the Jesuits were literate; indeed, their training made them masters of the written word. Writing was part of the general clerical culture of the period, but these missionaries belonged to a religious order that was renowned for using the power of the printing press to its best advantage. Thus the *Jesuit Relations* can be seen as the combined product of immersion in Native American society and an unparalleled ability to communicate with European audiences.

To gain full benefit from this historical document, some background is required on both the native nations mentioned in its pages and on the Jesuit chroniclers themselves. Even though the *Relations* are written, for the most part, in clear, down-to-earth prose, the transition from the mental and textual world of the seventeenth century to that of the present entails a certain amount of "decoding." I will begin with the Jesuits and the early modern Christian world that produced them.

THE SOCIETY OF JESUS IN EUROPE AND ABROAD

The Jesuits were members of a religious order, the Society of Jesus, and like the monks, nuns, and friars of other orders, they took special vows of poverty and obedience that distinguished them from regular parish priests. They were men who sought personal Christian perfection in a tightly organized association with branches (provinces) across Catholic Europe and headquarters in Rome. Whereas some orders specialized in teaching, hospital work, or monastic contemplation, the Jesuits' activities were multifaceted, encompassing education, literary and scientific activities, pastoral care, and overseas missions.

Founded by the Spanish ex-soldier Ignatius of Loyola in 1534, the Society of Jesus was firmly and powerfully established in Catholic Europe by the time it began sending missionaries to Canada. And yet it still exhibited a certain youthful dynamism in keeping with the reforming current then sweeping the church. The late sixteenth and early seventeenth centuries saw a religious revival sometimes known as the Counter Reformation or the Catholic Reformation. This tendency within Catholicism can, in some senses, be seen as a reaction to the abstract, Bible-centered religion of Protestantism. Thus it emphasized rituals and sacraments, the cult of the saints and of the Virgin Mary, clerical celibacy, religious orders, and the authority of the pope. In other aspects, this reinvigorated Catholicism seemed to run parallel to the Reformation. Reforming forces within the church fought against corruption and slackness among the clergy, as well as superstition and indifference on the part of their flocks. The Catholic Reformation summoned up a

great spirit of idealism, for it called on believers to renounce compla-
cency and remake the world.

The mood was at once grim and enthusiastic, with an inclination to
view conflict as part of a monumental struggle between good and evil.
"Heresy" (Protestant Christianity) and "paganism" (non-Christian religion) were external threats, but Christians also had to battle internal enemies: pride and other classic vices, as well as various evil temptations
associated with "the flesh." The suppression of sexuality, the exaltation
of celibacy, and the use of fasting, self-flagellation, and other ascetic
practices as a favored means of doing penance for sins while gaining
mastery over carnal temptation were all part of the struggle. For Catholics who sought to transcend the narrow limits of human existence,
heroic self-denial could be a means of making contact with the divine.
Such asceticism tended to be associated with mysticism — the celebration of the subjective experience of union with God — and in the seventeenth century mysticism had found a home in Catholic France, especially within the ranks of the Society of Jesus.

The Jesuits of the sixteenth and seventeenth centuries embodied
some of the central paradoxes of their day. Mystical and contemplative,
they could also be active, worldly, and ruthlessly rational in pursuit of
their goals. Instead of taking refuge from profane influences by retreating, after the fashion of medieval monks, behind protective monastic
walls, they went out to conquer the secular world. They started with the
young, particularly the sons of Europe's elite, who were attracted to the
order's colleges because of their high academic standards. Every Jesuit
was a college teacher at some point in his career, and each was well
equipped for the job thanks to his thorough training in classical learning
and rhetoric. (The allusions to ancient Greek and Roman literature scattered throughout the *Jesuit Relations* came naturally to missionaries ed-
ucated in this way.) Parents also appreciated the Jesuit colleges as highly
effective agencies of character formation. Precociously modern in their
sensitivity to the development of personality among children and adults,
the Jesuits specialized in human engineering.

In addition to operating schools, they also sponsored devotional societies for laypeople. They preached to illiterate peasants and gave spiritual advice to kings. For example, two Jesuits, Père La Chaise and Père
Le Tellier, were the confessors of Louis XIV. So effective was the order
that it quickly aroused the jealousy of rivals within the church and outside it. Blaise Pascal[2] and others connected with the Jansenist[3] faction

of French Catholicism denounced the Jesuits as political schemers, always ready to compromise on matters of doctrine in order to gain fame and influence. In Protestant Europe, the term *Jesuitical* became synonymous with devious ruthlessness.

Missions abroad to convert the "heretics" and "heathens" were part of the Jesuit program from the start. One of Ignatius of Loyola's first disciples, a young Portuguese priest named Francis Xavier, set the pattern. Following the maritime routes of Portugal's commercial empire in the East, Francis Xavier traveled first to India, where he baptized thousands of converts, and then to Japan and China, where he died a martyr's death. His letters to his colleagues back in Europe helped make the nascent Jesuit order famous. Widely circulated, these letters were read at least as much for their tales of exotic lands and strange customs as for their inspiring religious messages. (In this respect, they provided a model for the *Jesuit Relations* of New France.) After Francis Xavier came a succession of Jesuit missionary enterprises encompassing the globe and extending in time from the sixteenth century until the pope dissolved the Society of Jesus in 1773.

Some of the most interesting experiments in cross-cultural evangelizing occurred in the original mission field of Asia. There were spectacular, though short-lived, successes in Japan, but elsewhere progress was slow and limited. The Italian Jesuits Mateo Ricci (1552–1610) and Roberto di Nobili (1577–1656) are especially celebrated for devoting their lives to infiltrating the civilizations of China and India, respectively. Jesuits in these two countries accepted the daunting challenge of acquiring the languages and the cultural accoutrements necessary to gain acceptance in mandarin and Brahman circles. They also had to find ways to convey their Christian message to Asian audiences, a task that inevitably required some adaptation and compromise on points of doctrine and ritual. Their enemies in Europe made the most of the occasion to accuse the Jesuits of heterodoxy.

In Latin America, where they were also active, the Jesuits had less need to adapt to foreign cultures. There they accompanied the conquering empires of Spain and Portugal and consequently were in a better position to compel natives to adapt to their requirements. By the time Portuguese Jesuits arrived in Brazil in the sixteenth century, it had become

---

specific cases of conscience through interpretation of religious principles) was too permissive.

[3] Jansenists were Catholics who followed the Augustinian doctrines of Cornelis Jansen. Especially influential in seventeenth- and eighteenth-century France, they opposed the Jesuits theologically and politically.

a hell for Indians, who were routinely slaughtered and enslaved by rapacious settlers. The missionaries were courageous in denouncing oppression even as they gathered beleaguered natives together in special mission settlements for protection and indoctrination. Spanish Jesuits adopted a broadly similar approach in other parts of South America and Mexico. When the violence of, and exploitation by, fellow Spaniards posed the greatest obstacle to the spread of Christianity, it seemed essential to place Indians in protective mission settlements, called *reducciónes* in Spanish. The term implied that the resident natives had been "reduced" from their proud and untamed independence to a proper obedience to God's laws. Thus the success of the *reducción* system of Latin America, though it was established in opposition to colonialist oppression, depended on that same oppression to pressure natives into joining mission communities and to ensure that they stayed there. The Jesuits had their greatest success in seventeenth- and eighteenth-century Paraguay, where the Guaraní people faced exceptionally brutal Spaniards to the west and Brazilian slave raiders to the east. The missionaries here were able to impose an exacting regime of Christian prayers, sexual repression, and European-style agriculture on the natives, who found this disciplinary utopia preferable to the alternatives.

Coming to North America in the early seventeenth century, the French Jesuits could draw on the institutional memory of their order for guidance in this unfamiliar territory. Following the lead of Ricci and others, they began patiently studying the languages and cultures of the native peoples they encountered. Like the Jesuits of South America, they could be critical of colonialist exploitation and yet appreciative of the "secular sword" for its help in making "proud" and resistant Indian nations receptive to the Christian message. They set up *reducciónes* inspired by those in Latin America but never attained the degree of control exercised by the Jesuits of Paraguay. Lastly, they borrowed Francis Xavier's practice of writing letters for publication as their favored means of communicating their exploits to readers back home.

IROQUOIANS AND ALGONQUIANS

When they arrived on the banks of the St. Lawrence River in 1625, French Jesuits were entering a continent still very much under Indian control, even though the effects of European colonization were being felt all along the Atlantic coast and into the Great Lakes region. Dozens of independent native nations, each with its own distinctive culture, inhabited present-day eastern Canada and the northeastern United States.

Ethnohistorians (scholars who combine the methods of history and anthropology) tend to group the different peoples of the eastern woodlands into two main classifications, the Algonquians and the Iroquoians. The Jesuits had dealings with nations representing both these groups, and they soon learned that a wide linguistic gap separated the two. The Algonquians spoke various related dialects, but their grammatical structures and vocabularies bore no resemblance to those of the Iroquoian peoples. They also discovered a basic difference in their ways of life. Whereas the northern Algonquians generally depended on hunting, foraging, and fishing — and consequently lived in small, mobile bands — the Iroquoians cultivated corn and other crops, a practice that allowed them to live in concentrated, year-round settlements. The Iroquoian villages of what we now call northern New York and southern Ontario were quite populous, whereas small Algonquian bands ranged over much wider territories in the Canadian Shield region to the north and east. Even though some of the Iroquoian nations emerged as deadly enemies of the French, the Jesuits considered their mode of existence superior to that of the Algonquians, as it corresponded more closely to European cultural ideals.

Over the course of nearly two centuries of missionary work, the Jesuits had dealings with almost every Indian nation of the Northeast, but in the 1600s they directed most of their evangelizing efforts toward a handful of groups. Accordingly, the selection of texts in this book concentrates mainly on four nations: the Montagnais and Algonquins, both Algonquian speakers; and the Hurons and Iroquois, both Iroquoian peoples. The nomenclature can be confusing, since the name for a broad cultural/linguistic cluster is taken from the name of a particular ethnic group. Thus the Algonquins are only one of many Algonquian nations, as the Iroquois are one of several Iroquoian peoples.

To complicate matters further, the terms *Huron* and *Iroquois* actually designate confederacies formed prior to the arrival of the Europeans, when several distinct nations joined forces. Four tribes constituted the Huron confederacy: the Arendarhonons, Attignawantans, Attigneenongnahacs, and Tahontaenrats. They lived in close proximity to one another and had intermingled considerably by the time the Jesuits arrived. Consequently, the *Relations* usually refer to the Hurons as though they were a single entity with a uniform way of life. (I will follow their lead in this introduction.) By contrast, the Jesuits frequently referred to the Five Nations of the Iroquois League individually: the Mohawks, Oneidas, Onondagas, Cayugas, and Senecas. These peoples lived in widely separated locations across northern New York, and although their culture

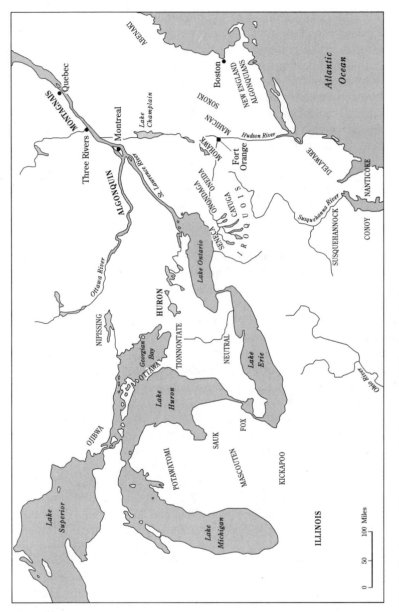

Native Nations and European Settlements, Mid-Seventeenth Century

was essentially the same, they had rather different relations with the French over the course of the seventeenth century. The selections in this book deal primarily with the Mohawks, the easternmost Iroquois tribe and the one that had the closest engagement with the French, both as deadly enemies and as devoted friends. From the beginning, New France posed a strategic threat to the Mohawks, and as the French forged an alliance with their traditional enemies, the Algonquins, the Mohawks became increasingly hostile. After decades of intermittent war, the Jesuits managed to convert many Mohawks, as well as some other Iroquois peoples, to Catholicism, and these Christian converts moved to live close to the French at Montreal. By about 1670, there were Iroquois settlements in Canada that were closely aligned with the French, as well as the five original Iroquois tribes, still occupying their New York homeland and unconnected with the French.

It is worth noting that, in a general sense, the lines of conflict and alliance had little to do with ethnic and cultural affinity. The Hurons and the Iroquois, though quite similar culturally, were militarily at odds through most of the period covered by the *Jesuit Relations,* whereas the Hurons, Algonquins, Montagnais, and French remained allies in spite of the great differences between them.

THE COLONIZATION OF NEW FRANCE

Long before the Jesuits appeared on the North American scene, French fishermen, explorers, and fur traders had already had extensive contact with the natives of the Northeast. The first year-round settlement was established in Acadia (present-day Nova Scotia, New Brunswick, and northern Maine) in 1604, and two Jesuits tried to establish a mission there between 1611 and 1613. By that time, the main thrust of French colonization had shifted farther west to the St. Lawrence River Valley, where Samuel de Champlain founded Quebec in 1608. When the Jesuits returned in 1625, they made Quebec their headquarters. Missionaries also followed the fur trade routes west to the land of the Hurons. From the beginning, then, the Jesuits appeared to native North Americans as part of a broader French presence. Accordingly, the relationships that developed between the Jesuits and the Iroquoians and Algonquians must always be seen as one aspect of a wider process of colonization. However much the Jesuits may have tried to shield converts from secular European influences, the whole missionary enterprise was affected by the larger pattern of relations between Indians and French.

The French had a unique approach to colonization. Partly because they came to the New World in comparatively small numbers and partly because they made their fortunes in Canada by trading for furs with native hunters, they had to come to terms with native cultures and interact extensively with Indian peoples. The French fully occupied only a narrow territory in the St. Lawrence Valley centering on the forts (later towns) of Quebec (1608), Three Rivers (1634), and Montreal (1642). Trade with peoples living far to the west was facilitated by the waterways of the Great Lakes, and because natives generally traded only with friends, this commercial penetration led to the formation of military-diplomatic alliances that helped extend French influence over vast regions. A great inland empire took shape in the second half of the seventeenth century, but it was an empire not of domination and subjection, but of multistranded commercial/diplomatic links between France and the different Indian nations of the Canadian hinterland.

Farther to the south, the English settled in larger numbers, and they came to depend heavily on agriculture for their food supply and export commodities. The New England and Chesapeake colonies developed a voracious appetite for Indian lands, an appetite that eventually led to war, extermination, and displacement. Whereas antagonism between natives and settler societies was a fundamental feature of colonization in English North America, in New France there were patterns of both cooperation and conflict. The French were not inherently kinder empire builders than the English, but their settlement of Canada did not require any substantial appropriation of Indian lands.

Nor was New France built on the subjugation of Indians through military conquest, as the Spanish colonies of South and Central America were. In Spain's New World empire, Indians owed the colonizers labor service and other forms of tribute as both a symbol of their subjection and a contribution to the Spanish economy. But in New France, the Indians were never really conquered. Violence and war were by no means absent from the colony's history, since military alliance naturally entailed conflict with nations outside the alliance, but the French were never in a position to impose their will by force of arms on the Indians in general. Allies, trading partners, and even, to some extent, defeated enemies, remained autonomous, though many of them came to recognize a certain French hegemony. Consequently, Jesuit missionaries had to work with natives who generally retained a high degree of independence, regardless of how entangled they became in the French network of alliance and trade.

Even though they were not displaced or conquered, the Indian nations of the eastern woodlands certainly experienced profound and wrenching change in the seventeenth century, and the *Jesuit Relations* bear witness to the powerful forces that swept the region as a result of the French presence. There were terrible epidemics of old-world diseases, as unfamiliar viruses and germs ravaged the Indians' vulnerable immune systems. Native economies were transformed by the demands of the fur trade, and metal implements and weapons brought from Europe gradually replaced traditional technologies. Political instability, conflict, and deadly wars were among the many indirect consequences of European intrusion. And, of course, the Jesuits themselves were determined to reshape native thinking and behavior in conformity with Christian principles. The overall impact of this program of "directed assimilation" may have been rather limited when compared to that of the undirected forces unleashed by the economic, technological, and biological forces of colonization. The Jesuit missionaries were witnesses to these profound historical processes, even though they did not control or fully understand them.

THE CANADIAN MISSIONS

There were two abortive beginnings to the Jesuit enterprise in New France—the Acadian expedition and a second, short-lived establishment at Quebec (1625–29)—both of them wrecked by English raiders. Two Jesuits returned to Quebec when the French reasserted control in 1632, with reinforcements following over the course of the decade. For more than a century beginning in the 1640s, the total number of Jesuits hovered between thirty and forty, with a larger, more variable number of *donnés*[4] and other laymen attached to the order as construction workers, canoeists, and artisans. Almost all the missionary priests were recruited from the Jesuit colleges of France. Service among the "savages" of North America was not an appealing prospect for most Jesuits, but a minority were inspired by what they had heard and read of this daunting assignment in a forbidding land and became desperate to "sacrifice themselves" (for that is how they generally understood the gesture) in New France. The majority of those who left France never returned, either

---

[4]*Donnés* were individuals, usually young men or boys, who helped the Jesuits with nonreligious duties. By the terms of their contracts, they had to remain chaste and serve without any pay other than their room and board.

because they finished their long careers in Canada or because (seven cases before 1663) they were killed in the Iroquois wars.

Although the Society of Jesus was never without powerful rivals, it was always the preeminent religious order in New France. The Jesuits operated a college for French Canadian boys at Quebec and eventually founded small establishments at Three Rivers and Montreal. They were well financed by revenues from their extensive seigneurial landholdings in Canada, supplemented by government subsidies and donations from benefactors. Aided by powerful friends at the center of France's empire, they took a leading role in the political life of the colony, particularly in the early decades. Even though colonial officials frequently opposed the Jesuits' interests from the 1660s on, the Jesuits managed to hold their own. They even survived the British conquest of 1760, as well as the storms raised by Enlightenment monarchies, which led to the expulsion of the Society of Jesus from the Portuguese and Spanish empires.

During the first few decades, missionary efforts had a dual focus: While some Jesuits tried to convert the Montagnais and Algonquins who frequented the posts at Quebec and Three Rivers, others traveled far into the interior to proselytize the Hurons, a populous nation that had emerged as the dominant force in the French system of trade and alliance. The natives clearly perceived the missionaries as emissaries from France and welcomed them because they already valued the French as suppliers of goods and as allies in their wars against the Iroquois. At first many were also interested in the Jesuits' stories of the origin of the universe and about the extraordinary life and teachings of Jesus. Some asked to be baptized, believing the ritual would initiate them into a curing society. Trouble arose when it became clear that Christianity was an exclusive and intolerant religion, one that branded other spiritual practices "diabolical" and declared various normal ways of behaving "immoral." When epidemics struck, the Hurons tended to blame the Jesuits, whose mysterious and antisocial behavior seemed to match the profile of malevolent sorcerers.

For many years, the Jesuit mission to New France was fraught with disappointment and frustration. In other parts of the world, Jesuits were used to working with a captive audience, such as vulnerable children in Europe and defeated Indians fleeing enslavement in Latin America. Here they lacked coercive power and so had to content themselves with learning the native languages, writing about their "superstitions," and performing surreptitious baptisms on ailing and dying infants, secure in the knowledge that the latter would go straight to heaven since they had not had time to sin. It was the absence of coercive authority, as much as anything, that made New France a hardship posting, though the colony's reputation was not enhanced by the dangers of incessant war. By the 1640s, the Iroquois, supplied with guns by the Dutch traders of Fort Orange (Albany, New York), were wreaking havoc with the Hurons, the Algonquins, and their French allies. One incidental result was that several missionaries were captured, tortured, and killed. All this pain and adversity was not without meaning for the Jesuits: It allowed them to identify with Christ on the cross and to assure themselves that out of affliction would come glory.

The missions did begin to show signs of success in the 1640s, when substantial numbers of adult natives accepted Catholicism. This was only, as the Jesuits readily admitted, because the Algonquins, Montagnais, and Hurons were being "crucified" themselves by the combined blows of epidemic disease, Iroquois attacks, and growing economic dependency. The desperate and often leaderless survivors of these disasters tended to be more open to proselytism. Just before the Hurons were effectively wiped out in 1649, whole villages had converted. Meanwhile, some of the Montagnais and Algonquin bands that frequented Quebec and Three Rivers also accepted baptism and came to live in highly regulated settlements that the Jesuits set up after the model of the South American *reducciónes*. This experiment in authoritarianism proved short-lived, however, since the natives involved either died off or deserted. Thereafter, the missionaries were careful to allow their converts a wide margin of independence, for the Indians of New France would not tolerate regimentation.

In the middle decades of the century, recurrent war with the Iroquois was crucial to the fate of the Jesuits and their missions. Finally, peace was secured in the 1660s, when, one by one, the Five Nations came to terms with the French and their native allies. King Louis XIV sent military forces to invade the country of the Mohawks, the last Iroquois holdouts, and the Jesuits used the threat of further offensives to persuade many Mohawks to adopt Christianity and move to loosely run mission communities near Montreal.

From that time on, there was less desperate drama in the chronicles of the Indian missions in North America. Some Jesuits tended to the spiritual needs of Iroquoian converts at mission settlements in the St. Lawrence Valley, while others took their message to the Algonquian bands of the Great Lakes hinterland. Jesuits were involved, to some extent, in late-seventeenth-century expeditions from Lake Michigan into the Mississippi River system, and they played a role after 1700 in the colonization of Louisiana. By that time, however, the *Jesuit Relations* were no longer being published.

THE *JESUIT RELATIONS* AND THEIR READERS

Through the most eventful years of their Canadian mission, the Jesuits published annual *Relations* for the benefit of audiences back home in France: pious well-wishers, potential donors, and simply curious readers. After some initial improvisation, a pattern emerged by which raw missionary reports were shaped into a finished volume. It began with detailed letters from priests in the field, the most important usually being the one brought down by the summer canoe brigade from the Huron country. The superior at Quebec would compile and edit these letters, paraphrasing some parts, copying others verbatim, and forwarding the whole package to France. When they reached Paris, headquarters for the Jesuit province of France, further editorial changes would be made, and then the texts would be sent to the printer, about a year after most of them had originally been drafted. In spite of the Jesuits' reputation as an international body directly in the service of the pope, the publication process, like the New France mission itself, was almost entirely a French operation. Some commentators make much of the fact that the *Relations* in their final form do not correspond to the unmediated reports of the missionaries in the field. This may be true, but all published works bear the marks of both author and editor. There is no reason to suppose that the Jesuit superiors and provincials altered the sense of the texts that passed through their hands.

European writings about the New World generally divide into two distinct genres, each with its own roots in classical literature: the travel narrative (*récit de voyage*), a personal chronicle of firsthand experience; and the ethnographic description, an impersonal, encyclopedic catalog of the customs and beliefs of some unfamiliar culture.[5] One of the peculiarities of the *Jesuit Relations* is that they combine both types of writing: Jacques Marquette's personal narrative of his trip down the Mississippi, for example, shares space with Jean de Brébeuf's systematic description of Huron society. Moreover, the Jesuits added another set of religious genre types. Drawing on the literary traditions of Christianity, they

---

[5] Gordon M. Sayre, *Les Sauvages Américaines: Representatio:is of Native Americans in French and English Colonial Literature* (Chapel Hill: University of North Carolina Press, 1997).

framed many of their texts as works of witness, prophecy, and hagiography. Moving with ease from one set of literary conventions to another, the Jesuits tried to appeal to a wide variety of tastes and interests. As Father François Le Mercier put it in the *Relation of 1669–70,* "I hope that there will be found here material to satisfy the curiosity of those who take pleasure in learning what occurs in foreign nations, and at the same time material to edify the piety and animate the zeal of apostolic men." [6]

There is very little hard data on the circulation and readership of the *Jesuit Relations.* We do know that the appearance of each successive volume was eagerly anticipated in some circles, as priests, nuns, and pious laypeople throughout France read them avidly. But how extensive was the readership among the more secular-minded? It's impossible to say for certain, though many scholars have speculated on the impact of the *Relations* on French views of North America and its native peoples. It has been suggested that they provided the ethnographic raw material, as well as a basically positive view of "uncivilized" humanity, that helped eighteenth-century thinkers such as Jean-Jacques Rousseau work out a revolutionary conception of human nature. However, few intellectual historians would now accept any direct connection between the *Jesuit Relations* and the Enlightenment's view of "savage man" in a state of nature. Travel writings by secular or Protestant figures such as Jean de Léry, Marc Lescarbot, and Baron Lahontan probably had a more immediate influence on Rousseau and his contemporaries. In general terms, however, it is fair to say that the *Relations* made a great and lasting contribution to European knowledge of Amerindian cultures.

The *Jesuit Relations* certainly had their critics at the time. Enemies of the Society of Jesus were legion: Protestants who viewed the Jesuits as the epitome of devious papist malevolence, secular deists who saw them as defenders of superstition, and, within the Catholic Church, Jansenists who differed on theological issues. Some rival religious orders also resented the fame and influence of the Jesuits. It was only natural that the Canadian mission reports would be attacked from these various hostile quarters. Friars of the Recollet order were particularly scathing, as the Jesuits had shouldered these pioneer missionaries out of the North American field between 1629 and 1670. Recollet writers such as Chrestien Le Clercq and Louis Hennepin mocked as extravagant "fictions" the tales of martyrdom and mystic visionaries that punctuate the *Relations.* Above all, they attacked the claim that Canadian natives had truly

---

[6] Quoted in J. H. Kennedy, *Jesuit and Savage in New France* (New Haven, Conn.: Yale University Press, 1950), 79.

converted to the Catholic faith. "There is scarce any Christianity among the Savages at this day," Hennepin wrote at the end of the seventeenth century, "except some particular Persons, and those in small numbers, very fickle and inconstant, ready at every moment for any small Interest to abandon their Religion."[7] Recollets took a more consistently dim view of the spiritual potential of Indians than did the Jesuits, and, like many modern historians, they doubted that conversions were either numerous or genuine. But, in fact, the *Jesuit Relations,* a few triumphant passages excepted, never really claim that native Canada had been fully Christianized. Indeed, they are filled with sighs of disappointment over setbacks and failures in the missionary enterprise, though, to be sure, these admissions of defeat are transformed, through the rhetorical skill of the Jesuits, into triumphs of missionary devotion. Moreover, the *Relations* do manage to maintain a positive tone by dwelling at length on the edifying piety of a few, obviously exceptional, converts. It was manipulative literary devices of this sort that the Recollets denounced; their critique seldom called into question the basic accuracy of Jesuit ethnography and historical chronicle.

CONFRONTING THE OTHER: THE PROBLEM OF CULTURAL AND HISTORICAL DIFFERENCE

Modern readers will be more likely to regard the *Jesuit Relations* as an instance of colonialist writing. Indeed, the missionaries' judgmental language may be shocking to students who have not been exposed to historical documents of the period. Questions of tone apart, it is clear that these texts about natives were written by Europeans for other Europeans. Thus, there is a great cultural gap separating observers and observed. Moreover, the Jesuits displayed their colonialist colors in assuming a one-way right to judge and evaluate various elements of the Algonquian and Iroquoian ways of life; they allowed for no reciprocal right of judgment over many European rules of doctrine and conduct that were, for the Jesuits, beyond criticism. Some native ways were considered bad, others good, but to these missionaries native society always remained an external object: the Other that defined itself by not being Us.

---

[7]Louis Hennepin, *A New Discovery of a Vast Country in America,* ed. R. G. Thwaites (1698; reprint, Chicago: A. C. McClurg, 1903), 587. See also the Recollet work sometimes attributed to Chrestien Le Clercq, *First Establishment of the Faith in New France,* trans. J. G. Shea (New York: J. G. Shea, 1881), 2:24–25.

A few qualifications are in order. The *Relations* are far too interesting to be categorized as colonialist texts, pure and simple. For one thing, these writings, though undoubtedly the work of Europeans, were generally the product of extensive consultation with Algonquians and Iroquoians. The native voice is by no means absent, even if it often comes across in a garbled and distorted form. Sometimes Indians are quoted extensively; more often their intellectual influence can be discerned in the way the Jesuit recorders recount events and describe customs. The missionaries were, of course, there to teach the Indians, not learn from them, and yet it seems unlikely that the years of immersion in a different culture would leave their outlook unaltered. Nowhere in the published *Relations* do any Jesuits admit to compromising their European principles, but, reading between the lines, it is possible to detect evidence of soul-searching and shifting points of view.

In addition to the cultural gap separating Jesuits and natives, we must also keep in mind the chronological gulf dividing us as modern readers from the seventeenth-century world in which these documents were written. Otherwise, it may be difficult to avoid the temptation to accuse the Jesuits of offenses (ethnocentrism is the most common charge) that are meaningless in the context of their times. Some historians discuss the missionaries and their writings in these ahistorical terms; others, equally ahistorical in my view, congratulate them on their prematurely "liberal" attitudes. It is true that the Jesuits were more likely than most of their contemporaries to say positive things about Indians, but they were not cultural relativists in anything resembling the manner of modern anthropology. Instead of trying to place them on some sort of single scale of tolerance and intolerance, we might better recognize the fundamental discontinuity between their way of thinking about cultural difference and ours.

In the mental universe of the *Jesuit Relations,* pluralism is a problem, a sign that something is amiss. Europeans of the seventeenth century were not troubled by a certain diversity of customs and manners in the different nations of the world; styles in costume and table etiquette were, for them, largely unimportant. But on basic questions—whether people lived in a fixed abode, how many husbands or wives they were permitted, their manner of worship—there were absolute rights and wrongs. Civilization and religion were singular as far as Europeans of that period were concerned.

As they attempted to understand the aboriginal societies of North America, missionaries such as Jean de Brébeuf and Paul Le Jeune would have been able to draw on ancient European traditions of ethnographic classification that went back to the early years of Christianity and, beyond that, to the pre-Christian world of classical antiquity. From the ancient Greeks came the polar opposition of civilization and barbarism or savagery. For them, civilized peoples had permanent homes, cities, and farming districts; they possessed some form of government, law, and civic order. To be a barbarian or savage was to lack these attributes. In the absence of law, savages tended to be utterly unrestrained in their behavior and disposed to violence. Civilization could take various forms, but nations either had it or they did not.

For these seventeenth-century Europeans, there was also a parallel religious dichotomy that opposed Christians and "pagans." (Complicating the scheme somewhat were the monotheistic religions such as Islam and Judaism—false but not pagan—but this was not an issue as far as native North America was concerned.) For Catholics of this period, Christianity was not just the best religion; it was the absolute truth. The behavioral norms of Christianity were requirements laid down by the creator of the universe, and therefore they were applicable to all humanity. God's existence should have been apparent to any rational being, and, in any case, He had revealed himself to everyone's ancestors at the time of creation and the Flood. Non-Christians were, therefore, "ignorant" or, depending on whether they had been exposed to Christian teaching, criminally defiant. It was often supposed that immorality was both a product of paganism and an obstacle to conversion.

Although terms such as *savage* and *barbarian* were generally accompanied by negative connotations, they also could have a positive implication. Since they represented the negation of Christian civilization, they could appear as a superior alternative when Europe seemed decadent and corrupt. The Jesuits, though uncritical of the ideals of their own society, were anything but complacent about the realities of nominally Christian Europe. They were painfully familiar with the shortcomings of civilization. Christian mythology provided them with an antidote to oversophisticated artificiality: This was the figure of the *innocent,* humanity before Adam and Eve had tasted the fruits of the tree of knowledge. Natives were sometimes presented as naked, prelapsarian humanity: the "noble savage" as a token of human possibilities before the Fall. Like other colonialist writings of the time, the *Jesuit Relations* frequently dwell on the natural virtues of American Indians, emphasizing their generosity, their bravery, their lack of affectation, and their immunity to greed and ambition.

Were the Jesuits really talking about Europe whenever they described and commented, favorably or unfavorably, on Algonquian and

Iroquoian societies? Were Indians merely a literary creation representing the opposite of the missionaries' own culture? Or did the Jesuits manage to overcome the limitations of their intellectual equipment and begin to see the world, at least to some degree, as a Huron or a Mohawk? These are some of the many issues likely to arise when you read and discuss the *Jesuit Relations*.

1

Montagnais Hunters
of the Northern Woodlands

The earliest published *Jesuit Relations* were written by Father Paul Le Jeune (1592–1664), the first superior of the New France mission. Le Jeune was raised as a Protestant but converted to Catholicism as a young man. He later joined the Society of Jesus and acquired years of experience as an educator and administrator in various Jesuit colleges in France before traveling to Canada at the age of forty. Administrative duties kept him at Quebec through most of his North American career, but he still had extensive contact with the Montagnais and Algonquin bands that spent the summer in the vicinity of the French fort. The earliest volumes of the *Jesuit Relations* are almost entirely Le Jeune's work, and they focus mainly on the Montagnais.

Thanks to half a century of fur trading, these hunting-gathering people had experienced considerable contact with the French by the time Le Jeune encountered them, and yet their ancestral way of life was only beginning to show the effects of European colonization. The Montagnais had developed finely tuned strategies for deriving a living from an inhospitable environment of spruce forests, low rocky hills, rivers, lakes, and wetlands. In summer they gathered several hundred strong along the St. Lawrence River, wherever the fishing and berrying were good. But autumn found them dispersing to inland hunting grounds, where they sought moose and other large mammals for their meat and hides, as well as beavers, the pelts of which were central to trade with the French.

The itinerant life of the Montagnais and Algonquins required not only an intimate knowledge of the landscape and its seasonal resources but also amazing technical sophistication. These peoples excelled above all in the technology of transportation. In summer the birch bark canoe carried them and all their possessions along the intricate network of rivers and lakes, yet it remained light enough for portages. When the waterways froze and snow covered the land, hunters donned their snowshoes and pulled their cargo on wooden toboggans.

Algonquin-Montagnais spiritual beliefs and practices were naturally of great interest to the Jesuits. Because these peoples saw different animals, as well as natural phenomena such as thunder and waterfalls, as possessing their own spirits and personalities, some anthropologists classify their religion as "animism." These peoples assumed that spirits could be helpful or harmful to humans, and the aim of Algonquian rituals was to propitiate these spirits — to deflect their malevolence or direct their powers toward human ends. They told stories of supernatural creatures and magical heroes as a means of conveying an understanding of the world. They consulted men or women known to possess special spiritual powers (shamans, or "jugglers," as the Jesuits derisively called them). They also looked for insight in their dreams and in ecstatic states induced by ceremonies such as the "shaking tent."

PAUL LE JEUNE WINTERS WITH MESTIGOIT'S BAND, 1633–1634

In the fall of 1633, not long after arriving in Canada, Father Le Jeune made a rather rash decision to follow a Montagnais band on its travels into the interior in search of game. The party was led by Mestigoit — Le Jeune calls him "my host" — and included a shaman, referred to by the missionary as "the sorcerer," and the shaman's brother, Pastedechouan. Le Jeune called the latter "the Apostate" because he had traveled to France several years earlier, converted to Christianity, and then reverted to the Montagnais religion upon his return to Canada. Their destination was the hunting grounds of the northern Appalachians, east of Quebec and south of the St. Lawrence. Le Jeune's aim in accompanying the band was to improve his knowledge of the native language and customs, while pressing his companions to abandon their "superstitions" and recognize the truth of Christianity. The missionary expedition ended up as an arduous struggle for survival, and far from making converts, Le Jeune seems to have impressed the Montagnais mainly with the incompetence and odd beliefs of the French. Still, the Jesuit did get to know the natives intimately, as his writings demonstrate.

There is an engagingly naive quality to these early writings of Paul Le Jeune. In retrospect, though the author does his best to maintain a stance of

Portrait of Father Paul Le Jeune (1591–1664)
Father Le Jeune was the first superior of the New France mission, and the pioneer author of the *Relations*.
National Archives of Canada/C-021404.

European superiority, he has difficulty disguising his own anxieties and uncertainties. It seems that the missionary found it unsettling to confront the Montagnais way of life, very much on its own ground and far from any European presence.

PAUL LE JEUNE

Journal [of a Winter Hunt][1]

1634

The Indians pass the winter in these woods, ranging here and there to get their living. In the early snows, they seek the beaver in the small rivers and porcupines upon the land; when the deep snows come, they hunt the moose and caribou, as I have said. From the twelfth of November of the year 1633, when we entered these vast forests, to the twenty-second of April of this year 1634, when we returned to the banks of the great river St. Lawrence, we camped at twenty-three different places. Sometimes we were in deep valleys, then upon lofty mountains, sometimes in the low flat country; but always in the snow. These forests where I was are made up of different kinds of trees, especially pines, cedars, and firs. We crossed many torrents of water, some rivers, several beautiful lakes and ponds, always walking over the ice. But let us come down to particulars and say a few words about each camping spot. My fear of becoming tedious will cause me to omit many things that I have considered trifling, although they might throw some light upon these memoirs.

Upon entering these regions, there were three cabins in our company: nineteen persons being in ours, sixteen in the cabin of the Indian named Ekhennabamate, and ten in that of the newcomers. This does not include the Indians who were encamped a few leagues[2] away from us. We were in all forty-five persons, who were to be kept alive on what it should please the holy providence of God to send us, for our provisions were getting very low.

[1] Selection titles are generally from the *Jesuit Relations*. Brackets indicate titles or parts of titles that were added by the editor.
[2] A league (French *lieue*) was a distance of approximately four kilometers, or two and a half miles.

JR 7:106–15, Paul Le Jeune, *Relation of 1634.*
(Source notes throughout use the abbreviation *JR*, followed by a volume and page reference, to designate Reuben G. Thwaites, ed., *The Jesuit Relations and Allied Documents,* 73 vols. [Cleveland: Burrows Brothers, 1896–1900].)

This is the order we followed in breaking up our camps, in tramping over the country, and in erecting our tents and pavilions. When our people saw that there was no longer any game within three or four leagues of us, an Indian who was best acquainted with the way to the place where we were going cried out in a loud voice outside the cabin one fine day, "Listen, men, I am going to mark the way for breaking camp tomorrow at daybreak." He took a hatchet and marked some trees, which guided us. They do not mark the way except in the beginning of winter, for when all the rivers and streams are frozen and the snow is deep, they do not take this trouble.

When there are a number of things to be carried, as often happens when they have killed a great many moose,[3] the women go ahead and carry a portion of these things to the place where they are to camp the following day. When the snow is deep, they make sledges of wood which splits and which can be peeled off like leaves in very thin, long strips. These sledges are very narrow, because they have to be dragged among masses of trees closely crowded in some places; but to make up for this, they are very long. One day, seeing the sledge of my host standing against a tree, I could scarcely reach to the middle of it, stretching out my arm as far as I could. They fasten their baggage upon these, and, with a cord that they pass over their chests, they drag these wheel-less chariots over the snow.

But not to wander farther from my subject, as soon as it is day each one prepares to break camp. They begin by having breakfast, if there is any; for sometimes they depart without breakfasting, continue on their way without dining, and go to bed without supping. Each one arranges his own baggage, as best he can, and the women strike the cabin, to remove the ice and snow from the bark, which they roll up in a bundle. Once packed, the baggage is thrown upon their backs or loins in long bundles, which they hold with a cord that passes over their foreheads, beneath which they place a piece of bark so that it will not hurt them. When everyone is loaded, they mount their snowshoes, which are bound to the feet so that they will not sink into the snow, and then they march over plain and mountain. They make the children start early and go on ahead, but even so they often do not arrive until quite late. These little

---

[3] In the original French, Le Jeune refers to the main quarry of the Montagnais as *les eslans,* which in the Thwaites edition is translated as "elk," although it seems highly unlikely that the hunters would have encountered elk in this region. Europeans at this time were still somewhat uncertain as to how to designate unfamiliar North American animals. Le Jeune refers to caribou as "wild asses."

ones have their packs, or their sledges, to accustom them early to fatigue; the adults try to stimulate them by making a contest to see who will carry or drag the most.

To paint for you the hardships of the journey, I have neither pen nor brush equal to the task. You would have to see them to understand, as this is a meal that must be tasted to be appreciated. We did nothing but go up and go down. Frequently we had to bend over double to pass under partly fallen trees, and step over others lying upon the ground whose branches sometimes knocked us over, gently enough to be sure, but always coldly, for we fell upon the snow. If there happened to be a thaw, oh God, what suffering! It seemed to me I was walking over a road of glass that broke under my feet at every step. The frozen snow, beginning to melt, would fall and break into blocks or big pieces, into which we often sank up to our knees, and sometimes to our waists. Falling was painful enough, but pulling oneself out was even worse, for our snowshoes would be loaded with snow and so heavy that, when we tried to draw them out, it seemed as if somebody were tugging at our legs to dismember us. I have seen some who slid so far under the logs buried in the snow that they could pull out neither their legs nor their snowshoes without assistance. So imagine someone on these paths, loaded down like a mule, and you may judge how easy is the life of the Indian.

In the discomforts of a journey in France, there are villages where one can refresh and fortify oneself, but the only inns that we encountered were brooks. We even had to break the ice in order to get some water to drink. It is true that we did not travel far each day, for that would indeed have been absolutely impossible for us.

When we reached the place where we were to camp, the women went to cut the poles for the cabin, and the men to clear away the snow. Now a person had to work at this building, or shiver with cold for three long hours upon the snow waiting until it was finished. Sometimes I put my hand to the work to warm myself, but usually I was so frozen that fire alone could thaw me. The Indians were surprised at this, for they were working hard enough to sweat. Assuring them now and then that I was very cold, they would say to me, "Give us your hands so that we may see if you are telling the truth"; and finding them quite frozen, they were touched with compassion and gave me their warm mittens and took my cold ones. This went so far that my host, after having tried it several times, said to me, "Nicanis,[4] do not winter anymore with the Indians, for

[4] Nicanis is the name the Montagnais gave to Father Le Jeune.

they will kill you." I think he meant that I would fall ill, and because I could not be dragged along with the baggage, they would kill me. I began to laugh and told him that he was trying to frighten me.

When the cabin was finished, about nightfall or a little before, they began to talk about dinner and supper all in one, for as we had departed in the morning with only a small morsel to eat, we had to have patience to reach our destination and to wait until the hotel was erected, in order to lodge and eat there. Unfortunately, on this particular day, our people did not go hunting as usual, and so it was for us a day of fasting as well as a day of work. . . .

PAUL LE JEUNE

On Their Hunting and Fishing

1634

The beaver is taken in several ways. The Indians say that it is the animal well beloved by the French, English, and Basques: in a word, by the Europeans. I heard my host say one day, jokingly, *Missi picoutau amiscou,* "The beaver knows how to make all things to perfection: It makes kettles, hatchets, swords, knives, bread; in short, it makes everything." He was making sport of our Europeans, who have such a fondness for the skin of this animal and who fight to see who will give the most to these barbarians to get it. They carry this to such an extent that my host said to me one day, showing me a very beautiful knife, "The English have no sense; they give us twenty knives like this for one beaver skin."[1]

In the spring, the beaver is taken in a trap baited with the wood it eats. The Indians are very clever in setting these traps, such that, when set off, they cause a heavy piece of wood to fall upon the animal and knock it out. Sometimes the dogs find a beaver outside its house, whereupon they will pursue it and capture it easily. I have never seen this chase but have been told of it; and the Indians highly value a dog which can scent and flush out this animal.

---

[1]The Montagnais had become acquainted with the English between 1629 and 1632, when the Kirke brothers had captured and occupied Quebec.

JR 6:296–99, 210–13, Paul Le Jeune, *Relation of 1634.*

During the winter they capture them in nets and under the ice. They cut an opening in the ice near the beaver's house and put into the hole a net with some wood which serves as bait. The poor animal, searching for something to eat, gets caught in a net made of good, strong, double cord; it must be hauled out quickly before it cuts the net to bits. Once it is taken from the water through the hole in the ice, they kill it with a big club. The other way of taking them under the ice is more noble. Not all the Indians use this method, only the most skillful. With their hatchets, they break apart the cabin or house of the beaver, which is indeed wonderfully made. . . .

The Indians do not throw to the dogs the bones of beavers or female porcupines; at least, not certain specified bones. In general, they are very careful that the dogs do not eat any bones of birds or of other animals that are caught in nets; otherwise they will never be able to catch any more except with the greatest difficulty. Yet they make a thousand exceptions to this rule, for it does not matter if the vertebrae or rump of these animals be given to the dogs, though the rest must be thrown into the fire. However, when a beaver has been taken in a net, it is best to throw its bones into a river. It is amazing how they gather and collect these bones, and preserve them with so much care, that you would say their hunt would be destroyed if they violated their superstitions.

As I was laughing at them and telling them that beavers do not know what is done with their bones, they replied: "You do not know how to catch beavers, and yet you want to tell us about it. Before the beaver is completely dead," they told me, "its soul comes to visit the cabin of the man who kills it, and looks very carefully to see what is done with his bones. If they have been given to the dogs, the other beavers would be warned, and so they would make themselves difficult to catch. But they are very glad to have their bones thrown into the fire or into a river. The trap which caught them is especially pleased with this."

I told them that the Iroquois, according to one who was with us, threw the bones of the beavers to the dogs, and yet they caught them very often; and that our Frenchmen captured far more game than they, though our dogs ate the bones. "You have no sense," they said. "Do you not see that you and the Iroquois cultivate the soil and gather its fruits, and not we, and that therefore it is not the same?" I began to laugh when I heard this irrelevant answer. The trouble is that I only stammer, I mix my words up, I pronounce badly, and so everything usually ends in laughter. What great difficulty there is in talking to a people without understanding their language. Furthermore, in their eat-all feasts it is very important to prevent the dogs from tasting even the least of it, but that is another subject. . . .

————

THE MONTAGNAIS DESCRIBED

The following passage is part of Paul Le Jeune's attempt to provide his readers with a systematic survey of Montagnais customs and culture. Normally, European writers of the time stuck to a single literary genre when they wrote about the natives of America: either an impersonal and "objective" ethnographic description or a first-person travel account. Le Jeune's Relation *of 1634 tends to blur the boundaries. The traveler's narrative featured on pages 23–26 contains paragraphs of ethnographic description, while the overview of Montagnais customs in this section keeps slipping into the personal narrative mode.*

PAUL LE JEUNE

On the Beliefs, Superstitions, and Errors of the Montagnais Indians

1634

I have already reported that the Indians believe that a certain being named Atahocam created the world and that one named Messou restored it. When I questioned the famous sorcerer and the old man with whom I passed the winter on this subject, they answered that they did not know who was the first creator of the world: that it was perhaps Atahocam, but that was not certain; that they only spoke of Atahocam as one speaks of a thing so far distant that nothing sure can be known about it; and, in fact, the word *Nitatachokan* in their language means "I relate a fable; I am telling an old story invented for amusement."

As to the Messou, they hold that he restored the world, which was destroyed in the Flood. Thus, it appears that they have some tradition of that great universal deluge which happened in the time of Noah, but they have burdened this truth with a great many irrelevant fables. This Messou went hunting, and his lynxes, which he used instead of dogs, having gone into a great lake, were held there. The Messou, seeking them everywhere, was told by a bird that it had seen them in the midst of this lake. He went in to get them out, but the lake overflowed, covering the earth and swallowing up the world. The Messou, very much astonished, sent a raven in search of a little piece of ground with which to rebuild this element [the earth], but he could not find any. He made an otter descend into the abyss of waters, but it could not bring back any. At last he sent a muskrat, which brought back a little morsel, and the Messou used this to rebuild this earth which we inhabit. He shot arrows into the trunks of trees, which made themselves into branches. He performed a thousand other wonders, avenged himself upon those who had detained his lynxes, and married a muskrat, by whom he had children who have repopulated this world. This is the way in which the Messou restored all things. I touched upon this fable last year, but, desiring to recapitulate all I know about their beliefs, I have repeated many things. Our Indian related to Father Brébeuf [see chapter 2] that his people believe that a certain Indian had received from the Messou the gift of immortality in a little package, with a strict injunction not to open it. While he kept it closed, he was immortal, but his wife, being curious and incredulous, wished to see what was inside this present. When she opened it, it all flew away, and since then the Indians have been subject to death.

They also say that all animals, of every species, have an elder brother, who is, as it were, the source and origin of all individuals, and this elder brother is wonderfully great and powerful. The elder of the beavers, they tell me, is perhaps as large as our cabin, although his younger brothers (that is, the ordinary beavers) are not quite as large as our sheep. Now these elder brothers of all the animals are the younger brothers of the Messou. As elder brother to all the beasts, this worthy restorer of the universe can certainly claim a distinguished lineage! If, while sleeping, someone sees the elder brother or progenitor of an animal, he will have a successful hunt; if he sees the elder brother of the beavers, he will take beavers; if he sees the elder brother of the moose, he will take moose, possessing the younger brothers through the favor of their senior, whom he has seen in the dream. I asked them where these elder brothers were. "We are not sure," they answered me, "but we think the elder brothers of the birds are in the sky, and that the elder brothers of the other animals are in the water."

They recognize two progenitors of the seasons. One is called Nipinoukhe; it is this one that brings the spring and summer. This name comes from *nipin,* which in their language means "springtime." The other is called Pipounoukhe, from the word *pipoun,* which means "winter"; it therefore brings the cold season. I asked them if this Nipinoukhe and Pipounoukhe were men or if they were animals of some other species, and in what place they usually dwelt. They replied that they did not know exactly what form they had, but they were quite sure they were living, for they heard them, they said, talking or rustling, especially at their coming, though they could not tell what they were saying. For their dwelling place they share the world between them, one keeping on one side, the other upon the other, and when the period of their stay at one end of the world has expired, each goes over to the locality of the other, reciprocally succeeding each other. Here we have, in part, the fable of Castor and Pollux.[1] When Nipinoukhe returns, he brings back with him the heat, the birds, the verdure, and restores life and beauty to the world; but Pipounoukhe lays everything to waste, being accompanied by the cold winds, ice, snows, and other phenomena of winter. They call this succession of one to the other Achitescatoueth, meaning that they exchange places.

Furthermore, they believe that there are certain spirits of light, or spirits of the air, which they call Khichikouai, from the word *khichikou,* which means "light" or "the air." The spirits, or Khichikouai, are acquainted with future events. They see very far ahead. This is why the Indians consult them, not all of them but certain shamans, who know better than the others how to impose upon and fool these people. I have chanced to be present when they consulted these fine oracles, and here is what I have observed.

Toward nightfall, two or three young men erected a tabernacle in the middle of our cabin. They stuck six poles deep into the ground in the form of a circle, and to hold them in place they fastened to the tops of these poles a large ring, which completely encircled them. This done, they enclosed this edifice with blankets, leaving the top of the tent open. It was all that a tall man could do to reach to the top of this round tower, capable of holding five or six men standing upright. Once this house was made, the fires of the cabin were entirely extinguished and the brands were thrown outside lest the flame frighten away the spirits, or Khichikouai, who were to enter this tent. A young shaman slipped in from below, turning back the covering which enveloped it, then replacing it when he had entered, for they must be very careful that there be no opening in

---

[1] Castor and Pollux are twin brothers of ancient Greek mythology.

this fine palace except from above. The shaman, having entered, began to moan softly as if complaining. He shook the tent gently at first; then, gradually becoming more animated, he began to whistle in a hollow tone as if from afar; then to talk as if speaking into a bottle; to cry like the owls of this country, which it seems to me have stronger voices than those of France; then to howl and sing, constantly varying the tones; ending by these syllables, *"ho ho, hi hi, gui gui, nioué,"* and other similar sounds, disguising his voice so that it seemed to me I was hearing puppets such as those that showmen use in France. Sometimes he spoke Montagnais, sometimes Algonquin, retaining always the Algonquin intonation, which is as vivacious as the Provençal dialect. At first, as I have said, he shook this edifice gently, but as he grew more animated, he fell into so violent an ecstasy that I thought he would break everything to pieces, shaking his house with so much force and violence that I was astonished at a man having so much strength. For, after he had once begun to shake it, he did not stop until the consultation was over, which lasted about three hours. Whenever he would change his voice, the Indians would at first cry out, *Moa, moa,* "Listen, listen," and then, as an invitation to these spirits, they said to them, *Pitoukhecou, pitoukhecou,* "Enter, enter." At other times, as if they were replying to the howls of the shaman, they drew this aspiration from the depths of their chests, *ho, ho.* I was seated like the others looking on at this wonderful mystery, and though forbidden to speak, I had not vowed obedience to them, and so I did not fail to intrude a little word into the proceedings. Sometimes I begged them to have pity on this poor shaman who was killing himself in this tent; at other times I told them they should cry louder, for the spirits had gone to sleep.

Some of these barbarians imagined that this shaman was not inside, that he had been carried away, without knowing where or how. Others said that his body was lying on the ground and that his soul was up above the tent, where it spoke at first, calling these spirits and throwing from time to time sparks of fire. Now to return to our consultation. The Indians, having heard a certain voice that the shaman counterfeited, uttered a cry of joy, saying that one of these spirits had entered; then addressing themselves to him, they cried out, *Tepouachi, tepouachi,* "Call, call"; that is, "Call your companions." Thereupon the shaman, pretending to be one of the spirits and, changing his tone and his voice, called them. In the meantime our sorcerer, who was present, took his drum and began to sing with the shaman who was in the tent, and the others answered. They made some of the young men dance, among others the Apostate, who did not wish to hear of it, but the sorcerer made him obey.

At last, after a thousand cries and howls, a thousand songs, and having danced and thoroughly shaken this fine edifice, the Indians believed that the spirits, or Khichikouai, had entered, and the sorcerer consulted them. He asked them about his health — for he was sick — and about that of his wife, who was also sick. These spirits, or rather the shaman who counterfeited them, answered that, as to his wife, she was already dead, that it was all over with her. I could have said as much myself, for one needed not be a prophet or a sorcerer to guess that, inasmuch as the poor creature was already visibly on death's door. In regard to the sorcerer, they said that he would live to see another spring. Now, knowing his disease — which was pain in the abdomen, or rather an infirmity resulting from his licentiousness and lewdness, for he is vile to the last degree — I said to him, seeing that he was otherwise healthy and that he drank and ate very heartily, that he would not only see the spring but also the summer, if some other accident did not overtake him. I was not mistaken.

After these interrogations, these fine oracles were asked if there would soon be snow, if there would be much of it, if there would be moose, and where they could be found. They answered — or rather the shaman, always disguising his voice — that they saw a little snow and some moose far away, without indicating the place, having the prudence not to commit themselves. . . .

PAUL LE JEUNE

On the Good Things Which Are Found among the Indians

1634

If we begin with physical advantages, I will say that they possess these in abundance. They are tall, erect, strong, well proportioned, agile; there is nothing effeminate in their appearance. Those little fops that are seen elsewhere are only painted images of men, compared with our Indians. I was once inclined to believe that pictures of the Roman emperors represented the ideal of the painters rather than men who had ever existed, so strong and powerful are their heads; but I see here upon the shoulders of these people the heads of Julius Caesar, of Pompey, of Augustus, of Otto, and of others that I have seen in France, either drawn upon paper or in relief on medallions.

As to the mind of the Indian, it is of good quality. I believe that souls are all made from the same stock and that they do not differ substantially. Hence, the well-formed bodies and well-regulated and well-arranged organs of these barbarians suggest that their minds too ought to function well. Education and instruction alone are lacking. Their soul is a naturally fertile soil, but it is loaded down with all the evils that a land abandoned since the birth of the world can produce. I naturally compare our Indians with [European] villagers, because both are usually without education, although our peasants are slightly more advanced in this regard. Nevertheless, people who come to this country always confess and frankly admit that the Indians are more clever than our ordinary peasants.

Moreover, if it is a great blessing to be free from a great evil, our Indians should be considered fortunate. For there are two tyrants, ambition and avarice, who distress and torture so many of our Europeans but have no dominion over these great forests. Because the Indians have neither civil regulation, nor administrative offices, nor dignities, nor any positions of command — for they obey their chief only through goodwill toward him — they never kill one another to acquire these honors. Also, they are content with basic subsistence, and so not one of them gives himself to the Devil to acquire wealth.

They profess never to get angry, though not because of the beauty of this virtue, for which they have not even a name, but rather for their own contentment and happiness. In other words, they want only to free themselves from the bitterness caused by anger. The sorcerer said to me one day, speaking of one of our Frenchmen, "He has no sense, he gets angry; as for me, nothing can disturb me. Let hunger oppress us, let my nearest relations pass to the other life, let the Iroquois, our enemies, massacre our people; I never get angry." What he says cannot be taken as an article of faith, for as he is haughtier than any other Indian, so I have seen him annoyed more often than any of them. It is true also that he often restrains and governs himself by force, especially when I expose his foolishness. I have only heard one Indian pronounce this word, *Ninich-catihin,* "I am angry," and he said it only once. But I noticed that people were wary of him, for when these barbarians are angry, they are dangerous and unrestrained.

Whoever professes not to get angry ought also to make a profession of patience. The Indians surpass us to such an extent in this respect that we ought to be ashamed. I saw them, in their hardships and in their

Indian Women and Children
As imagined by a European illustrator who probably never set foot in North America.
Courtesy of the Newberry Library, Chicago.

labors, suffering cheerfully. My host, wondering at the great number of people who I told him were in France, asked me if the men were good, if they did not become angry, if they were patient. I have never seen such patience as is shown by a sick Indian. Others may yell, storm, jump, and dance, but he will scarcely ever complain. When I was with them and there was danger of great suffering, they would say to me, "We shall be sometimes two days, sometimes three, without any food to eat. Take courage, *Chibiné,* let your soul be strong to endure the pain and the hardship; try not to feel sad, as otherwise you will fall sick. Watch us. See how we keep laughing even though we have little to eat." One thing alone casts them down: That is when they see the approach of death, for they fear it beyond measure. Take away this apprehension from the Indians, and they will endure all kinds of degradation and discomfort and all kinds of trials and suffering very patiently. . . .

They are very much attached to each other and cooperate admirably. You do not see any disputes, quarrels, enmities, or reproaches among them. Men leave the household arrangements to the women without interfering with them. The women cut up and divide the food, deciding how much to give to each member of the family as they please, without any objections or anger on the part of the husband. When our provisions were disappearing rapidly under the management of a thoughtless young woman who accompanied my host, I never heard him ask her to explain what had happened to the food. I never heard the women complain because they were not invited to the feasts, because the men ate the good pieces, or because they had to work continually, gathering firewood, erecting the cabins, dressing the skins, and busying themselves with other hard work. Everyone does his own chores, gently and peacefully, without any disputes. It is true, however, that they have neither gentleness nor courtesy in their utterance; and a Frenchman could not assume the accent, the tone, and the sharpness of their voices without getting angry. Yet they do not become irritated.

HOW TO SETTLE DISPUTES AND DISCIPLINE CHILDREN

Paul Le Jeune received an early lesson in how the Algonquians handled assaults and injuries and how their children were disciplined. It was in 1633, on the occasion of a visit by a party of Algonquins and Nipissings who had traveled down the Ottawa and St. Lawrence rivers to trade with the French at Quebec.

PAUL LE JEUNE

What Occurred in New France in the Year 1633

1633

. . . One of them was looking very attentively at a little French boy who was beating a drum. As the Indian approached close to see him better, the little boy struck him a blow with one of his drumsticks and made his head bleed badly. Immediately all the people of his nation who were looking at the drummer took offense upon seeing this blow given. They went and found the French interpreter and said to him: "One of your people has wounded one of ours. You know our custom well; give us presents for this wound." As there is no government among the Indians, when one among them kills or wounds another, he is (assuming he escapes immediate retaliation) released from all punishment by giving a few presents to the friends of the deceased or wounded one. Our interpreter said: "You know our custom: When any of our number does wrong, he is punished. This child has wounded one of your people, and so he shall be whipped at once in your presence." The little boy was brought in, and when they saw that we were really in earnest, that we were stripping this little boy, pounder of Indians and of drums, and that our switches were all ready, they immediately asked that he be pardoned, arguing that he was only a child, that he had no mind, that he did not know what he was doing. As our people were going to punish him nevertheless, one of the Indians stripped himself entirely, threw his robe over the child, and cried out to the man who was going to do the whipping: "Strike me if you will, but you will not strike him"; and thus the little one escaped. All the Indian nations of these parts — and those of Brazil, we are told — cannot punish a child, nor allow one to be chastised. How much trouble this will give us in carrying out our plans of teaching the young!

2

Jean de Brébeuf on the Hurons

Thanks mainly to the Jesuits, there is probably no group of native North Americans whose culture and history in the period of initial contact with Europeans is better documented than that of the Hurons. Their large population and stable village habitat made them a more promising target for evangelization than the dispersed, nomadic Montagnais bands Paul Le Jeune had pursued through the forests. Accordingly, the Jesuits devoted the bulk of their resources between 1634 and 1649 to converting these Iroquoian people, an emphasis reflected in the ample coverage the Hurons receive in the *Relations* from that period. Huron material will appear in other parts of this compilation, but this chapter is excerpted entirely from Jean de Brébeuf's "Huron" *Relation of 1636*.

A martyr tortured and killed during the Iroquois invasion of 1649, Brébeuf achieved the status of a canonized saint of the Catholic Church. For our purposes, however, he is more noteworthy as a close observer of Huron culture — a missionary who spent the greater part of his adult life living among the Hurons, hundreds of miles from European settlements. Brébeuf lived among the Hurons from 1626 to 1629 and then returned in 1634 at the head of a party of three Jesuits and six laymen to establish the mission on a solid footing. Apart from some brief assignments to other Canadian locations, Brébeuf was attached to the Huron mission from its beginning to its end (1649). In this thoroughly Huron cultural environment, one in which Christianity and other aspects of European culture had little impact for many years, the missionary had only to look around him to learn about native ways. His knowledge was deepened, however, through long conversations with Huron friends and acquaintances, who told him of their metaphysical and cosmological views and patiently explained the reasons for various customs and rituals. Like other missionaries of the time, Brébeuf wrote scathingly of these "foolish delusions" when he addressed European readers, and yet it seems he reported what he saw and heard as faithfully as he could. If one reads his words attentively, the voices of his Huron interlocutors, faint and garbled though they may be in places, can nonetheless be heard.

The *Relation of 1636,* portions of which appear below, represents Brébeuf's attempt to provide a systematic and exhaustive overview of Huron ethnography in the style of the well-established European genre of the "customs and manners of the savages." The full text occupies an entire volume and constitutes the longest and most ambitious piece of ethnographic description in all the *Jesuit Relations.* It covers a wide range of topics, including law, politics, and marriage, although naturally Brébeuf's main interest was in matters connected to religious beliefs and rituals.

LANGUAGE

Our selections begin with a discussion of the Huron language. Training in Latin and Greek was part of the education of every Jesuit, but Brébeuf was particularly adept at languages, acquiring a basic knowledge of several North American dialects to go with his fluency in Huron. (In spite of modest disclaimers to the contrary, he spoke Huron well, though not perfectly as of 1636.) This chapter in his Relation *represents the missionary's contribution to contemporary European discussions on the origins and diversity of languages. The science of comparative linguistics was in its infancy then, as intellectuals tried to reconcile empirical knowledge of the languages of the world with biblical accounts of the Tower of Babel. Theoreticians wondered, for example, whether there had been one original and "natural" language, which different existing languages reflected to varying degrees. Brébeuf's discussion is shaped by these issues and by the practical difficulties of a missionary struggling to translate European religious concepts into a language not built around Christian concepts.*

JEAN DE BRÉBEUF
Of the Language of the Hurons
1636

This is only to give a little foretaste of the language, and to notice some of its peculiarities, in anticipation of a grammar and a complete dictionary.

They have a letter to which we have nothing to correspond — we express it by khi[chi]; the Montagnais and the Algonquins also use it. They are not acquainted with *B, F, L, M, P, X, Z;* and *I*[1] and *V* are never consonants for them. The greater part of their words is composed of vowels. They lack all the labial letters. This is probably the reason why they all open their lips so awkwardly, and why we can scarcely understand them when they whisper or speak in a low voice.

As they have hardly any virtue or religion, or any learning or government, they have consequently no individual words suitable for signifying these things. Hence it is that we are at a loss in explaining to them many important matters, depending upon a knowledge of these things.

Compound words are more often used by them and have the same effect as an adjective and a noun joined together would have with us: *andatarasé,* fresh bread; *achitetsi,* a foot long. The variety of these compound nouns is very great, and that is the key to opening the secret of their language. They have, like us, different genders and, like the Greeks, different numbers, besides a certain relative declension, which always includes in itself the possessive pronoun, *meus, tuus, suus* [mine, yours, his/hers]—for example, *iatacan,* my brother; *aiatacan,* my brothers; *satacan,* your brother; *tsatacan,* your brothers; *otacan,* his brother; *atotacan,* his brothers.

As to cases, they have them all, or supply them by very appropriate particles. The astonishing thing is that all their words are universally conjugated—for example, *assé,* it is cool, *assé chen,* it was cool; *gaon,* old, *agaon,* he is old, *agaonc,* he was old, *agaonha,* he is growing old; and so on. It is the same with that word *iatacan,* which means "my brother," *oniatacan,* we are brothers, *oniatacan ehen,* we were brothers. There is a richness here which is lacking in some other areas. A relative noun for them always includes the meaning of one of the three persons of the possessive pronoun, so that they cannot say simply father, son, master, servant, but are obliged to say one of these three: my father, your father, his or her father. To facilitate the task of translating prayers, I have designated one of their nouns to stand for the word "Father," but we nevertheless find it impossible to get them to say properly in their language, "In the name of the Father, and of the Son, and of the Holy Ghost." Would you judge it proper, until a better expression is found, to substitute instead, "In the name of our Father, and of His Son, and of their Holy Ghost?" Certainly it seems that the three persons of the most holy Trinity would be sufficiently expressed in this way. . . .

Now in connection with this name "Father," I must not forget the difficulty there is in teaching people to say "Our Father who art in

---

[1] In the seventeenth century, the letters *I* and *J* were often used interchangeably.

Heaven" when they have none on earth. To speak to them of a deceased person whom they have loved is to insult them. A woman, whose mother had died a short time before, almost lost her desire to be baptized because the command "Thou shalt honor thy father and thy mother" had been inadvertently quoted to her.

As for the verbs, what is most remarkable in their language is (1) that they have some verbs for living things and different ones for inanimate objects, (2) that they vary their tenses in as many ways as did the Greeks; their numbers also — in the first person, there is both a dual number and a plural, and, beyond that, there is a further distinction: thus, to say "we set out, you and I," we must say *kiarascwa,* and to say "we set out, he and I," *aiarascwa.* Likewise in the plural, "we, several of us, set out," *awarascwa;* "we set out with you," *cwarascwa.*

Besides all this, there is to be noticed a double conjugation, and I believe that this is common to all American languages. The one is simple and absolute, like our Latin and French conjugations. For example, the verb *ahiaton,* meaning "to write," is conjugated absolutely in this way: *iehiaton,* I write; *chiehiatonc,* you [singular] write; *ihahiatonc,* he writes; *awahiatonc,* we write; *scwahiatonc,* you [plural] write; *attihiatonc,* they write. The other method of conjugation may be called the reciprocal, inasmuch as the action signified by the verb always has some person or thing as its object; thus, instead of saying, as we do in three words, "I love myself," the Hurons say only, *iatenohwe;* "I love you" [singular], *onnonhwe;* "I love you both," *inonhwe;* "I love you" (several), *wanonhwe;* and so on.

What I find most extraordinary is that there is a feminine conjugation, at least in the third person, both for the singular and the plural; we have not yet learned very much about this. Here is an example of it: *ihaton,* he says; *iwaton,* she says; *ihonton,* they [masculine] say; *ionton,* they [feminine] say. The principal distinguishing feature of this feminine conjugation is the lack of the letter *H,* in which the masculine abounds; perhaps this is to give the women to understand that there ought to be nothing rough or coarse in their words or their manners, but that grace and the law of gentleness ought to be upon their tongues, following that saying of the Sage, "In her tongue is the law of kindness."[2] That is enough of that subject for now, unless you wish to hear something about their style. They frequently use comparisons, weather lore, and proverbs. Here is one of their most remarkable: *Tichiout etoatendi,* "Behold," they

---

[2] Prov. 31:26; Latin in original.

say, "the falling star," when they see someone who is fat and prosperous; for they hold that once upon a time a star fell from the sky in the form of a fat goose. . . .

———

RELIGION, MYTH, AND RITUAL

Brébeuf was naturally preoccupied with Huron beliefs and practices relating to the supernatural and the metaphysical, and although he sometimes wrote of it in disdainful terms, the Jesuit obviously studied Huron religion with the utmost care and seriousness. Clearly, his account is based on direct observation, supplemented by conversations with unnamed Hurons. Like other European missionaries of the period, Brébeuf was always looking for parallels to Christian myths about creation and the Flood. Such echoes would suggest that the Hurons had once been aware of the true God and, though the memory had dimmed with time, it might be revived.

JEAN DE BRÉBEUF

What the Hurons Think about Their Origin

1636

It is astonishing to see so much blindness in regard to the things of Heaven, in a people who do not lack judgment and knowledge in reference to those of earth. This is what their vices and brutality have merited from God. There are some indications, as can be seen in certain details in their fables, that in the past they had some knowledge of the true God that was more than merely natural. Even if they had only that insight which nature can provide, still they ought to have been more reasonable on this subject unless, as the Apostle [Paul] says, "Because that, when they knew God, they glorified him not as God, neither were they thankful; but became vain in their imaginations, and their foolish heart was darkened."[1] Since they were unwilling to acknowledge God in their

---

[1] Rom. 1:21; Latin in original.

habits and actions, they have lost the thought of him and have become worse than beasts in his sight for the lack of respect they display.

To begin with fundamental beliefs, most of them take pride in deriving their origin from heaven. Their conviction is based on the following fable, which passes among them for the truth.

They recognize as head of their nation a certain woman whom they call Aataentsic, who fell from heaven, they say, into their midst. For they think the heavens existed long before this wonder occurred, but they cannot tell you when or how its great bodies were drawn from the abysses of nothingness. They even suppose that above the vault of heaven there was, and still is, a land like this one, with woods, lakes, rivers, and fields, as there are here on earth, and with peoples who inhabit them. There is some disagreement as to the manner in which this fortunate fall occurred. Some say that one day, as she was working in her field, she perceived a bear. Her dog began to pursue it, and then she herself went after it. The bear, seeing himself closely pressed and seeking only to escape the teeth of the dog, fell by accident into a hole. The dog followed him. Aataentsic approached this precipice and, finding neither the bear nor the dog in view, despaired and threw herself into the hole after them. However, her fall happened to be more favorable than she had expected. For she fell down into the waters of the earth without being hurt, even though she was pregnant. After this, the waters dried up little by little, and the earth appeared and became habitable.

Others attribute this fall to another cause, which seems to have something to do with Adam, though the story is predominantly falsehood. They say that the husband of Aataentsic, being very sick, dreamed that it was necessary to cut down a certain tree from which the people who dwelt in Heaven obtained their food. Eating the fruit of this tree, he believed, would cure him immediately. Aataentsic, knowing the desire of her husband, took his ax and went off to accomplish the task. She had no sooner dealt the first blow than the tree at once melted, almost under her feet, and fell to the earth. She was so astonished that, after carrying the news to her husband, she returned and threw herself after it. As she fell, the Turtle happened to raise its head above water and perceived her. Not knowing what to do at the sight of this astonishing wonder, she called together the other aquatic animals to get their advice. They immediately assembled, and she showed them what she had seen, asking what they thought she should do. The majority voted to refer the matter to the beaver, who, as a courtesy, left it to the Turtle's judgment. The latter finally concluded that they should all promptly set to work, dive to the bottom of the water, bring up soil to her, and put it on her back. No sooner said than done, and the woman fell very gently on this island. She was pregnant when she fell, and after a time she gave birth to a daughter, who almost immediately became pregnant herself. (If you ask them how this could happen, you will make them very uncomfortable. "The fact is," they tell you, "that she was pregnant." Some throw the blame upon some strangers who landed on this island. Try, I pray you, to make this agree with what they say: that before Aataentsic fell from the sky there were no men on earth!) Be that as it may, she brought forth two boys, Tawiscaron and Iouskeha, who, when they grew up, quarreled with one another. (Does this not relate in some way to the murder of Abel?) They came to blows, but with very different weapons. Iouskeha had the horns of a stag; Tawiscaron used only some wild rose hips, in the belief that, as soon as he struck his brother with them, [his brother] would fall dead at his feet. But it happened quite differently than he had expected, and instead Iouskeha struck him so hard in the side that he bled profusely. This poor wretch immediately fled, and from his blood, which was sprinkled across the land, certain stones sprang up, like those we employ in France to strike a gun, which the Indians call even today Tawiscara, from the name of this unfortunate man. His brother pursued him and killed him. This is what most of the Hurons believe concerning the origin of these nations.

There are some Hurons whose imaginations do not soar so high and who are not so ambitious as to believe that they derive their origin from Heaven. They say that in the beginning of the world, the land was quite covered with water, with the exception of a little island on which was the sole hope of the human race: a single man whose sole companions were a fox and a little animal like a marten, which they call Tsouhendaia. The man, not knowing what to do upon finding himself isolated on such a small piece of land, asked the fox to dive into the water to see if there were any bottom to it. He had no sooner wet his paws than he drew back, fearing that this experiment would cost him his life. Whereupon the man became indignant: "Tessandion, you have no sense," he said to him, and kicked him into the water, where he drank a little more than his fill. However, [the man] did not give up his plan, and he persuaded the little animal that remained as his sole companion, until it finally resolved to plunge in. Not realizing that the water was shallow, it jumped in and crashed violently against the bottom. When it resurfaced, its snout was all covered in mud. The man, very glad at this happy discovery, exhorted the animal to continue bringing up soil to increase the size of the islet. This it did and with so much diligence that the little island ceased to be an island and changed into the vast country that we see today. If you

again press the Hurons at this point to explain this man's existence —
Who gave him life? Who put him upon this little island? How could he
become the father of all these nations if he was alone and had no companion?—you will gain nothing by asking all these questions. You will
only receive this solution (and it would not be bad, if only their religion
were good): "We do not know; this is what we were told; our fathers
never taught us any more about it." What would you say to that? All that
we do is to bear witness to them that we feel compassion for their gross
ignorance. We take the occasion, if they seem capable of understanding,
to explain some of our mysteries, showing them how fully they conform
to reason. They listen very willingly and are well satisfied with this.

But to return to Aataentsic and Iouskeha; they hold that Iouskeha is
the sun and Aataentsic the moon, and yet that their cabin is situated at
the ends of the earth — that is, near our Ocean Sea.[2] (For beyond that is
a lost world as far as they are concerned; before they had any commerce
with the French, they never dreamed that there was under heaven any
land but their own. Now that they have been disabused of this idea, many
still believe that their world and ours are two quite separate entities,
made by the hands of different workmen.) They say that four young men
once undertook a journey to find out for themselves. They found
Iouskeha quite alone in his cabin, and he received them very kindly. After an exchange of formal greetings, following the customs of the country, he advised them to conceal themselves in a corner; otherwise he
would not answer for their lives. Aataentsic was sure to play a trick on
them if they did not keep on their guard. That fury herself arrived toward evening. She noticed that there were new guests in the house, and,
as she can assume any form she wishes, she made herself into a beautiful girl, handsomely adorned with a beautiful necklace and beadwork
bracelets, and asked her son where his guests were. He replied that he
did not know what she meant, and so she left the cabin. Iouskeha took
the opportunity to warn his guests, and thus their lives were saved. Although their cabin is so very distant, [Aataentsic and Iouskeha] are nevertheless both present at the feasts and dances which take place in the
villages. Aataentsic is regularly trounced there, and Iouskeha blames
these beatings on a certain horned *oki*[3] named Tehonrressandeen; but
at the end of the tale, it turns out that it is Iouskeha himself who, under
that disguise, has thus insulted his own mother.

[2] Atlantic Ocean.
[3] "Spirit," other-than-human person.

Moreover, they consider themselves greatly obliged to this person-age [Iouskeha]. In the first place, according to some Hurons — the ones who disagree with the beliefs mentioned above — it is to him that we owe the many fine rivers and beautiful lakes. In the beginning of the world, they say, the earth was dry and arid. All the waters were collected under the armpit of a large frog, so that Iouskeha could not have a drop unless the frog gave it to him. One day he resolved to free himself, he and all his posterity, from this bondage. In order to attain this end, he made an incision under the armpit, whence the waters came forth in such abundance that they spread throughout the whole earth, and hence the origin of rivers, lakes, and seas. Is that not a subtle solution to an is-sue debated by our schools [of philosophy]? They hold also that without Iouskeha, their kettles would not boil, as he learned from the Turtle the process of making fire. Were it not for him, they would not have such good hunting and would not find it so easy to capture animals in the chase. For they believe that animals did not roam free at the beginning of the world, but that they were shut up in a great cavern, where Iouskeha guarded them. (Perhaps there may be some allusion here to the fact that God brought all the animals to Adam.) At any rate, one day he decided to turn them loose, in order that they might multiply and fill the forests; however, he did so in such a way that he might easily dispose of them when he wished. This is what he did to accomplish his end: As they emerged from the cave, one by one, he wounded them all in the foot with an arrow. However, the wolf dodged the shot, and that is why, they say, they have great difficulty in hunting him.

Further than that, they regard [Iouskeha] as the ancients once did Ceres.[4] According to them, it is Iouskeha who gives them the grain they eat; it is he who makes it grow and brings it to maturity. If they see their fields verdant in the spring, if they reap good and abundant harvests, and if their cabins are crammed with ears of corn, they owe it to Iouskeha alone. I do not know what God has in store for us this year, but to judge from the rumors going round, we are seriously threatened with a great infertility. It is said that Iouskeha has been seen, quite dejected and thin as a skeleton, and carrying a poor ear of corn in his hand. Some add that he was holding the leg of a man and was tearing at it with sharp teeth. All this, they say, is an indubitable sign of a very bad year. But the amusing thing is, no one can be found in the country who will say, "I have seen him" or "I have spoken to a man that has seen him," and yet

---

[4] Roman goddess of agriculture.

everyone believes this as if it were an indisputable fact, and no one takes the trouble to look into the truth of it. If it should please the divine Goodness to give the lie to these false prophets, it would be no small advantage in adding authority to our faith in this country, and in opening the way to spread the holy Gospel. We have received and are receiving every day so many favors from Heaven that we have reason to hope for this one as well, if it is for the glory of God.

JEAN DE BRÉBEUF

That the Hurons Recognize Some Divinity; Of Their Superstitions and of Their Faith in Dreams

1636

As these poor Indians are men, they have not been able to deny the existence of God altogether. Because they are given to vice, however, they are only able to form conceptions of him that are unworthy of his greatness. They have neither sought nor recognized him except on the surface of created things, in which they have hoped to find fortune or dreaded misfortune. They address themselves to the earth, the rivers, the lakes, the dangerous rocks, and, above all, to the sky, in the belief that these things are animate and that some powerful spirit or demon resides there.

They are not contented simply to make wishes; rather, they often accompany these with a sort of sacrifice. I have noticed two kinds of these. One type is to render them [the spirits] propitious and favorable, and the other is to appease them when they have received what they imagine to be some disgrace from them or believe they have incurred their anger or indignation. Here are the ceremonies they employ in these sacrifices. They throw some tobacco into the fire, and if it is, for example, to the sky that they address themselves, they say, *Aronhiaté onné aonstaniwas taitenr,* "O sky, here is what I offer thee in sacrifice. Have pity on me, assist me." If it is to implore health, *Taenguiaens,* "Heal me." They have recourse to the sky for almost all their needs, and respect the great bodies in it above all creatures, and remark in it in particular something divine. Indeed, it is, after man, the most vivid image we have of divinity. There is nothing which represents divinity to us so clearly. We perceive its omnipotence in all the prodigious effects the heavens cause here on earth, its immensity in the sky's vast extent, its wisdom in the orderly movement of the heavenly bodies, its goodness in the benign influences it sheds continually over all creatures, and its beauty in the sun and in the aspect of the stars. I say this to show how easy it will be, with time and divine aid, to lead these peoples to a knowledge of their Creator, since they already give special honor to a part of His creation which is such a perfect image of Him. And, furthermore, I may say it is really God whom they honor, though blindly, for they imagine in the heavens an *oki,* that is to say, a demon or power which rules the seasons of the year, which holds in check the winds and the waves of the sea, which can render favorable the course of their voyages and assist them in every time of need. They even fear his anger and invoke him as a witness in order to render their faith inviolable when they make some promise of importance, or agree to some bargain or treaty of peace with an enemy. Here are the terms they use: *Hakrihoté ekaronhiaté tout Icwakhier ekentaté,* "The sky knows what we are doing today." And they think that if, after this, they should violate their word or break their alliance, the sky would certainly chastise them. . . .

The Hurons hold that fish are possessed of reason, as are the deer and moose as well, and that is why they do not throw to the dogs either the bones of the latter when they are hunting or the refuse of the former when fishing; otherwise, the others would be warned and would hide themselves and not let themselves be caught. Every year they marry their nets, or seines, to two little girls, who must be only six or seven years of age, to ensure that they still retain their virginity, a very rare quality among them. The celebration of these nuptials takes place at a fine feast, where a net is placed between the two virgins. This is to make it happy to catch fish. Still, I am very glad that virginity receives among them this kind of honor, as it will help us someday to make them understand the value of it. Fish, they say, do not like the dead, and hence they abstain from going fishing when someone related to them dies. . . .

They have a faith in dreams which surpasses all belief. If Christians were to put into execution all their divine inspirations with as much care as our Indians carry out their dreams, no doubt they would very soon become great saints. They look upon their dreams as ordinances and irrevocable decrees; to delay the execution of them would be a crime. An Indian of our village dreamed this winter, shortly after he had fallen asleep, that he ought straightway to make a feast. Though it was the middle of the night, he immediately arose and came and woke us to borrow one of our kettles.

The dream is the oracle that all these poor peoples consult and listen to, the prophet which predicts future events, the Cassandra which warns of misfortunes threatening them, the physician who treats them in their sicknesses, the Aesculapius[1] and Galen[2] of the whole country: It is their most absolute master. . . .

[1]Ancient Roman god of medicine and healing.
[2]Ancient Greek physician and medical writer.

JEAN DE BRÉBEUF

Concerning Feasts, Dances . . . and What They Call Ononharoia

1636

I do not intend to detail everything our Indians are accustomed to do in connection with their dreams, for that would require too long a list of delusions. I shall content myself with saying that their dreams usually relate either to a feast, or to a song, or to a dance, or to a game, or to a certain sort of mania that they in fact call *ononharoia,* which is to say "turning the brain upside down." If it should happen that someone of some importance falls sick, the captain goes to inquire on behalf of the elders what he has dreamed until at last he draws from the man what it is that he desires for his health. Then everyone makes an effort to find it for him. If they do not have it, it must be found. From this mode of conduct, and from the fact that they exercise hospitality among themselves gratuitously, taking nothing except from us, from whom they always expect something, I entertain the hope that they will one day become capable of Christian charity.

The *ononharoia* is for the sake of mad persons and it begins when someone says that they must go through the cabins to tell that they have dreamed. That very evening, the troop of maniacs goes about among the cabins and upsets everything. On the morrow they return, crying in a loud voice, "We have dreamed," without saying what [the dream was about]. The people in each cabin guess what this object might be and present it to the companions, who refuse nothing until the right thing is guessed. You see them come out burdened down with hatchets, kettles, bead necklaces, and similar presents, after their fashion. When they [the maniacs] have found what they sought, they thank the person who has given it to them, and after having received further accoutrements to this mysterious present — such as some leather or an awl, if it were a shoe — they go away in a body to the woods, and there, as they say, they cast their madness out of the village, and the sick person begins to get better. And why not? He has what he was seeking for, or what the Devil required. . . .

All their feasts may be reduced to four kinds. *Athataion* is the feast of farewells; *Enditeuhwa* of thanksgiving and gratitude; *Atouront aochien* is a feast for singing as well as for eating; and *Awataerohi* is the fourth kind, made for deliverance from a sickness of that name.

The ceremonies here are almost like those of the Montagnais, and for that reason I refer for the most part to the *Relations* of preceding years.

I blush to say that they engage in [feasts] often whole days and whole nights, for they must, by the end, empty the pot. And if you cannot swallow all the food provided for you in one day, if you cannot find anyone who will help you finish it in return for some present, then, when the others have done their duty, you will be left there in a little enclosure, where no one but yourself will enter for twenty-four whole hours. A feast is a matter of importance, they cry, driving away those who arrive after the eating has begun and when the distributor has filled everyone's bowl, in which usually there is enough to keep one eating from morning until night. And whoever finishes first has to be served again and again, until the kettle is empty. Is it not true, on hearing of all this, and of several other traits of gluttony, which I omit out of respect for good taste, to say, "For the kingdom of God is not meat and drink."[1] Such is indeed the kingdom which the Devil has usurped over these poor blind beings. May it please our Lord to have pity on them and to deliver them from this tyranny.

But the most magnificent of these feasts are those they call *Atouronta aochien,* that is, singing feasts. These feasts will often last a full twenty-four hours; sometimes there are thirty or forty kettles, and as many as thirty deer will be eaten. This last winter, one was held in the village of Andiataé, of twenty-five kettles, in which there were fifty great fish, larger than our largest pike in France, and one hundred and twenty others of the size of our salmon. Another took place at Contarrea, of thirty kettles, in which there were twenty deer and four bears. Moreover, there

---

[1] Rom. 14:17; Latin in original.

is usually a large company. Eight or nine villages will often be invited, or even the whole country. In the latter case, the master of the feast sends to each captain as many sticks as the number of persons he invites from each village.

Sometimes they hold these feasts purely for display and to gain renown. They are also held when they take a new name, principally when they resuscitate, as they put it, the name of some deceased captain who has been held in esteem in the country for his valor and his conduct of public affairs. Above all, they hold a feast when they prepare to take up arms and go to war.

The largest cabin of the village is chosen to receive the company. They do not hesitate to inconvenience themselves for each other on these occasions. It is considered so important that when they build a new village, one cabin is made much larger than the others for this very purpose. Some are as much as twenty-five or thirty fathoms[2] in length. When the company is assembled, they sometimes begin to sing before eating, though occasionally they eat first in order to sing more heartily. If the feast is to last, as is often the case, the whole day, one portion of the kettles is emptied in the morning and the other is reserved for the evening. During these songs and dances, some will make motions of striking down their enemies, as if in sport. Most commonly their cries are *hen, hen,* or *hééééé,* or else *wiiiiii.* They ascribe the origin of these mysteries to a certain superhuman giant whom one of their men wounded in the forehead when they dwelt by the shores of the sea. The man was offended because the giant failed to reply with the customary response, *kwai,* to his polite greeting. To punish the Hurons for this wound, the monster cast among them the apple of discord. After having recommended to them war feasts, *ononharoia,* and this refrain *wiiiii,* he buried himself in the earth and disappeared. Might this indeed have been some infernal spirit?

[2] In the original French, Brébeuf uses the term *brasse,* an old French measure roughly equivalent to an English fathom. One *brasse* was equal to 5 feet, or 1.6 meters.

LAW AND GOVERNMENT

In his chapter on law and political organization, Brébeuf challenges a view commonly held among the political philosophers of early modern Europe: that authority is the essential attribute of government and that, in its absence, humans inevitably descend into a state of violent anarchy. Many of

his readers would have considered the Hurons "savages" and would there-
fore have assumed that they were utterly lacking in restraint. The Jesuit
points out that although the Hurons have no powerful leaders, or even the
concept of submission to authority, they do display a high degree of self-
control and mutual benevolence.

JEAN DE BRÉBEUF

Of the Polity of the Hurons and of Their Government

1636

I do not claim here to put our Indians on the same level as the Chinese, Japanese, and other perfectly civilized nations, but only to distinguish them from the condition of beasts (to which the opinion of some has reduced them) and to rank them among men, and to show that among them there is even some sort of political and civic life. It is quite important, in my opinion, to note that they live assembled in villages, with sometimes as many as fifty, sixty, or a hundred cabins (that is to say, three hundred to four hundred households); that they cultivate the fields, from which they obtain sufficient food to maintain themselves year-round; and that they live together in peace and friendship. I certainly believe that there is not, perhaps, under heaven a nation more praiseworthy in this respect than the Nation of the Bear.[1] Setting aside a few evil-minded persons, such as one meets almost everywhere, they have a gentleness and affability almost incredible for savages. They are not easily annoyed, and, moreover, if they have received wrong from anyone, they often conceal the resentment they feel; at least one finds here very few who allow themselves any display of anger or vengeance.

They maintain such perfect harmony by visiting one another frequently, by helping one another in time of sickness, and by their feasts and their marriage alliances. When they are not busy with their fields, hunting, fishing, or trading, they spend less time in their own cabins than in those of their friends. If they fall sick or desire anything for their health, there is a rivalry as to who will show himself most obliging. If they have any unusually good delicacy, as I have already said, they offer

---

[1] The Attignawantans, or "Nation of the Bear," were one of the four tribes that made up the Huron confederacy.

a feast for their friends and hardly ever eat it alone. In their marriages there is this remarkable custom: They never marry anyone related to them in any way, either directly or collaterally; instead, they always make new marital alliances, which is very helpful in maintaining goodwill. Moreover, by this habit of visiting one another — given that they possess, for the most part, rather good minds — they arouse and influence one another wonderfully.

Consequently, almost none of them are incapable of conversing or of reasoning very well, and in good terms, on matters within their knowledge. The councils, too, held almost every day in the villages on almost all matters, improve their capacity for speaking. Anyone who wishes may be present and may express his opinion, though it is the elders who are in the ascendant and it is their judgment that decides issues. Let it be added also that propriety, courtesy, and civility, which are, as it were, the flower and charm of ordinary human conversation, are not lacking among these people. They call a polite person *Aiendawasti*. To be sure, you do not observe among them any of those hand kissings, compliments, and vain offers of service which do not pass beyond the lips. Yet they do render certain civilities to one another and preserve, through a sense of propriety, various ceremonies in their visits, dances, and feasts. Neglect of such courtesy and propriety would lead to immediate censure, and if anyone made such blunders repeatedly, he would soon become a byword in the village and would lose all his influence.

When they meet, the only salutation they give is to call the other by name, or say "my friend," "my comrade," or "my uncle," if it is an elder. If an Indian finds himself in your cabin when you are eating, and if you present to him a dish of food that you have scarcely touched, he will content himself with tasting it and will hand it back to you. But if you give him a dish for himself, he will not put his hand to it until he has shared it with his companions, and the latter would usually take only a spoonful. Admittedly, these are small things, but they nevertheless demonstrate that these peoples are not quite so rude and unpolished as one might suppose.

Furthermore, if laws are like the governing wheel regulating a community — or, to be more exact, are the soul of a commonwealth — it seems to me that, in view of the perfect understanding that reigns among them, I am right in maintaining that they are not without laws. They punish murderers, thieves, traitors, and witches, and although they are not as severe with murderers as their ancestors were, still there is little disorder in this connection. This leads me to conclude that their procedure is scarcely less effective than is the death penalty in other places.

The relatives of the deceased not only prosecute the individual who committed the murder but address their complaint to his entire village, which must make restitution. For this purpose, they must provide up to sixty presents as soon as possible, the least of which must be the value of one new beaver robe. The captain presents these himself in person, and makes a long harangue at each present that he offers, so that entire days sometimes pass in this ceremony. There are two sorts of presents. The first nine, which they call *andaonhaan,* are put into the hands of the relatives to make peace and to take away from their hearts all bitterness and desire for vengeance that they might feel toward the person of the murderer. Others are placed on a pole which is raised above the head of the corpse, and are called *Andaerraehaan,* which means "that which is put on the pole." Each of these presents has a special name. There are those of the first nine, which are the most considerable, sometimes consisting of a thousand porcelain beads each.

The captain, raising his voice in the name of the guilty person, and holding in his hand the first present, speaks as if the hatchet were still in the death wound: *Condayee onsahachoutawas:* "Here," says he, "is what he uses to withdraw the hatchet from the wound, and makes it fall from the hands of him who would wish to avenge this injury." At the second present [he says], *Condayee oscotaweanon,* "There is something with which he wipes away the blood from the wound in his head." By these two presents he signifies his regret for having killed him, and that he would be quite ready to restore him to life, if it were possible.

Yet, as if the blow had rebounded on their native land, and as if the country had received the greatest wound, he adds the third present, saying, *Condayee onsahondechari,* "This is to restore the country." [At the fourth present he says,] *Condayee onsahondwaronti, etotonhwentsiai,* "This is to put a stone upon the opening and the cleft in the ground that was made by this murder."

Metaphor is largely in use among these peoples, and unless you accustom yourself to it, you will understand nothing in their councils, where they speak almost entirely in metaphors. They claim by this fourth present to reunite all hearts and wills, and even entire villages, which have become estranged. For it is not here as it is in France and elsewhere, where the public and a whole city do not generally take part in the quarrel of an individual. Here you cannot insult any one of them without the whole country resenting it and taking up the quarrel against you, and even against an entire village. Hence arise wars, and it is more than sufficient reason for taking arms against some village if it refuses to make satisfaction by proper presents for the killing of one of your friends.

The fifth present is made to smooth the roads and to clear away the brushwood: *Condayee onsa hannonkiai,* that is to say, "In order that one may go henceforth in perfect security over the roads, and from village to village." The four others are addressed immediately to the relatives, to console them in their affliction and to wipe away their tears. *Condayee onsa hoheronti:* "Behold," says he, "here is something for him or her to smoke," speaking of his father or his mother, or of the one who would avenge his death. They believe that there is nothing so suitable as tobacco to appease the passions; that is why they never attend a council without a pipe, or calumet, in their mouths. The smoke, they say, gives them intelligence and enables them to see clearly through the most intricate matters. Also, following this present, they offer a seventh to completely restore the mind of the offended person: *Condayee onsa hondionroenkhra.* The eighth is to give a beverage to the mother of the deceased, and to heal her of the serious illness caused by the death of her son: *Condayee onsa aweannoncwa d'ocweton.* Finally, the ninth is, as it were, to stretch out a mat for her, on which she may rest herself and sleep during the time of her mourning: *Condayee onsa hohiendaen.*

These are the principal presents; the others are, as it were, an excess of consolation and represent all the things that the dead man would use during life. One will be called his robe, another his belt, another his canoe, another his paddle, his net, his bow, his arrows, and so on. After this, the relatives of the deceased regard themselves as perfectly satisfied.

Long ago, the parties did not come to terms so easily and at so little expense. In addition to these presents paid for by the public, the guilty person was obliged to endure an indignity and punishment that some will perhaps consider almost as terrible as death itself. The dead body was placed upon poles, and the murderer was compelled to remain underneath so that all the putrid matter which exuded from the corpse fell upon him. Then they put beside him a dish of food, which was soon filled with the filth and corrupt blood which little by little fell into it, and merely to get the dish pushed back ever so little would cost him a present of seven hundred beads, which they called *hassaendista.* The murderer remained in this position as long as the relatives of the deceased pleased. Even then, to escape it he had to make a rich present called *akhiateandista.* If, however, the relatives of the dead man avenged themselves for this injury by the death of him who struck the blow, all the punishment fell on them, and they also had to make presents to those who were the first murderers, without the latter being obliged to give any satisfaction. This is to show how much they regard vengeance as detestable, for the blackest crimes, such as murder, appear as nothing in comparison with it. Vengeance wipes them all away and brings upon itself all the punishment that they merit. So much for murder. Wounding also has to be healed by presents, such as necklaces or hatchets, depending on how serious the wound is.

They also punish sorcerers (that is, those who use poison or cause death by spells) severely, and this punishment is authorized by the consent of the whole country, so that whoever catches them in the act has full right to cleave their skulls and rid the world of them, without fear of being apprehended or obliged to give any satisfaction for it.

As for thieves, they are not tolerated, even though the country remains full of them. If you find anyone possessed of anything that belongs to you, you can in good conscience play the despoiled king and take what is yours, and [anything else besides], leaving him as naked as your hand. If he is fishing, you can take his canoe, his nets, his fish, his robe, all he has. It is true that in such cases the strongest prevails; still, such is the custom of the country, and it certainly holds some to their duty.

Besides having some sort of laws maintained among themselves, there is also a certain order established as regards foreign nations. Firstly, concerning commerce, several families have their own private trade, and the first man who discovers it is considered master of a trade route. The children share the rights of their parents in this respect, as do those who bear the same name. No one else goes into it without permission, and this is given only in consideration of presents. The master allows only as many or as few as he wishes to share in the trade. If he has a good supply of merchandise, it is to his advantage to go trading with only a few companions, for thus he secures all that he desires in the country [where he goes to trade]. It is this [ownership of trade routes] which constitutes their most prized possession, and, if anyone should be bold enough to pursue trade without permission of the owner, doing his best to transact business in secret, and if he is surprised en route, he will be treated as no better than a thief. He will carry nothing back to his house but his own body, unless he is accompanied by a strong escort, in which case he may return safely with his baggage. There will be complaints but no further prosecution.

Even in wars, where confusion often reigns, they do not fail to keep some order. They never undertake war without reason, and the commonest reason for taking up arms is when some nation refuses to give satisfaction for the death of someone and fails to furnish the presents required by the agreements made between them. They take this refusal as an act of hostility, and the whole country embraces the quarrel. In particular, the relatives of the dead person consider themselves obliged in honor to resent it and raise a force to attack the perpetrators. (I shall not speak of their conduct in war, nor of their military discipline. That is better treated by Monsieur de Champlain, who was personally involved and held command among them. Moreover, he has spoken of it fully and very pertinently, as in all matters which concern the manners of these barbarous nations.[2] I will only say that if God gives them the grace to embrace the faith, I shall change and reform some of their procedures.)

It begins with an individual who raises a band of young men who gather, so it seems, for the purpose of avenging a private quarrel and the death of a friend, rather than for the honor and preservation of the nation. Then, if they succeed in capturing some of their enemies, they treat them with all the cruelty they can devise. Five or six days will sometimes pass in satiating their rage, burning the prisoners over a slow fire, and, not satisfied with seeing their skins entirely roasted, they cut open the legs, the thighs, the arms, and the most fleshy parts of the body and thrust into the wounds glowing brands or red-hot hatchets. Sometimes in the midst of these torments they compel them to sing — those who have the strength do so hurling forth a thousand imprecations against those who torment them.

On the day of their death they must repeat the performance, if they have strength, and sometimes the kettle in which they are to be boiled will be on the fire, while these poor wretches are still singing as loudly as they can. This inhumanity is altogether intolerable; indeed, many people are unwilling to attend these fatal banquets. After having at last brained the victim, if he was a brave man, they tear out his heart, roast it on the coals, and distribute pieces of it to the young men, as they think that this makes them courageous. Some make an incision in their own neck and cause some of his blood to run into it. They say that mingling the blood in this way has the power to ensure that they can never be surprised by the enemy, as they will always be aware of their approach, however secret it may be.

They put him in the kettle piece by piece, and although at other feasts the head — whether of a bear, a dog, a deer, or a large fish — is reserved

<hr />

[2] Samuel de Champlain, soldier, explorer, and founder of the French colony of Canada, wrote extensively about the native nations, particularly the Hurons, whom he accompanied during several expeditions against the Iroquois. Somewhat baffled by a native culture of warfare that emphasized individual initiative rather than authoritarian discipline, conceal-ment and surprise rather than open maneuvers, and the taking of prisoners rather than the capture of territory, he judged the Hurons deficient soldiers. See H. P. Biggar, ed., *The Works of Samuel de Champlain* (Toronto: Champlain Society, 1929), 3:53–79.

for the captain, in this case the head is given to the lowe
company. Indeed, some people are horrified to taste thi.
other portion of the body, whereas others eat it with pleas
seen Indians in our cabin speak with gusto of the flesh of an Iro
praise its quality in the same terms as they would praise the fle
deer or a moose. This is certainly very cruel, but we hope, with ti.
sistance of Heaven, that the knowledge of the true God will entirely b.
ish from this country such barbarity.

For the security of the country, they surround the principal villages
with a strong palisade of stakes, in order to sustain a siege. They maintain paid informants in the neutral nations, and even among enemy nations, by means of whom they are secretly warned of any plots. They are,
indeed, so careful and circumspect on this point that if there is some
tribe with whom they have not entirely broken, they allow them complete freedom of movement through their country. Nevertheless, for
greater security, they assign them to special cabins, to which they must
retire. If they were found elsewhere, they would be treated severely.

As regards the authority of commanding, here is what I have observed. All the affairs of the Hurons come under one of two headings:
The first are essentially affairs of state — whether they concern either
citizens or foreigners, the public or the individuals of a village — such as
feasts, dances, games, lacrosse matches, and funeral ceremonies. The
second are affairs of war. There are different captains for each of these
affairs. In the large villages there will be sometimes several captains, for
both civil administration and for war, and they divide among themselves
the families of the village into so many captaincies. One even finds captains to whom all these governments report, because their intelligence,
popularity, wealth, or other qualities have made them particularly
influential in the country. There are none, however, chosen to be greater
than the others. The first rank is held by those who have acquired it by
their intelligence, eloquence, magnificence, courage, and wise conduct.
Consequently, the affairs of the village are referred principally to which-
ever of the captains possesses these qualifications. The same is true with
regard to the affairs of the whole country, in which the men of greatest
intelligence are the leading captains. Usually there is one only who bears
the burden of all, and it is in his name treaties of peace are made with foreign peoples. Even the country bears his name: For example, when one
speaks of *Anenkhiondic* in foreign councils, it is understood to mean the
Nation of the Bear. Formerly only worthy men were captains, and so
they were called *Enondecha,* the same name by which they call the country, nation, or region, as if a good captain and the country were one and

ᴇ same thing. But today they are not as careful in the selection of their ᴘtains, and so they no longer give them that name, although they still ᴀll them *atiwarontas, atiwanens, ondakhienhai,* "big stones, the elders, the sedentary ones." Nevertheless, as I have said, the men who hold the first rank in the local affairs of the villages, as well as in those of the whole country, are still those who have the greatest merit and intelligence. Their relatives are like so many lieutenants and councillors.

They reach this degree of honor partly through succession and partly through election. Their children do not usually succeed them, but rather their nephews and grandsons. The latter do not inherit these petty royalties, like the dauphins of France or children inheriting from their fathers. Instead, they are accepted by the whole country only if they possess the proper personal qualifications and agree to accept the position. There are some men who refuse these honors, either because they lack aptitude in speaking or sufficient discretion or patience, or because they like a quiet life, for these positions entail service more than anything else. A captain must always be ready to heed the call of duty. If a council is held five or six leagues away for the affairs of the country, he must go, winter or summer, and whatever the weather. If there is an assembly in the village, it takes place in the captain's cabin, and if there is anything to be made public, he must announce it. The very limited authority he usually has over his subjects is not a powerful attraction to make him accept this position. These captains do not govern their subjects by means of command and absolute power, as they have no force at hand to compel them to their duty. Their government is only civil, and they merely represent what is to be done for the good of the village or of the whole country. Beyond that, everyone does as they please. There are, however, some who know well how to secure obedience, especially when they possess the affection of their subjects. Some, too, are kept from these positions because of the memory of ancestors who have served the country badly. Captains are accepted only by dint of presents that the elders accept in their assembly and put into the public coffers. Once a year, in the springtime, these resuscitations of captains take place, unless some special cases delay or hasten the matter. I should like here to ask those who have a low opinion of our Indians, what they think of this method of conducting affairs. . . .

JEAN DE BRÉBEUF

Of the Order the Hurons Observe in Their Councils

1636

. . . All having arrived, they take their seats, each in his own quarter of the cabin, those of the same village or of the same nation near one another in order to consult together. If it happens that someone is absent, the question is raised as to whether the assembly would still be legitimate, and sometimes the absence of one or two persons leads to the whole gathering being dissolved and adjourned to another time. But if all are gathered, or if, notwithstanding, they think it their duty to proceed, the council is opened. It is not always the chiefs of the council who do this, as they can be excused on grounds of difficulty in speaking, indisposition, or even their dignity.

After salutations, thanks for the trouble taken in coming, thanksgivings rendered (I know not to whom) that everyone has arrived without accident, that no one has been surprised by enemies, nor has fallen into any stream or river, nor has been injured — in brief, that everyone has arrived well — all are exhorted to deliberate maturely. Then the affair to be discussed is brought forward, and the distinguished councillors are asked to give their advice.

At this point, the deputies of each village or nation consult in a low tone as to what they will reply. Then, when they have consulted well together, they give their opinions in order and decide according to the plurality of opinions. In all this, some things are worthy of remark. The first is their manner of speaking, which is unlike common speech and has a special name: *acwentonch.* It is common to all Indians; they raise and quaver the voice, like the tones of a preacher in olden times, but slowly, decidedly, and distinctly. They even repeat the same argument several times. The second remarkable thing is that the persons giving their opinions summarize the issue, as well as all the previous arguments, before giving their own views.

An interpreter once told me that these nations had a private language in their councils, but I have learned by experience that this is not so. I know that they do have some special terms, as there are in all kinds of arts and sciences, and as there are in the palaces, the schools, and so on.

JR 10:254–61, Jean de Brébeuf, *Relation of 1636.*

It is true that their speeches are at first very difficult to understand, on account of an infinity of metaphors, circumlocutions, and other rhetorical devices. For example, speaking of the Nation of the Bear, they will say, "The bear has said such and such, or has done so and so, or the bear is cunning, is bad, or the hands of the bear are dangerous." When they speak of the man who arranges the Feast of the Dead, they say "he who eats souls," and when they speak of a nation, they often name only the principal captain. Thus, speaking of the Montagnais, they will say, "Atsirond says: . . . ," using the name of one of their captains. In short, it is in these ways that they elevate their style of language and try to speak well. Almost all of them have minds that are naturally sound; they reason very clearly and do not stumble in their speeches, and so they make a point of mocking those who trip over their tongues. Some of them seem to be born orators.

After someone has given his opinion, the head of the council repeats, or causes to be repeated, what he has said. Consequently, matters must be clearly understood, so often are they repeated. This was very fortunate for me, since, at the council [mentioned in another part of the *Relation*] where I made them a present to encourage them to take the road to Heaven, one of the captains repeated what I had said, and dilated upon it and amplified it better than I had done, and in better terms. In truth, owing to our limited knowledge of this language, we say not what we wish but what we can.

Each speaker ends his speech with these words: *Condayauendi ierhayde cha nonhwicwahachen,* which means, "That is my thought on the subject under discussion," and then the whole assembly responds with a very strong respiration drawn from the pit of the stomach, *haau.* I have noticed that when anyone has spoken to their liking, this *haau* is given forth with much more effort.

Another remarkable thing is their great prudence and moderation of speech. I would not dare to say they always practice self-restraint, for I know that sometimes they sting each other, yet you always remark a singular gentleness and discretion. I have not attended many of their councils, but every time I have been invited, I have come away astonished at this feature. . . .

THE HURON FEAST OF THE DEAD

The climax of the "Huron" Relation comes with this splendid description of the great Feast of the Dead, a ceremony that united (in theory) all the Huron people approximately every twelve years. Brébeuf was privileged to witness a solemn Feast of the Dead in 1636, and his account of that event is written in the form of a first-person narrative, rather than in the more impersonal, encyclopedic style he maintains in other chapters. He makes no attempt to disguise the fact that he was impressed by the spectacle surrounding the mass interment in a central grave of the bones of deceased villagers brought from all corners of Huronia. In contrast with his accounts of other "pagan ceremonies," the editorial comments punctuating this one are almost all favorable. Brébeuf seemingly was swept away by the elaborately orchestrated pageantry of the ritual. His positive portrait also can be attributed to his Counter Reformation religious sensibility, with its weakness for images of skeletons, putrefying corpses and everything calculated to give Christians a vivid reminder of what the future had in store for their bodies. In this connection, he valued the Huron ceremony for the lessons it inadvertently provided for Christians. As far as the natives themselves were concerned and the prospects for conversion, Brébeuf found encouragement in every aspect of Huron mourning customs, for all the affection and care lavished on the remains of dead relatives constituted, in his mind, so many signs of belief in an afterlife. His expectation in 1636 was that people who recognized the immortality of the soul in general terms could not fail eventually to see the need for Christian salvation.

JEAN DE BRÉBEUF

Of the Solemn Feast of the Dead

1636

The Feast of the Dead is the most renowned ceremony among the Hurons. They call it a feast because, as I shall now fully relate, when the bodies are taken from their cemeteries, each captain makes a feast for the souls in his village. The most considerable and most magnificent ceremony is that of the master of the feast, who is for that reason called, par excellence, the master of ceremonies.

JR 10:278–303, Jean de Brébeuf, *Relation of 1636.*

General Feast of the Dead among the Huron and Iroquois
A European engraver created this image from the description provided by the
Jesuit author, Joseph-François Lafitau, in his book, *Customs of the American In-
dians Compared with the Customs of Primitive Times* (1724).
Courtesy of the Newberry Library, Chicago.

This feast abounds in ceremonies, but you might say that the principal ceremony is that of the kettle. Because the latter is so important, the Feast of the Dead is hardly ever mentioned, even in the most important councils, except under the name of "the kettle." They appropriate to it all the terms of cookery, so that, in speaking of hastening or of postponing the Feast of the Dead, they will speak of stirring up, or of dampening, the fire beneath the kettle, and, employing this way of speaking, one who should say, "The kettle is overturned," would mean that there would be no Feast of the Dead. . . .

Twelve years or thereabouts having elapsed, the elders and notables of the country assemble to decide on a definite time to hold the feast that will be convenient for the whole country and the foreign nations that may be invited. Once the decision is taken, preparations are made to transport all the bodies to the village where the common grave is located, each family seeing to its dead with a care and affection that can hardly be described. If they have relatives who died in any other part of the country, they spare no trouble in fetching them. They take them from the cemeteries, bear them on their shoulders, and cover them with the finest robes they have.

In each village they choose a fair day and proceed to the cemetery, where those called *Aiheonde,* who had charge of the funerals, take the bodies from the tombs in the presence of the relatives, as the latter renew their tears and feel afresh the grief they had on the day of the funeral. I was present at this spectacle and willingly invited all our servants, for I do not think one could see in the world a more vivid picture or more perfect representation of what man is. It is true that in France our cemeteries preach a powerful message and that all those bones piled up one upon another without discrimination — those of the poor with those of the rich, those of the mean with those of the great — are so many voices continually proclaiming to us the thought of death, the vanity of the things of this world, and contempt for earthly life. Still, it seems to me that what our Indians do on this occasion touches us still more and makes us see more closely and apprehend more vividly our wretched state. For, having opened the graves, they display before you all these corpses, and they leave them thus exposed in a public place long enough for the spectators to learn, once and for all, what they will be someday.

The flesh of some is quite gone, and there is only a sort of parchment on their bones; other bodies look as if they had been dried and smoked, and show scarcely any signs of putrefaction; and still others are swarming with worms. When the relatives have gazed upon the bodies to their satisfaction, they cover them with handsome new beaver robes. Finally, after a time, they strip them of their flesh, taking off skin and flesh that they throw into the fire along with the robes and mats in which the bodies were wrapped. They leave the bodies of the recently dead in the state in which they are, simply covering them with new robes.

Of the latter, they had [in this village] only one old man, of whom I have spoken before, who died this autumn on his return from fishing: This swollen corpse had only begun to decay a month ago, with the first warmth of spring. The worms were swarming all over it, and the corruption that oozed out of it gave forth an almost intolerable stench, and yet they had the courage to take away the robe in which it was enveloped, clean it as well as they could, and, taking it up in their bare hands, put the body into a fresh mat and robe, and all this without showing any horror at the corruption.

Is that not a noble example to inspire Christians, who ought to have much more elevated thoughts, to undertake acts of charity and works of mercy toward others? After that, who would be afraid of the stench of a hospital, and who would not take special pleasure in finding himself at the feet of a sick man all covered with sores, in the person of whom he beholds the Son of God?

As they had to remove the flesh from all these carcasses, they discovered that two bodies contained a kind of amulet. One of these I saw myself, a turtle's egg with a leather strap, and the other, which some of our fathers handled, was a little turtle the size of a nut. These excited the belief that they had been bewitched and that there were witches in our village, which led some people to decide to leave at once. Indeed, two or three days later, one of the richest men, fearing that some harm would come to him, moved his cabin to a place two leagues from us, to the village of Arontaen.

The bones having been well cleaned, they put some of them into bags, some into fur robes, loaded them on their shoulders, and covered these packages with another beautiful hanging robe. As for the whole bodies, they put them on a sort of litter and carried them with all the others, each into his cabin, where each family made a feast to its dead.

Returning from this feast with a captain (who is very intelligent and who will someday be very influential in the affairs of the country), I asked him why they called the bones of the dead *Atisken*. He gave me the best explanation he could, and I gathered from his conversation that many of them think we have two souls, both of them being divisible and material, and yet both reasonable. One of them separates itself from the body at death yet remains in the cemetery until the Feast of the Dead, after which either it changes into a dove or, according to a common belief, it goes away at once to the village of souls. The other is more attached to the body and, in a sense, provides information to the corpse. It remains in the grave after the feast and never leaves, unless someone bears it again as a child. He pointed out to me, as proof of this metempsychosis,[1] the perfect resemblance some people have to a deceased person. A fine philosophy, indeed! That, at any rate, is why they call the bones of the dead *Atisken,* "the souls."

A day or two before setting out for the feast, they carried all these souls into one of the largest cabins of the village, where some of them were hung on the cabin poles and the rest were put on display inside. The captain entertained them and made them a magnificent feast in the name of a deceased captain, whose name he bore. I was present at this feast of souls and noticed four things in particular there. First, the presents which the relatives made for the feast, and which consisted of robes, beaded necklaces, and kettles, were strung on poles along both sides of the cabin. Secondly, the captain sang the song of the deceased captain, just as the latter had asked it to be sung on this occasion. Thirdly, all the guests were allowed to help themselves to any of the dishes and could even take food home with them, contrary to the usual custom at feasts. Fourthly, at the end of the feast, by way of compliment to the man who had entertained them, they imitated what they call the call of the souls and went out of the cabin crying *haéé, haé.*

The master of the feast, and even Anenkhiondic, chief captain of the whole country, sent several pressing invitations to us. You might say that the feast would not have been a success without us. I sent two of our fathers, several days beforehand, to view the preparations and to find out the exact date of the feast. Anenkhiondic gave them a very hearty welcome, and on their departure conducted them himself to see the pit a quarter of a league from the village, showing them, with great demonstrations of affection, all the preparations for the feast.

The feast was to take place on the Saturday of Pentecost, but some problems arose, and, because of uncertainty about the weather, it was postponed until Monday. The seven or eight days before the feast were spent in assembling the souls, as well as the foreigners who had been invited. Meanwhile, from morning until night, the living were continually making presents to the young people, in consideration of the dead. In one place, women were shooting with the bow for a prize, which was a quillwork belt, or a necklace or string of beads. In other parts of the village, the young men were throwing batons. The prize for victory in this

---

[1] The passing of the soul from one body to another after death.

contest was an ax, some knives, or even a beaver robe. Every day more souls arrived. It is heartening to see these processions, sometimes of two or three hundred persons, everyone carrying their souls — in other words, their bones — done up in parcels on their backs and under a handsome robe, as I indicated above. Some had arranged their parcels in the form of a man, ornamented with beaded necklaces and elegant garlands of long red fur. On setting out from the village, the whole band cried out *haéé, haé,* and repeated this cry of the souls along the way. According to them, this cry greatly consoles them. Without it, this burden of souls would weigh very heavily on their backs and cause them a pain in the sides for the rest of their lives.

They go in short stages. Our village took three days to cover the four leagues to Ossossané (which we call La Rochelle), where the ceremonies were to take place. As they near a village, they cry again *haéé, haé,* and the whole village comes to meet them, and many more gifts are given on this occasion. Everyone has his prearranged place in one of the cabins, and everyone knows where his souls are to be lodged, and so it is done without confusion. At the same time, the captains hold a council to discuss how long the band shall sojourn in the village.

All the souls of eight or nine villages had reached La Rochelle by the Saturday of Pentecost, but the fear of bad weather compelled them, as I said, to postpone the ceremony until Monday. We were lodged a quarter of a league away, at the old village, in a cabin where there were fully a hundred souls attached and hung upon the poles, some of which smelled a little stronger than musk.

About noon on Monday, they came to inform us that we should hold ourselves in readiness, for they were going to begin the ceremony. The bundled-up souls were then taken down, the relatives unwrapped them to say their last adieus, and then the tears flowed afresh. I admired the tenderness of one woman, the daughter of a captain who was a very important man in the country before he died at an advanced age, toward her dead father and children. She combed the hair of her father and handled his bones, one after the other, with as much affection as if she wished to restore him to life. She placed by his side his *Atsatonewai,* that is, his package of council sticks, which are all the books and papers of the country. As for her little children, she put beaded bracelets on their arms and bathed their bones with her tears. The others could scarcely tear her away, but they insisted, as it was time to depart. The man who bore the body of this old captain walked at the head; the men followed and then the women, walking in this order until they reached the pit.

Let me describe the arrangement of this place. It was about the size of the Place Royale in Paris. There was in the middle of it a great pit, about ten feet deep and five fathoms in diameter. All around it was a scaffold and a well-constructed sort of theater, nine or ten fathoms in diameter and nine or ten feet high. Above this staging rose many poles, trimmed and well arranged, with cross poles to attach the bundles of souls. Since the whole bodies were to go in the bottom of the pit, they had been placed the preceding day at the edge of the hole, under the scaffold, stretched out upon bark or mats fastened to stakes at about the height of a man.

People arrived with their corpses at about one in the afternoon and divided themselves into their different cantons, and subdivided by family and village. They laid on the ground their parcels of souls, almost as earthen pots are displayed [in France] at a village fair. They unfolded also their bundles of robes and all the presents they had brought, and placed them upon poles, which extended from 500 to 600 fathoms [2,500 to 3,000 feet], so there were as many as twelve hundred presents. These remained thus on exhibition two full hours, in order to give foreigners time to view the wealth and magnificence of the country. I did not find the crowds as numerous as I had expected; probably there were no more than two thousand persons. About three o'clock, everyone put away their various articles and folded up their robes.

Meanwhile, each captain took his turn to give the signal [to his people], and immediately they came running, all loaded with their bundles of souls, as if assaulting a town. They climbed to the theater on the ladders hung all round it, and hung their packages on the poles, each village having its designated section. That done, all the ladders were taken away, but a few captains remained there and spent the rest of the afternoon until seven o'clock announcing the presents, which were made in the name of the dead to certain specified persons.

"This," said they, "is what such and such a dead man gives to such and such a relative." About five or six o'clock, they lined the bottom and sides of the pit with fine, large, new robes, each of ten beaver skins, in such a way that the robes extended more than a foot out of it. As they were preparing the robes that were to be employed for this purpose, some people went down to the bottom and brought up handfuls of sand. I asked what this ceremony meant and learned that they believe that this sand helps them win at games of chance. Of those twelve hundred presents that had been displayed, forty-eight robes served to line the bottom and sides of the pit; and each whole body, besides the robe in which it had been wrapped, had another one, and sometimes even two more, to cover it. . . .

At seven o'clock, they took the whole bodies down into the pit. We had the greatest difficulty in getting near. Nothing has ever depicted for me so well the confusion there is among the damned. On all sides you could have seen them unloading half-decayed bodies, and on all sides was heard a horrible din of confused voices of people speaking without making themselves understood. Ten or twelve men were in the pit arranging the bodies side by side all around them. In the very middle of the pit, they put three large kettles, which could be of use only to souls: One had a hole through it, another had no handle, and the third was in no better condition. I saw very few beaded necklaces, though it is true that they put many on the bodies. This is all that was done on that day.

All the people passed the night on the spot. They lighted many fires to cook their meals. We withdrew for the night to the old village, intending to return the next morning at daybreak, when they were to throw the bones into the pit. But an accident occurred, and, as a result, we did not arrive in time, though we made great haste. One of the souls, which was not securely tied or was perhaps too heavy for the cord that fastened it, had fallen into the pit. This noise awakened the company, who immediately ran and crowded up on the scaffold, where they emptied indiscriminately all the bundles into the pit, though they kept the robes in which they had been wrapped. We had only set out from the village at that time, but the noise was so great that it seemed almost as if we were there. As we drew near, we saw nothing less than an image of Hell. The large space was quite full of fires and flames, and the air resounded in all directions with the confused voices of these barbarians. Eventually, the noise ceased and they began to sing, but in tones so sorrowful and lugubrious that it represented to us the horrible sadness and the abyss of despair into which these unhappy souls are forever plunged.

Almost everything had been thrown in by the time we arrived, for it was done almost in the blink of an eye; everyone had been in a great hurry, thinking there would not be room enough for all the souls. However, we saw enough of it to judge of the rest. There were five or six men in the pit, using poles to arrange the bones. When the pit was within about two feet of being full, they turned back over the bones the robes that bordered the edge of the pit, and covered the remaining space with mats and bark. Then, in no special pattern, they heaped the pit with sand, poles, and wooden stakes. Some women brought some dishes of corn, and that day, and the following days, several cabins of the village provided baskets full of it, which were thrown upon the pit.

We have fifteen or twenty Christians interred with these infidels. We said for their souls a *De profundis,* with a strong hope that, if divine benevolence continues to shower its blessings upon these peoples, this festival will cease to be held, or will only be for Christians, and will take place with ceremonies as sacred as the ones we saw are foolish and useless. They are even now beginning to be a burden to them, on account of the excesses and superfluous expenses connected with them.

The whole morning passed in gift giving. Most of the robes in which the souls had been wrapped were cut into pieces and thrown from the height of the theater into the midst of the crowd, for anyone who could get them. It was very amusing when two or three people seized hold of a beaver skin, for then it had to be cut into as many pieces, and thus they found themselves almost empty-handed, for the fragment was scarcely worth the picking up. I admired the enterprising ingenuity of one Indian: Instead of running after these flying pelts, he would approach people disputing possession of a skin and offer them some tobacco, a precious commodity in short supply in the country this year, and thus he settled the matter to his own profit and advantage.

Before going away from the place, we learned that on the night they had made presents to foreign nations on behalf of the master of the feast, our names had been mentioned. And indeed, as we were going away, Anenkhiondic came to present to us a new robe of ten beaver skins, in return for the necklace [wampum] that I had given them as a present in open council to open for them the way to heaven. They had felt themselves under such obligation for this gift that they wished to demonstrate their gratitude at a great assembly. I did not accept it, however, telling him that, as we had made this present only to lead them to embrace our faith, they could not render us greater service than by listening to us and believe in Him who made all things. He asked me then what I desired he should do with the robe, and I replied that he might dispose of it as he wished, which perfectly satisfied him. . . .

3

Disease and Medicine

The *Jesuit Relations* are a good source of information on the spread of old-world diseases among the native populations of North America, a tragic and crucially important dimension of the history of early European contact. They are even more valuable for the light they shed on Indian and European views of sickness and health in the seventeenth century and on these cultures' respective approaches to combating disease. Although the Jesuits seldom attempted to quantify the population loss through epidemics (which historians now estimate at upwards of 50 percent), their anecdotes and reports of "flourishing villages" transformed into "hospitals" help us grasp the immense suffering that ensued when Indians first encountered the germs and viruses that were the Old World's invisible agents of conquest. We now know that diseases such as smallpox, influenza, and measles can have a devastating effect on populations that have never been exposed to them. Unlike the natives of North America, Europeans of the seventeenth century carried acquired immunity in their bloodstreams. Thus they were much less likely to contract these familiar diseases, and when they did fall ill, they tended to recover more readily than the unprotected Indians.

The Jesuits of New France knew nothing of germs, viruses, and immunity. Though knowledgeable by the standards of their day, they lived centuries before modern science systematically classified diseases, discovered how they spread, and developed preventive and curative drugs. They brought to New France various medicines, including sugar, widely regarded as a cure-all in the seventeenth century, and they were eager to learn about native herbal remedies as well. They also had recourse to the surgeon's art in serious cases, bleeding their colleagues or prescribing purges, treatments based on the prevalent theory that illness resulted from an excess of fluids in the body. The Jesuits did not see themselves as doctors, however. Their priority was saving souls, and when epidemics struck, they put most of their efforts into baptizing the dying rather than relieving the suffering of the living — a strategy that did not make a favorable impression on their native hosts.

As the Jesuits struggled to explain to their readers, and to themselves, the terrible epidemics that devastated the nations of North America, they tended to focus more on the ultimate question of why, rather than on the immediate question of how, disease spread. Seeing individuals and whole nations struck low, they perceived signs of God's plan to punish the wicked, test the resolution of the virtuous, or simply gather souls to heaven. Since God worked through nature, explanations could be found in both religion and science, just as relief could be sought through prayer and medicine.

Native peoples such as the Hurons, who are featured in most of the documents that follow, also attributed illness to both natural and supernatural causes, though they did not separate the two as rigidly as did Christians. Their spiritual/medical specialists (shamans) had no aim other than to help the sick recover, and they approached the task with a wide array of therapeutic techniques. Often they administered medicines derived from the roots, bark, or leaves of particular plants and trees. Many native healers were skilled at setting broken bones, and others could perform surgery to extract arrows and bullets from wounded warriors. The Jesuits mention these achievements in passing but do not dwell on them, as such "natural" medicines did not trouble the missionaries. By contrast, accounts of other types of healing procedures that were tinged with non-Christian spirituality ("superstition") occupy a major portion of the *Relations,* mainly because the Jesuits regarded these techniques with horrified fascination.

Many Huron medical procedures, as described in the *Relations,* involved the mind as well as the body, for these natives did not see illness as a purely physical problem. With what seems today a rather sophisticated appreciation of the interconnection of feelings, attitudes, and bodily well-being, they would frequently try to cure sickness through ceremonies that recognized and gave dramatic expression to a person's repressed desires. Although the Jesuits report on these rituals in wonderful detail, they had little understanding of the psychological dynamics involved and were shocked by the eroticism that often surfaced.

Equally surprising to the missionaries was the collective dimension of Huron medicine. In Europe, illness was an individual problem, and the sick person inhabited a narrowly bounded sphere into which, ideally, only the doctor and family caregivers were admitted. As much as possible, the patient was isolated from the noise and bustle of normal life. The Hurons, by contrast, kept their sick in the midst of the busy longhouse environment. More fundamentally, they conceived of the patient as an integral part of larger collectivities: family, household, clan, village.

Thus many curative rituals involved that larger society, whether in feasting, playing games of chance, bestowing presents, or otherwise participating in the healing of the sick.

The Jesuits' disapproval of most aspects of native medicine is quite apparent in the selections that follow, and the contrast with their rather positive view of the Indians' funeral customs is quite striking. Even though the missionaries sometimes mocked native therapies (with unintended irony, in view of their own reliance on techniques such as bleeding), their disapproval did not stem from a concern that these were ineffective. On the contrary, they worried most when "pagan ceremonies" did cure illness. Since a spiritual element pervaded so much of Huron medicine, success suggested the assistance of supernatural forces that, because they did not derive from God, must be diabolical. Apart from their fundamental opposition to devil worship, the Jesuits also objected to native curing customs as an obstacle to conversion, since many Hurons who showed a promising interest in Christianity reverted to "infidelity" when they had medical problems.

HURON MEDICAL PRACTICES

The selections in this chapter begin with some general observations on Huron medical practices taken from Jean de Brébeuf's Relation of 1636. Also included are two excerpts from Father Jérôme Lalemant's Relation of 1639. One of these discusses the use of gambling to cure disease, while the other describes ondinonc, *the treatment of ailments by addressing repressed desires.*

JEAN DE BRÉBEUF
[Cure by Lacrosse][1]
1636

The *aoutaerohi* is a remedy for only one particular kind of disease, which they also call *aoutaerohi*. This term comes from the name of a little demon as large as the fist, which they say is in the body of the sick person, especially in the part that pains him. They find out that they are sick with

[1] Brackets indicate that the three titles in this section of Chapter 3 were inserted by the editor.

this disease by means of a dream, or by the intervention of some sorcerer. One day I went to visit a woman who thought herself sick of *aoutaerohi,* and when I assigned another cause for her illness and laughed at her *aoutaerohi,* she called out to this demon, *aoutaerohi hechrio Kihenkhon: "aoutaerohi,* I pray you that this man may know who you are and that you will make him feel the ills that you make me suffer." To drive away this demon, they make feasts accompanied with songs, which very few of them know how to sing properly. . . .

There are as many as twelve kinds of dances that constitute the many sovereign remedies for sickness. Only a dream or else the *Arendiowane,* or sorcerer, can determine whether this or that is the proper remedy for a given disease.

Of three types of games that are popular among these peoples — lacrosse, dish, and straw — the first two, they say, are wonderful for the health. Is this not worthy of compassion? Imagine a poor sick person, fevered of body and almost dying, and some miserable sorcerer prescribes, as a cooling remedy, a game of lacrosse! Or perhaps the patient himself has dreamed that he must die unless the whole country plays lacrosse for his health. Then, no matter how insignificant the person may be, you will see a fine field where village contends against village for lacrosse supremacy, with wagers of beaver robes and beaded necklaces spurring them on.

Sometimes, also, one of these shamans will say that the whole country is sick, and he calls for a game of lacrosse to heal it. No more needs to be said; word quickly spreads, and all the captains of every village order that all the young men do their duty in this respect; otherwise some great misfortune will befall the whole country. The game of dish is also greatly valued for medical purposes, especially if the patient has dreamed of it. . . .

JÉRÔME LALEMANT

[Cure by Gambling]

1639

One of the latest pieces of foolishness that occurred in this town was on behalf of a sick man of a neighboring town who either dreamed or was ordered by a doctor of the country that a game of dish must be played to restore his health. He spoke to the captains, who immediately assembled the council, fixed the time, and chose the town to be invited for this purpose, and the choice fell on our town. An envoy from that place was sent here to make the overtures, the proposal was accepted, and preparations began on both sides.

This game of dish consists of tossing some wild plum stones in a wooden dish, each stone colored white on one side and black on the other. Victory or loss is determined [by the combination of whites and blacks], according to the rules of the game.

It is more than I can do to depict the diligence and activity of our barbarians in preparing themselves and in seeking all the means and omens to ensure good luck and success in their game. They gather together at night to practice shaking the dish to ascertain who has the best hand and to display their lucky charms and exhort them. At last, they lie down to sleep in the same cabin, having previously fasted and for some time abstained from their wives. All this is done in order to have some favorable dream so that in the morning they can relate what happened during the night.

Finally, they collect all the things that they have dreamed can bring good luck and fill carrying bags with them. In addition, they search everywhere for people who have talismans to bring luck in gambling, as well as those with *ascwandics,* or personal demons, and get them to accompany the person who holds the dish and remain close to him when he shakes it. Should there be some old men whose presence is regarded as helpful in strengthening the virtue of their talismans, they do not simply take the charms with them, but go so far as to load these men upon the shoulders of the young men and carry them to the place of the assembly. And inasmuch as we pass in the country for master sorcerers, they do not fail to urge us to pray and to perform all sorts of ceremonies in order to make them win.

As soon as they arrive at the appointed place, the two parties take their places on opposite sides of the cabin and fill it from top to bottom, above and below the *andichons* (sheets of bark that form a sort of bed canopy or roof). This runs parallel to a lower platform that rests on the ground and which they sleep upon at night. The *andichons* are placed upon horizontal poles which run the whole length of the cabin. The two players are in the middle, together with their assistants, who hold the talismans. Anyone in attendance wagers whatever he wishes with someone else, and so the game begins.

It is then that everyone begins to pray or mutter I know not what words, with gestures and eager motions of the hands, eyes, and the whole face. All this to attract good luck and to urge their demons to take courage and not let themselves be tormented. Some are appointed to utter execrations and to make contrary gestures, with the aim of driving ill luck back to the other side and frightening the opponents' spirit.

This game was played several times this winter, all over the country. I do not know why, but the people of the towns where we have residences have been completely without luck. One town lost thirty wampums of a thousand beads each, which in this country would be equivalent to fifty thousand pearls or pistoles[1] in France. But it is worse than that, for, hoping always to win back what they have lost, they stake tobacco pouches, robes, shoes, and leggings — everything they have — so that, if they remain unlucky, which they did in this case, they return home as naked as the hand, having sometimes lost even their breechclouts.

They do not leave, however, until the patient has thanked them for the health he has recovered through their help, always professing himself cured at the end of all these fine ceremonies, although frequently he does not survive for long afterward.

The funny part is that, after suffering these losses and returning home, our barbarians come and reproach us, saying, "What is the use of believing?" It is plain to see, they say, that our sole intention is to ruin the places where we have made our abode, and thus gradually destroy the whole country. Since we have been with them and have spoken to them of God, they no longer dream, their talismans and *ascwandics* have no more power, they are unlucky in everything, in sum, there is no evil that does not accompany them. . . .

[1]The pistole was a coin in circulation in France at this time. Lalemant is not trying to establish an exact currency conversion but rather to convey a sense of the magnitude of the loss.

JÉRÔME LALEMANT

[Satisfying the Soul's Desires]

1639

For two years, an old man of this town named Taorhenche had a cancer on his arm, which, starting from his wrist, expanded to the shoulder and then began to enter his body. It was said that previously he had neglected none of the ceremonies — or, rather, superstitions — practiced in the country to recover his health. Last winter, a little before his death, he gave the captains to understand that he desired something as consolation and as a final effort to cure him. The council was assembled, and some individuals were appointed to go and discover his wishes. These turned upon five or six points: a number of dogs of a certain shape and color with which to make a three-day feast, a quantity of flour for the same purpose, some dances and similar performances, but principally he wanted the ceremony of the *andacwander,* a coupling of men and girls, which occurs at the end of the feast. He specified that there should be twelve girls, plus a thirteenth for himself.

The answer being brought to the council, he was furnished immediately with what could be given at once, thanks to the liberality and voluntary contributions of individuals who happened to be present and therefore heard about the request. These peoples' glory, on such occasions, in despoiling themselves of their most precious possessions. Afterward, the captains went through the streets and public places, and into the cabins, announcing in a loud voice the desires of the sick man and exhorting people to satisfy them promptly.

They are not content to go on this errand once; instead they repeat it three or four times, speaking in such a way as to give the impression that the welfare of the whole country is at stake. Meanwhile, they take care to note the names of the girls and men who present themselves to carry out the principal desire of the patient. And when the feast assembles, their names are announced, after which follow the congratulations of all those present, and the choicest morsels are carried to the men and women appointed to appear in that wretched performance which is to finish the feast. After that come the thanks of the sick man for the health that has been restored to him, as he professes himself entirely cured by this remedy.

This wretched play continued for two days, and on the third it was not enacted, although it should have been, according to the original plan and intention of the patient. They tried to make us believe that it was we who had caused this breach by displaying the displeasure and pain that we felt. Be that as it may, the whole ceremony took place without the sick man feeling any better in consequence, and soon afterward he died. In his last feast before death, he said that he died willingly, having only one regret, that he would no longer be honored, as he had been all his life, with the delicious foods served at feasts. This soul was too much attached to the things of the flesh to enjoy those of the spirit. . . .

We learned that there are hardly any heads of family in these countries who do not have some dances, feasts, and other ceremonies for the cure of their illnesses and the success of their affairs, but all these were taught them by the demons, either in the manner that we shall presently describe or through appearing to them in dreams, sometimes in the form of a raven or some other bird, sometimes in the form of a serpent . . . or of some other animal, which speaks to them and reveals the secret of good fortune, to recover their health when they fall ill or to have success in their enterprises. And this secret is called *ondinonc,* which means a desire inspired by the demon. And, in fact, if you ask someone who has a desire of this sort the cause of that desire, he will simply reply, *Ondays ihatonc oki haendaerandic:* "The thing under the form of which my familiar demon appeared to me gave me this advice."[1]

These *ondinoncs* are always accompanied by feasts or dances. The ceremonies, and even the songs that are sung there, are mostly dictated by the demon, who gives all his instructions with warnings and threats that all will be lost if they are not carried out exactly, down to the smallest detail. Consequently, when the captains announce the desires of the sick or other persons who have dreamed, and when they say that it is the *ondinonc* of a certain person, everyone immediately goes to great lengths to satisfy the individual involved. This seems entirely confirmed by the formula observed by the captains when they take to the person the things called for at the first assembly: "Listen, [name of the recipient]," they cry, "and you, voice of 'demon' (that is, the being which inspired you), here is what such and such a person gives." And, as they say this, they toss the presents onto the patient.

This is the pattern followed in a ceremony that took place while I was writing the above. It was on behalf of a sick woman, and in fulfillment of one of her desires fifty persons performed a special dance lasting three hours. Three days were spent in preparation for this dance, and on the day it was to take place, the captains made no less than five public announcements: first to proclaim that it was time to begin washing their bodies, then to say they should grease them, later that they should adorn themselves with one piece of finery, then with another. You would have thought that the town was on fire and that everything was about to be consumed. The final announcement was made to urge all the people

---

[1]As explained earlier, the Jesuits used the term *demon* as a translation for the Huron word *oki* (spirit). In this sentence, Lalemant refers to a "familiar demon," which, shorn of the diabolical sense added by the missionary, might be translated as "personal guardian spirit."

to attend and to get there before the arrival of those who were to dance. Before the latter came a captain bearing the rest of the desires of the patient, who made his declaration in the form mentioned earlier. There followed, a little distance behind, the company of dancers, men and women, at whose head marched two masters of ceremonies, singing and playing continually on a turtle. This turtle is not a real turtle, but only a shell and skin so arranged as to make a sort of drum, in which certain stones or pits have been put to make an instrument like that which children in France play with. There is something mysterious about this semblance of a turtle, to which these people attribute their origin. We shall know in time what there is to it.

The masters of ceremony now place themselves at the head of the patient, who is in the middle of the cabin, and then move apart, one remaining at her head, the other going to her feet. All the others who dance form a sort of flock, wheeling round and round the patient, not ceasing while the masters of ceremony sing and play on the turtle. It seemed impossible to take greater care or create more mystery, or that anyone could play their part with more earnest attention, and yet the sick woman only complained that they had not observed all the forms and that she would not recover; and, in fact, she grew worse.

––––––––––

THE INFLUENZA EPIDEMIC OF 1637

In the fall of 1636, the Huron villages where Jesuits resided were struck with a "fever," most likely a strain of influenza originating in New England. The missionaries and their servants were inconvenienced for a time, but the Hurons were devastated. The disease spread slowly over the course of the winter, but with the return of spring, it flared up anew. Village after village succumbed, and the number of the dead multiplied. As the Hurons' desperation increased, they followed their shamans' urging to undertake extraordinary curative rituals. Quite reasonably, they believed that the unprecedented medical emergency had something to do with the presence of the French missionaries in their midst, and, accordingly, some Hurons approached the Jesuits to find out what the latter and their god required as the condition of ending the plague. Father Brébeuf set out the far-reaching changes the Indians would have to make to their way of life to satisfy the Christian deity, but as the headman Aënons indicated in his eloquent reply, compliance was impossible. Fear and perplexity then changed to anger, and plans were formulated (though never carried out) to kill all the Jesuits as hostile sorcerers.

We begin with the Jesuits' efforts to treat their own sick. Father François Le Mercier, and not the superior, Jean de Brébeuf, is the narrator.

FRANÇOIS LE MERCIER

The Malady with Which Our Little Household Has Been Afflicted

1637

... Father Jogues was no sooner out of danger than Father Chastellain fell ill. He was harassed by a burning fever, which made him very restless and which possessed him until the seventh of October. The father superior twice bled him very successfully, and he also bled Dominique [a lay employee], who was sick with a purple fever and who sank so low that we gave him extreme unction.[1] Father Garnier's fever was not so violent, and we did not consider it otherwise dangerous, except that it occasioned him great weakness. The father superior tried twice to bleed him, but the blood would not flow. This was God's way of guiding his hand in this time of need. Through all this, they endured a great deal, and we felt much compassion for them, for we could give them but slight relief. If a bed of feathers often seems hard to a sick person, I leave Your Reverence to imagine how comfortable they could be upon a bed made of nothing but a mat of rushes spread over some bark, with at most a blanket or a piece of skin thrown over it. In addition to this, one of the most annoying things, and one which it was almost impossible to remedy, was the continual noise, both within and outside the cabin. ...

On the first day of October, I began to feel some symptoms; by evening I had a fever, and, like the others, I had to surrender to the illness. But I got off too cheaply, suffering only three attacks, though the second one was so violent that I condemned myself to a bleeding; my blood was obstinate, however. God reserved for me a more natural remedy, which appeared at the end of the third attack and enabled me to say the holy

---

[1] One of the Catholic last rites.

Mass the next day. However, I was of almost no use to our fathers for another six or seven days. The Indians wondered at the orderly way we cared for our sick and at the regimen we put them on. It was a curious thing to them, for they had never yet seen French people ill.

I have not told Your Reverence that Tonneraouanont, one of the famous sorcerers of the country, came to see us when he heard that we were sick. To hear him talk, he was a personage of merit and influence, although in appearance he was a very insignificant object: small, hunchbacked, extremely misshapen, and wearing a piece of a robe — some greasy and patched old beaver skins — over his shoulder. This is one of the oracles of the whole country, who had this winter made entire towns bend to his decrees. He had come at that time to blow upon some sick people of our village. . . . In order to make our mouths water and to better sell his remedy, he said, "I am not an ordinary man; I am like a demon, which is why I have never been sick. In the three or four times that the country has been afflicted with an epidemic, I did not trouble myself at all about it, and I never feared the disease, for I have remedies to preserve me. Hence, if you will give me something, I will undertake in a few days to get all your sick back on their feet."

The father superior, in order to prolong the jest, asked what he desired. "You must give me," said he, "ten cylindrical glass beads, and one extra for each patient." . . . He told us that he would teach us the roots that must be used, or if we wished to proceed more quickly, he could take care of the cures himself. He would pray and have a special sweat — in a word, perform all his usual charlatan's tricks — and in three days our sick would be cured. He made a very plausible speech.

The father satisfied him, or rather instructed him on this point. He gave the sorcerer to understand that we could not approve this sort of remedy, that the prayer he offered availed nothing and was only a compact with the Devil, for he had no knowledge of or belief in the true God, to whom alone it is permitted to address vows and prayers. However, as far as natural remedies were concerned, we would willingly employ them, and we would be grateful if he would teach us some of them. He did not insist further upon his sweat, but named us two roots that were, he said, very efficacious against fevers; and he showed us how to use them. . . .

FRANÇOIS LE MERCIER

The Help We Have Given to the Sick of Our Village

1637

On the twelfth, Father Pijart made a trip to Khinonascarant, three little hamlets two leagues from us. There he encountered a man who seemed about to die. He took the opportunity to instruct him and speak to him of baptism. The sick man listened to him willingly at first, and even indicated that he would be glad to be baptized. But his wife, coming unexpectedly, turned him from his purpose, telling him that it would not be proper for him to go to heaven, since none of his relatives were there. She told the father that he need not go to any further trouble, especially as the sick man was not in possession of his faculties and did not know what he was saying. And so matters went no further, though fortunately for him, his sickness was not fatal. It is a thing altogether worthy of compassion to see how some of them take the speeches we give them about heaven. On one occasion, an Indian told the father superior that they were not very well pleased when we asked the sick where they wished to go after death, to Heaven or to Hell. "That is not right," said he. "We ourselves do not ask such questions, for we always hope that they will not die and that they will recover their health." Another one said, "For my part, I have no desire to go to heaven; I know no one there, and the French who are there would not care to give me anything to eat." For the most part, they think of nothing but their stomachs and of the means for prolonging this miserable life. . . .

Meanwhile, the Devil was playing his pranks elsewhere and, speaking through the mouth of the sorcerer Tonneraouanont, was turning aside these peoples from applying to God. For some time, this little hunchback had been declaring that the whole country was sick, and he had prescribed a medicine, in the form of a game of lacrosse, for its recovery. This order had been announced through all the towns, the captains had set about having it executed, and the young people had not spared themselves. But it was all in vain: The disease continued to spread, gaining strength as it went. By the fifteenth of October we counted in our little village thirteen or fourteen sick. Our sorcerer did not yet feel ready to undertake the cure of the whole country, though he

JR 13:124–27, 130–33, François Le Mercier, *Relation of 1637.*

did make one rash promise to help his own village of Onnentisati. Not satisfied to give some hope that no one there would be sick, he absolutely guaranteed it, basing his assurance on the power that he, as a demon, claimed to have over the contagion. He was immediately given what he needed to make a feast. Word of this boast spread everywhere and was accepted as truth, and all the people of Onnentisati were then considered fortunate and out of danger. This constrained us to address ourselves to God, and to implore his divine goodness to confound the Devil in the person of this wretch, and to obtain glory for himself from this public affliction. And the next day, the fourteenth, we made a vow to say for this purpose thirty Masses in honor of the glorious patriarch, Saint Joseph. It was not long before we had something with which to close the mouths of those who boasted to us of their prowess, for this town was not spared any more than the others. There were a great many sick there, several of whom died and, as we hope, went to heaven.

On the same day, we baptized in our village an Indian named Onendouerha and his wife, both of whom were very ill. Some days before, they had asked for baptism with a great deal of fervor and thoroughly satisfied the father superior when it became necessary to instruct them individually. Yet both are still in good health. It is a source of grief to us that because we have not yet any wholly converted towns, we afterward get nothing but empty words from these new Christians, whom we baptized only when they appeared to be on death's door. [If they recover], the torrent of old customs and common superstitions bears them away. We are daily expecting that it will please God to take care of this, and we hope soon to be granted this favor from heaven. . . .

FRANÇOIS LE MERCIER

Ossossané Afflicted with the Contagion

1637

On the next day, the thirtieth [of October], we made a vow, we and our servants, both for the welfare of our whole village and for the preservation of our little household. The father superior pronounced it at the Mass, in the name of all, holding in his hand the holy Sacrament of the altar. We bound ourselves to say each three Masses, one in honor of our

JR 13:162–73, 234–43; *JR* 14:50–55, François Le Mercier, *Relation of 1637.*

Lord, another in honor of the Blessed Virgin, and a third in honor of Saint Joseph, and we resolved to renew the vow the next year on the day of the Immaculate Conception of the same Virgin. As for our domestics, they promised three special Communions and to say their beads twelve times. For our part, we now have every reason to praise God, who has granted to us all the favor of passing the winter in very good health, although the greater part of the time we have been among the sick and the dead, and although we have seen many fall sick and die, merely through the communication that they had with one another. The Indians were astonished at it, and are still astonished every day, saying in reference to us, "Those people are not men; they are demons." God will grant them, if it shall please Him, grace to recognize that someday. "It is of the Lord's mercies that we are not consumed, because his compassions fail not."[1] It is through His mercy alone that we are not reduced to dust with the others and that Heaven ceaselessly pours out upon us its stream of favors and blessings. Our poor village continued to be afflicted until spring and is almost entirely ruined. We are not surprised at this, for the greater part of them showed that their belief consisted only in fine words, and that in their hearts they have no other God than the belly and anyone who will promise them absolutely to restore them to health in their illnesses.

On the fourth of December, having learned the news from Ossossané that the disease was spreading there and that some of its people had recently died, the father superior sent Father Charles Garnier and me there. We made this journey joyously and with all the more confidence in God, as I was convinced that my knowledge of the language was insufficient. On our arrival, we instructed and baptized a poor man who, it was believed, could not live through the night. We did not make a long sojourn there, as we had orders to be present at the Feast of the Conception of our Lady, and had it not been for that, we would not have readily left the sick, who were as many as fifty by actual count. We visited each of them individually, always giving them some little word of consolation. We were made very welcome, all greeting us with very kindly faces. The journey the father superior had made there having inclined to us the hearts and affections of all, most of them regarded us only as persons from whom they expected some consolation, and likewise something to relieve them in their sickness. A few raisins were very acceptable, and we were careful not to forget these. The few of them that we have are only for the Indians, and Your Reverence would not believe how readily they take these little sweets.

[1] Lam. 3:22; Latin in original.

I will say here in general that they have often given us admission to the sick, and if it happened that, while instructing them, they fell into a stupor, a little sugar or some good preserved fruit in a spoonful of warm water enabled us to revive them. I will even add that some little innocents were baptized in their last moments, unknown to and against the wishes of their parents, under the pretext of wishing to give them some of these sweets. We baptized eight people during this journey, four adults and four little children. It was a providence of God for us, who were still new in this profession, to find almost everywhere persons who favored our purpose and who aided us greatly in obtaining from the patients what we desired. Among others, one of the more influential men of the village served us as interpreter in instructing one of his daughters, doing so voluntarily and with great affection. He did even more than we wished; and when we would have been satisfied to draw a simple "yes" or "no" from the patient, he desired her to repeat, word for word, the instruction we gave her. Before departing, we saw the captain, Anenkhiondic, and some of the elders, and we told them of the vow that the people of our village had made in order to stop the progress of the disease. They manifested a great desire to do the same and charged us to report to the father superior that they were quite prepared to do all that he should judge proper on this occasion. Their love of life made them speak in this way, and, indeed, they will make the same promise the others did, and with even more ostentation, but when it comes to the execution of what they have promised, they will prove to be no better than the others.

Meantime, while we were at Ossossané, the father superior and our fathers at Ihonatiria were not idle. As if the sick there were not enough to keep them fully occupied, the inhabitants of Oenrio (a village one league distant from us), seeing themselves assailed by the malady, manifested a desire to have recourse to God. The father superior went to see them and sound them out. He baptized a little child on his arrival. At the same time, the captain had the council assemble and invited the father. Without preliminaries, he asked [the father superior] what they had to do that God might have pity on them. The father superior answered them that the principal thing was to believe in [God] and to be firmly resolved to keep His commandments, touching especially upon some of their customs and superstitions, which they must renounce if they purposed to serve him.

Among other things, he proposed to them that henceforth, since they were thus inclined, they should give up their belief in their dreams, their marriages should be binding and for life, and they should observe conjugal chastity. They should also understand that God forbade vomiting feasts; those shameless assemblies of men and women (I would blush to speak more clearly); eating human flesh; and those feasts they call *aoutaerohi,* which they make, they say, to appease a certain little demon to which this name is given. These are the points that the father especially recommended to them, and then he spoke to them about the vow our Indians of Ihonatiria had made, to build a little chapel next spring wherein to praise and thank God, if it pleased his divine goodness to deliver them from this malady.

The father was listened to by all with close attention, but these conditions astonished them greatly, and Onaconchiaronk, whom we call the old captain, spoke in reply. "My nephew," he said, "we have been greatly deceived. We thought God was to be satisfied with a chapel, but I see he demands much more." And the captain Aënons, going still farther, said, "*Echon,* I must speak to you frankly: I believe your proposition is impossible. The people of Ihonatiria said last year that they believed, but only so that they would be given tobacco. All that did not please me. For my part, I cannot dissemble; I express my sentiments frankly. I consider that what you propose will only prove to be a stumbling block. Besides, we have our own ways of doing things, and you have yours, and all the other nations have their own ways. When you speak to us about obeying and acknowledging as our master him whom you say made heaven and earth, I believe you are talking of overthrowing the country. Your ancestors assembled in earlier times and held a council where they resolved to take as their God the one whom you honor, and they ordained all the ceremonies that you observe. As for us, we have learned different ones from our own Fathers." . . .

[By January 1637, the epidemic was ravaging the large Huron town of Ossossané. Jean de Brébeuf hurried there to provide what relief he could and to combat "superstitious" remedies.]

On the 17th, the epidemic, continuing to rage at Ossossané, forced the father superior to resume the assistance we had been giving the sick there. He took with him Father Isaac Jogues and Mathurin, who performed some very successful bleedings. . . .

He arrived at Ossossané, where he found the demons at large and a poor people in deeper affliction than ever, giving their attention to the follies of a certain Tehorenhaegnon, who boasted of having a secret remedy for this kind of disease, which he had learned from the "demons" themselves, after twelve or thirteen days of fasting in a little cabin which he had made for this purpose on the shore of the lake. Accordingly, the inhabitants of Ossossané, hearing of what he could do and seeing that presents were offered to him on all sides in order to gain his goodwill and to get from him some relief, sent to him some of their chief men to entreat him very humbly to have pity upon their misery and to proceed to their village to see the sick and to give them some remedies. Tehorenhaegnon evinced a willingness to comply with their request, but being unable (or rather not deigning) to go there in person, he sent an associate, named Saossarinon, to whom he communicated all his power and to whom he gave his bow and arrows to represent his person.

As soon as he arrived, one of the captains proclaimed in a loud voice, throughout the town, that all the sick should take heart, for Tehorenhaegnon promised to drive the disease away very soon, and that, not being able to come in person, he had sent Saossarinon with the power to give them all manner of satisfaction. He ordained that on three consecutive days three feasts should be made, promising that all those who attended and observed all the ceremonies should be protected from the disease.

Toward evening, the people assembled in the very cabin of our host, which is one of the largest in the town. Our fathers stayed there in order to observe all that might happen. The company was composed only of men — the women were to have their turn afterward — and all the families were represented. Before beginning the ceremony, one of the captains climbed to the top of the cabin and cried aloud to this effect: "Come now, see us here assembled. Listen, you demons whom Tehorenhaegnon invokes, behold us about to make a feast and have a dance in your honor. Come, let the contagion cease and leave this town. If you still have a desire to eat human flesh, repair to the country of our enemies. We now associate ourselves with you, to carry the sickness to them and to ruin them." This harangue ended, and they began to sing. Meanwhile, Saossarinon went to visit the sick and made the rounds of all the cabins. But the feast did not take place until daybreak; the entire night was passed in a continual uproar. Sometimes they sang, and at the same time they beat out a loud rhythm on pieces of bark, and sometimes they arose and began to dance, each one striving to dance well, as if his life depended upon it.

The substitute of Tehorenhaegnon was to have put in an appearance at this cabin, but he found so much to do in other cabins that daylight overtook him in his progress. Meanwhile, they awaited him with great impatience, and as they were singing, one after another, there was one of them who began speaking: "Come, great *Arendiowane,* come; behold the day beginning to dawn." Not to keep them waiting longer, [Saossarinon] passed by some of the remaining cabins. At his arrival a profound silence prevailed. A captain walked before him, holding in one hand the bow of Tehorenhaegnon as a sign of the power possessed by this deputy, and in the other a kettle filled with a mysterious water with which he sprinkled the sick. As for [Saossarinon], he carried a turkey's wing, with which he fanned them gravely and at a distance after he gave them something to drink. He performed the same ceremonies for the sick of this cabin, then, having inspired the whole company with courage and hope, he withdrew. The feast took place, and afterward the men left the place to the women, who also came, singing and dancing in their turn. As for a feast, the women had none.

On the twentieth, Saossarinon himself made the second feast. There the aid of the demons was invoked in the same words as upon the preceding day, and after eating, someone said that the physician had already cured twelve people. This news caused great rejoicing among the company. The captain Andahiach thanked him and his master Tehorenhaegnon, as well as all the captains of the town of Andiataé, declaring that the whole town would be under obligation to them and begging them to continue their favors. The third feast did not take place for lack of fish.

On the twenty-first, Saossarinon returned to Andiataé, at his departure taking into partnership with himself and Tehorenhaegnon one Khioutenstia and one Iandatassa, to whom he taught the secrets of his art and communicated his power. As a token of the latter, he left them each a turkey's wing, adding that henceforth their dreams would prove true. He also asked them to send word, after a few days, on the success of their remedies. Four or five days later, all the cabins were visited to ascertain the number cured and the number sick, in order to inform Tehorenhaegnon. According to their calculations, there were twenty-five cured and twenty-five sick. Word was sent immediately to this personage at Andiataé. Tehorenhaegnon sent Saossarinon the next day to try to cure the rest, but Saossarinon would not take the trouble to go and visit the sick. Instead he gave orders that they should drag themselves, or that they should be carried, to him in the cabin of one Oonchiarré, where there were already a great many sick people. But this plan went very badly for him, and this second time no good effects were seen from his remedies, for some would not go there because they felt too weak. That very night a woman of the cabin died and the next morning another one, who had been carried there. The father superior instructed the latter and baptized her with a great deal of satisfaction. Moreover, he did so well that those gentlemen, the substitutes of Tehorenhaegnon, were obliged to throw aside their turkey wings and renounce their office. . . .

[The epidemic was in its last stages by the summer of 1637, and, as Father Le Mercier's chronicle for the month of June reports, the Hurons were generally convinced that the Jesuits were using sorcery to destroy them.]

. . . Your Reverence can see that our poor Indians are not yet free from sickness. If God does not mercifully intervene, the great heat that prevails here at this season is not likely to dissipate this bad air. There are two villages that are especially afflicted, Andiataé and Onnentisati, where the two greatest sorcerers of the country, Sondacouané and Tehorenhaegnon, reside. During the winter they had already lost a great deal of their credit with the sick of other villages, and now they are more than ever discomfited, seeing that their sweats, feasts, potions, and prescriptions are of no avail with their countrymen. Recently, Sondacouané has taken it into his head to forbid to the sick the "French snow"—this is what they call sugar—and has persuaded some that it is a species of poison. It is easy to see who is the real source of this prohibition. The Devil knows well enough how much these little sweets have already aided us in wresting from his hands so many souls that he held captive. He has made every effort this winter to stop our mouths and prevent us from preaching to these barbarous people the grandeur and infinite mercy of the Master whom we serve. But because his designs did not succeed (for God granted us the favor of baptizing two hundred and thirty or forty persons), he has recently stirred up new tempests against us. They are still saying, almost as much as ever, that we are the cause of the malady. These reports are partly founded upon the fact that it is in this season much more fatal than it was during the severe cold of the winter, and consequently most of those we baptize die. Besides this, a certain Algonquin captain has now given our Hurons to understand that they were mistaken in thinking that the devils caused them to die, that they should blame only the French, and that he had seen a woman who appeared to be French and who was infecting the whole country with her breath and her exhalations. Our Indians imagine that it is the sister of the late Etienne Brulé,[2] who is avenging her brother's death. This sorcerer added that we ourselves meddle in witchcraft and that we use for

---

[2] Etienne Brulé was a young Frenchman who had gone to live among the natives and was killed, under rather mysterious circumstances, at a Huron village in 1632.

that purpose images of our saints. When the images are displayed, certain tainted influences issue forth and sink into the chests of those who look at them, which is why it is no surprise that they later fall ill with the disease. The prominent men and chiefs of the country do not appear to share this belief, but they fear that some fool will commit an act of violence that will cause them to blush. We are in God's hands, and all these dangers do not make us forfeit a moment of our joy. It would be too great an honor for us to lose our lives while employed in saving some poor soul. . . .

FRANÇOIS LE MERCIER

Of the Hurons Baptized This Year, 1638

1638

The greatest of our difficulties was to discover those who were sick, as this search was so distasteful to them. "You care for only the sick and the dead," they said to us. Indeed, we made the rounds of the cabins incessantly, for often someone was taken sick and carried away in less than two days. Our most common occupation was that of physician, with the object of increasingly discrediting their sorcerers and their imaginary treatments. And yet we had nothing to give them as medicine save a little piece of lemon peel — French squash, as they call it — or a few raisins in a little warm water, with a pinch of sugar. This little help, however, with the blessing of God added, accomplished wonders, and, according to them, it restored health to many. . . .

SMALLPOX AMONG THE HURONS, 1639

There was no mistaking the epidemic that entered the Huron lands late in the summer of 1639: The oozing red sores, lassitude, and fever were sure signs of smallpox. In Europe, smallpox was disfiguring and killing people by the thousands, but in the biological "virgin soil" of the Americas, it mowed down native populations with shocking efficiency. It seems clear that far more Hurons perished in 1639 than in the plague that struck them two years earlier. It appears that the epidemic originated in New England and was carried to the St. Lawrence Valley by visiting Indians, who in turn passed it on to Hurons who had gone down to trade with the French. Nevertheless, the Hurons were inclined to blame the Jesuits, since the missionaries had already provided grounds, during the influenza outbreaks of 1637, for suspecting that they were engaged in genocidal black magic. As was the case during the earlier epidemic, there were calls to execute the Jesuits and liquidate the French alliance.

JÉRÔME LALEMANT

Of the Persecutions Excited against Us

1640

It was when the Hurons returned from their journey to Quebec that [smallpox] entered the country, our Hurons having thoughtlessly mingled with some Algonquins whom they met on the way up here, most of whom were infected with [it]. The first Huron who introduced it came ashore just beside our house, newly built on the edge of a lake, and from there he carried it to his own village, about a league distant from us, and then promptly died. It would take no great prophet to predict that the illness would soon be spread abroad through all these regions, for the Hurons, regardless of any plague or contagion, live in the midst of their sick, sharing and mingling with them as if they were in perfect health. And indeed, within a few days, almost everyone in the cabin of the deceased was infected, and then the disease spread from house to house, from town to town, and eventually affected the entire country. . . .

Because the towns nearest our new house were the first ones attacked and the most severely afflicted, the Devil did not fail to seize the opportunity to reawaken all the hoary delusions and revive the former complaints against us, attributing to our living here all their misfortunes and especially all their sickness. They no longer speak of anything else, crying aloud that the French must be massacred. These barbarians excite one another to that effect. The death of those they love deprives them of reason and heightens their rage against us in every town, so that the best informed among them can hardly believe we are able to survive so horrible a storm. They observed, with some basis in reason, that since our arrival in these lands, those who were nearest to us happened to be those most ruined by the diseases and that the towns that welcomed us now appear utterly exterminated. Certainly, they said, the same fate will befall all the others if the course of this misfortune is not stopped by the massacre of those who were the cause of it. This was a common opinion, not only in private conversation but in the general councils held on this account, where the plurality of voices voted for our death, with only a few elders kindly obliging us with a verdict of banishment.

At the same time, this false imagination seemed to be powerfully confirmed by the fact that they saw us going through the country using every means possible to gain access to the cabins and taking unheard-of pains to instruct and baptize the most seriously ill. No doubt, they said, we must have a secret understanding with the disease (for they believe that it is a demon), since we alone were all full of life and health, though we constantly breathed nothing but a totally infected air, staying whole days close by the side of the most foul-smelling patients, for whom everyone felt horror. No doubt we carried misery with us, since, wherever we set foot, either death or disease followed us.

In consequence of all these sayings, many held us in abomination. They expelled us from their cabins and did not allow us to approach their sick, especially the children, not even to lay eyes on them. In a word, we were dreaded as the greatest sorcerers on earth.

Wherein truly it must be acknowledged that these poor people are in some sense excusable. For it has happened very often, and has been remarked more than a hundred times, that where we were most welcome and baptized the greatest number of people was in fact where the greatest number died. Conversely, in the cabins to which we were denied entrance, though they were sometimes extremely sick, at the end of a few days one saw every person happily cured. We shall see in heaven the secret, but ever adorable, judgments of God herein. . . .

A MEDICAL DUEL: FATHER ALLOUEZ
AND THE POTAWOTAMIS

In 1666 Father Claude Allouez toured the western Great Lakes, meeting with people such as the Potawotamis, who had only recently established contact with the French. As was so often the case, a devastating epidemic (it is

not clear what the disease was) soon followed. In the revealing passage that
follows, Allouez reports on the different ways in which he and the Pota-
wotami shamans tried to cure the sick, drawing on therapeutic techniques
derived from both European and native medical traditions. Note that in the
Jesuit's mind, the drama revolved not around the conflict of infection and
medicine, but around a contest between the shaman and the missionary to
determine how the disease would be understood. Allouez saw himself as
locked in combat with diabolical forces, and the visible triumph of God was
his top priority.

CLAUDE ALLOUEZ

Of the Mission to the Potawotamis

1666–1667

In late winter, a young man, in whose canoe I had a place on my journey
to this country, was seized with the contagious disease that was then
prevalent. I tried to show him as much kindness as he had shown me ill
usage on the journey. As he was a man of considerable importance, they
tried every sort of magical nonsense to cure him. Eventually, they came
to me claiming to have extracted two dog's teeth from his body. "That is
not what causes his illness," I told them, "but rather the tainted blood
which is in his body," for I judged that he had pleurisy. Meanwhile, I began to instruct him in good earnest, and on the next day, finding him well
prepared, I gave him holy baptism with the name of Ignatius, hoping that
great saint would confound the evil spirits and the shamans. In fact, I
bled him and showed the blood to the shaman, who was present at the
time. "Here," I said, "is what is killing this sick man. With all your affected arts, you should have drawn from him every drop of this corrupt
blood and not some alleged dog's teeth." But the shaman, perceiving
that this bleeding had greatly relieved the patient, wanted the glory of
curing him for himself. To that end, he made him take some kind of medicine that produced such a bad effect that the patient seemed as though
dead and remained so for three hours. This result was proclaimed
throughout the village, and the shaman, much surprised by the turn of
events, confessed that he had killed the poor man and begged me not to

forsake him. Indeed, he was not abandoned by his patron saint Ignatius, who restored him to life in order to confound the superstitions of these infidels. This young man was not yet cured when his sister fell ill of the same disease. We enjoyed greater access to her in the discharge of our duties after what had happened to her brother, and so I had every opportunity to prepare her for baptism, and in addition to that grace, the Blessed Virgin, whose name she bore, procured her recovery.

But she was scarcely out of danger when the same disease struck her cousin, who was in the same cabin. He appeared to me more dangerously ill than the other two had been, which made me hasten to baptize him after the necessary instruction. He was already feeling better, by virtue of this sacrament, when his father took it into his head to make a feast, or rather a sacrifice, to the sun to ask for his son's recovery. I came upon them in the midst of the ceremony and immediately took my sick neophyte in my arms, endeavoring to convince him that God alone was the master of life and death. He immediately acknowledged his error and made atonement to God through the sacrament of penance. Then I spoke to his father and everyone else involved in the sacrifice, saying, "Now I despair of this patient's recovery, since you have had recourse to others than He who holds in his hands both life and death. You have killed this poor man by your impiety. I give up all hope for him." He did indeed die sometime afterward, and I trust that God may have accepted his temporal death as penance for his offense, so that [God] will not deprive him of the everlasting life which this man will have obtained by the intercessions of Saint Joseph, whose name he bore.

4

Diplomacy and War

The Jesuit missions of New France were conducted throughout the seventeenth century in an atmosphere of tension, war, and shifting alliances involving the French and the various native nations. Accordingly, the *Relations* are packed with news of war and peace — daring raids, hopeful negotiations, surprise ambushes, captivity, torture, and redemption — all recounted in the style of romantic adventure with an overlay of pious sentiments. In some cases, armed conflict pitted Christian forces (French and/or native converts) against "infidels" (usually Iroquois), allowing the Jesuit chroniclers to adopt the rhetoric of crusader narratives. What makes the *Relations* uniquely valuable sources on Indian war and diplomacy is the richness of detail, the anecdotes of battlefield adventures, the captivity stories, and the verbatim accounts of diplomatic speeches. These are not the usual colonialist accounts of brave Europeans fighting and subduing faceless "savages," but rather stories in which the natives themselves feature centrally.

Unlike the Spanish in Mexico and South America, the French did not come to America as Christian conquerors. They never secured the submission of the native peoples of New France. Instead, they established a place for themselves in the existing native alliance system. Eventually, French Canada would emerge as the strongest power in the region, even as the hegemonic power, but its ascendancy was never complete, and antagonisms that had originated before the arrival of the French continued. By all accounts, native wars became more intense and deadly in the seventeenth century, due partly to the adoption of European weaponry but also to the pressures and upheavals occasioned by epidemics, trade, and other effects of contact. Generally, the main lines of conflict separated the Five Nations of the Iroquois in the south from a northern alliance encompassing the Hurons, Algonquins, Montagnais, and French. One tribe of Iroquois, the Mohawks, lived closest to the St. Lawrence and therefore inflicted the greatest damage on the Algonquins and French.

PEACE NEGOTIATIONS AT THREE RIVERS, 1645

The long war between the Iroquois and the northern nations was interrupted by occasional truces and periods of peace, although these were seldom stable, nor did they usually involve all the belligerents. One such truce was established from 1645 to 1647 between the Mohawks and their enemies, principally the Algonquins and French. The St. Lawrence River had been the main theater of Mohawk raids, but it also served as the site of peace overtures, culminating in a general conference in July 1645 at the French fort of Three Rivers. The peace proved temporary and may never have been intended as more than a short breathing space in which to effect a prisoner exchange.

Father Barthélemy Vimont's account of the meeting emphasizes the eloquence of the main Mohawk emissary, Kiotseaeton. The Jesuits were famous in seventeenth-century France as experts in the theory, practice, and teaching of rhetoric, and so Vimont's praise should be seen as the appreciation of a master. Vimont listened to the speaker's words through an imperfect interpreter, for at that time none of the Jesuits fully understood the Mohawk tongue. But diplomatic oratory in this multilingual part of the world was designed to bridge the language gap through the use of gestures, repetition, and symbols. As in all native ceremonies, gift giving played a central role. With every point he makes verbally, Kiotseaeton presents a length of patterned beadwork — the French called this a collier *or* porcelaine, *translated here as "wampum" or "belt"— which is an item of value but also a mnemonic device that fills some of the functions of alphabetic writing. The diplomat's speeches, mimed before the audience to make them vivid and memorable and rendered concrete through the use of wampum belts, are largely metaphorical.*

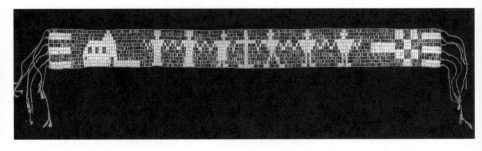

A Huron Wampum Belt
Huron wampum belt showing details of Huron missionary life.
McCord Museum of Canadian History, Montreal.

Treaty of Peace between the French, Iroquois, and Other Nations

1644–1645

On the fifth day of July, the Iroquois prisoner who had been set at liberty and sent back to his own country, as I have said in the foregoing chapter, made his appearance at Three Rivers accompanied by two men of note among those peoples who had been delegated to negotiate peace with Onontio (thus they name Monsieur the governor[1]) and all the French, as well as all the Indians who are our allies.

A young man named Guillaume Couture, who had been taken prisoner with Father Isaac Jogues and who had since then remained in the Iroquois country, was with them.[2] As soon as he was recognized, everyone embraced him, for he was looked upon as a man risen from the dead. It was a joy to all who had thought he had died or, at least, that he had been in danger of passing the remainder of his days in most bitter and cruel captivity. As soon as he landed, he informed us of the design of the three Indians with whom he had been sent back. When the most important of the three, named Kiotseaeton, saw the French and the Indians hastening to the bank of the river, he stood up in the bow of the shallop that had brought him from Richelieu to Three Rivers. He was almost completely covered with porcelain beads. Motioning with his hand for silence, he called out: "My brothers, I have left my country to come and see you, and at last I have reached your land. I was told, on my departure, that I was going to seek my death and that I would never again see my country. But I have willingly exposed my life for the sake of peace. I come therefore to learn the intentions of the French, of the Hurons, and of the Algonquins. I come to make known to you the thoughts of all my country." When he had said this, the shallop fired a

---

[1] Charles Huault de Montmagny (known to the Iroquois as Onontio) was governor of New France from 1636 to 1648.

[2] Guillaume Couture, a young surgeon working for the Jesuits, had been captured along with Father Isaac Jogues in an Iroquois ambush in 1642. (See the selection on page 160.)

JR 27:246–73, Barthélemy Vimont, *Relation of 1644–45.*

shot from its swivel gun, and the fort replied with a discharge of cannon, as a sign of rejoicing.

When those ambassadors had landed, they were conducted into the room of the Sieur de Chamflour,[3] who gave them a very cordial reception. They were offered some light refreshments, and after they had eaten and smoked, Kiotseaeton, who continued as spokesman, said to all the French who surrounded him, "I find much kindness in your houses. Since setting foot in your country, I have observed nothing but rejoicing. I see very well that the one who dwells in heaven wishes to arrange something very important. The minds and thoughts of men differ too much to fall into accord; it is Heaven that will bring all together." On the same day, a canoe was sent to Monsieur the governor to inform him of the arrival of these new guests.

Meanwhile, both they and the prisoners who had not yet been released had full liberty to wander wherever they wished. The Algonquins and Montagnais invited them to their feasts, and gradually they became accustomed to conversing together. Sieur de Chamflour treated them very well. One day he said to them that they should consider themselves at home here among us, that they had nothing to fear, that they were in their own house. Kiotseaeton replied to this compliment by a very well pointed and neat retort. "I beg you," he said to the interpreter, "to say to that captain who speaks to us that he tells a great falsehood with respect to us; at least it is certain that what he says is not true." And thereupon he paused a little to let the wonder grow. Then he added: "That captain tells me that I am here as if in my own country. That is very far from the truth. I would be neither honored nor treated with such consideration in my own country, while here everyone honors and cherishes me. He says that I am as if in my own house, but that is a lie. I am badly treated in my house, and here I fare well every day — I am continually feasting. Therefore I am not as if I were in my own country or in my own house." He indulged in many other repartees which clearly showed that he had wit.

Finally, Monsieur the governor came from Quebec to Three Rivers, and after having seen the ambassadors, he gave audience to them on the twelfth of July. This took place in the courtyard of the fort, over which large sails had been spread to keep off the heat of the sun. Here is how

---

[3] François de Chamflour was commander of the French post of Three Rivers.

Novae Franciae Accurata Delineatio, 1657
This illustrated map of New France, published in Italy, was probably the work of
Francesco-Giuseppe Bressani, one of very few foreign Jesuits, and the only Ital-
ian, to serve in the Canadian mission field.
Courtesy of the University of Western Ontario.

the places were arranged: On one side was Monsieur the governor, accompanied by his people and by Reverend Father Vimont, superior of the mission. The Iroquois sat at his feet, on a great piece of hemlock bark. They had stated before the assembly that they wished to be on his side, as a mark of the affection that they bore to the French. Opposite them were the Algonquins, the Montagnais, and the Attikamegues.[4] The other two sides were closed in by some French and some Hurons. In the center was a large space, somewhat longer than wide, in which the Iroquois caused two poles to be planted, with a cord stretched between them on which to hang and tie the words that they were to bring us — that is to say, the presents they wished to make us, which consisted of seventeen beaded wampums. A portion of the latter were on their bodies, while the remainder were tied up in a small pouch placed quite near them.

When all had assembled and had taken their places, Kiotseaeton, a tall man, rose to his feet and regarded the sun. He then cast his eyes over the whole company, took a wampum in his hand, and began to speak in a loud voice. "Onontio, lend me your ear. I am the mouth for the whole of my country. You listen to all the Iroquois in hearing my words. There is no evil in my heart. I have only good songs in my mouth. We have a multitude of war songs in my country, but we have cast them all to the ground. We no longer have any but songs of rejoicing." Thereupon he began to sing, and as his countrymen responded, he walked about the great space as if on the stage of a theater. He made a thousand gestures, looking up to heaven, gazing at the sun, rubbing his arms as if he wished to draw from them the strength that moved them in war. After he had sung awhile, he said that the present that he held in his hand thanked Monsieur the governor for having saved the life of Tokhrahenehiaron when, last autumn, he pulled him from the fire and from the teeth of the Algonquins. But he complained gracefully that he had been sent back all alone to his own country. "If his canoe had been upset, if the winds had caused it to sink, if he had been drowned, you would have waited long for the return of the poor injured man, and you would have accused us of a fault which you yourselves have committed." When he had said this, he fastened his wampum at the appointed spot.

Drawing out another, he tied it to the arm of Guillaume Couture, saying aloud: "It is this collar that brings you back this prisoner. I would not have said to him, while he was still in our country: 'Go, my nephew. Take a canoe and return to Quebec.' My mind would not have been at rest. I

4 The Attikamegues were Algonquin bands from north of Three Rivers.

would always have been thinking over and over again to myself, 'Is he not lost?' In truth, I would have no sense, had I acted in that way. He whom you have sent back had all the difficulties in the world on his journey." He began to express these, but in so pathetic a manner that no actor in France could not have equaled the ingenuity of that barbarian. He took a stick, placed it on his head like a bundle, then carried it from one end of the square to the other, representing what that prisoner had done on the rapids and the fast-flowing waters. Arriving at these points, he had transported his baggage, piece by piece. [Kiotseaeton] went backward and forward, showing the portages and returns of the prisoner. He ran against a stone, retreating more than he advanced in his canoe, because alone he could not maintain it against the current. He lost heart and then regained his strength. In a word, I have never seen better or more expressive acting. "And yet," said he, "if you had helped him to pass the rapids and the bad roads, and then if, while stopping and smoking, you had watched him from afar, you would have greatly consoled us. But I know not where your thoughts were, to send a man back quite alone amid so many dangers. I did not do that. 'Come, my nephew,' I said to him whom you see before your eyes, 'follow me, I wish to take you back to your country, at the risk of my life.'" That is what was said by the second wampum, which he tied next to the first.

The third bore witness that they had added something of their own to the presents that Monsieur the governor had given to the captive whom he had sent back to their country, and that those presents had been distributed to the nations who are allied to them, to arrest their hatchets and to cause the weapons and paddles to fall from the hands of those who were embarking to go to war. He named all those nations.

The fourth present was to assure us that the thought of their people killed in war no longer affected them, that they cast their weapons under their feet. "I passed by the place where the Algonquins massacred us last spring," he said. "I saw the spot where the fight took place in which they captured these two prisoners here. I passed by quickly, for I did not wish to see the blood that had been shed by my people. Their bodies still lie in that place. I turned away my eyes for fear of exciting my anger. Then, striking the earth and listening, I heard the voice of my ancestors massacred by the Algonquins. When they saw that my heart was capable of seeking vengeance, they called out to me in a loving voice: 'My grandson, my grandson, be good; do not get angry. Think no longer of us, for there is no means of bringing us back from death. Think of the living — that is the important thing — save those who still live from the sword and fire that pursue them. One living man is better than many dead ones.'

Having heard those voices, I passed on, and I came to you, to deliver those whom you still hold."

The fifth was given to clear the river and to drive away enemy canoes, which might impede navigation. He made use of a thousand gestures, as if he had collected the waves and had caused a calm, from Quebec to the Iroquois country. . . .

The tenth was given to bind us all very closely together. He took hold of a Frenchman, placed his arm within his, and with his other arm he clasped that of an Algonquin. Having thus joined himself to them, he said, "Here is the knot that binds us inseparably. Nothing can part us." This belt was extraordinarily beautiful. "Even if the lightning were to fall upon us, it could not separate us, for if it cuts off the arm that holds you to us, we will at once seize each other by the other arm." And thereupon he turned around and caught the Frenchman and the Algonquin by their two other arms and held them so closely that he seemed unwilling ever to leave them.

The eleventh invited us to eat with them. "Our country is well stocked with fish, with venison, and with game. It is everywhere full of deer, elk, beaver. Give up," said he, "those stinking hogs that run among your houses, that eat nothing but filth. Come and eat good meat with us. The path is clear. There is no longer any danger." He accompanied his discourse with appropriate gestures.

He lifted the twelfth belt to dispel the clouds in the air, so that all might see quite plainly that our hearts and theirs had nothing hidden, that the sun and the truth might spread their light everywhere.

The thirteenth was to remind the Hurons of their goodwill. "Five days ago," he said (and by this he meant five years), "you had a sack filled with wampum and other presents, all ready to come and seek for peace. Who made you change your minds? That sack will upset, the presents will fall out and break, they will be lost, and you will lose your nerve."

The fourteenth was to urge the Hurons to speak without delay, not to be bashful like women, and that they should resolve to go to the Iroquois land, passing by way of the country of the Algonquins and the French.

The fifteenth was to show that they had always desired to bring back Father Jogues and Father Bressani. They had thought that Father Jogues had been taken from them and they turned over Father Bressani to the Dutch because that was what he wanted.[5] "If he had been patient,

---

[5] Isaac Jogues and Francesco-Giuseppe Bressani were two Jesuits captured in two separate Mohawk raids while traveling the canoe routes connecting Quebec and the Huron country. Jogues was taken in 1642 and, after months of torture and slavery, escaped to the Dutch at Fort Orange (Albany). (See pages 155–71.) Bressani fell into Mohawk

I would have brought him back. How can I know now where he is? Perhaps he is dead, possibly drowned. It was not our intention to put him to death. If François Marguerie and Thomas Godefroy had remained in our country," he added, "they would have been married by this time, we would be but one nation, and I would be one of you."[6] (Father Jogues listened to this speech, then told us with a smile: "The stake was all prepared; had not God preserved me, they would have put me to death a hundred times. This good man says whatever he pleases." Father Bressani told us the same thing on his return.)

The sixteenth was to welcome them to this country when they came here and to protect them from the hatchets of the Algonquins and the cannons of the French. "When we brought back your prisoners some years ago, we thought that we would be your friends, but we heard arquebus and cannon shots whistling by on all sides. That frightened us and we withdrew, but we are brave in war, and so we decided to give proof of our courage the following spring. We made our appearance in your territory and captured Father Jogues, together with some Hurons."

The seventeenth present was the very beaded necklace that Honatteniate wore in his country. This young man was one of the two prisoners last captured. His mother, who had been Father Jogues's aunt in the Iroquois country, sent his necklace to whoever had given her son life. When that good woman learned that the good father whom she called her nephew was in this country, she greatly rejoiced, and her son still more so, for he had always seemed sad until Father Jogues came down from Montreal, and then he began to breathe freely and be merry.

When this great Iroquois had said all that is mentioned above, he added: "I am going to spend the remainder of the summer in my country in games, in dances, in rejoicing for the sake of peace, but I fear that, while we dance, the Hurons will come to taunt and annoy us." That is what occurred at that assembly. Everyone admitted that this man was impassioned and eloquent. I gathered only some disconnected fragments from the mouth of the interpreter, who spoke only in a rambling manner and did not follow the order observed by this barbarian.

He [Kiotseaeton] sang some songs between his gifts, he danced for joy — in a word, he showed himself to be an excellent actor for a man

---

hands in 1644; his fingernails were torn out and one finger was amputated before the Dutch ransomed him. At the time of these peace talks, he was probably at sea, on his way to Europe.

[6]François Marguerie and Thomas Godefroy were French interpreters and wilderness travelers, prototypes of the famous *coureurs de bois*. Captured while hunting near Three Rivers, they remained prisoners of the Mohawks from February to June 1641.

who has learned only what nature has taught him, without rule and without precept. The day ended with the Iroquois, the French, the Algonquins, the Hurons, the Montagnais, and the Attikamegues all dancing and rejoicing with much gladness.

On the following day, Monsieur the governor gave a feast to all members of those nations who were present at Three Rivers, to exhort them all together and to banish all distrust that might set them at variance. The Iroquois manifested their satisfaction in every way. They sang and danced according to their custom, and Kiotseaeton strongly urged the Algonquins and Hurons to obey Onontio and to follow the French in their thoughts and intentions.

On the fourteenth of the same month, Monsieur the governor replied to the presents of the Iroquois with fourteen gifts, each of which had its meaning and carried its particular message. The Iroquois accepted them all with marks of great satisfaction, which they manifested by three loud cries, uttered in unison from the depths of their chests, at each word or at each present that was given them. Thus was peace concluded with them, on condition that they should commit no act of hostility against the Hurons, or against the other nations allied to us, until the chiefs of those nations who were not present had treated with them.

When this matter had been brought to a happy conclusion, Pieskaret[7] arose and made a present of some furs to the ambassadors, exclaiming that it was a rock or a tombstone that he placed on the grave of those who had been killed in the last fight so that their bones might no longer be disturbed and that the remembrance of what had happened might be forgotten, with no further thought of revenge.

Then Noel Negabamet[8] arose and lay down in the middle of the square five large moose hides. "There," he said to the Iroquois, "is something to protect your feet and your legs, lest you hurt them on your return journey, should any stone remain on the path that you have made smooth." He also gave them five others to serve as shrouds for those who had been killed in battle and to allay the grief of their relatives and friends, who could not bear to have them left unburied. He said, moreover, that as he and his people at Sillery were of one heart with their elder brother, Monsieur the governor, they joined their present with his. Finally, three shots were fired from the cannon to drive away the foul air of war and to rejoice at the happy advent of peace.

---

[7] Pieskaret (baptized Simon) was an Algonquin chief famous for his war exploits against the Iroquois.

[8] Noel Negabamet was a leader of the Christian Montagnais of Sillery, near Quebec.

Sometime after this meeting, an ill-disposed Huron accosted the Iroquois captain who had been the agent and spokesman throughout, and sought to inspire him with distrust of the French. But the captain nobly replied to him in these terms: "My face is painted and daubed on one side, while the other is quite clean. I do not see very clearly on the side that is daubed over, but on the other side my sight is good. The painted side is toward the Hurons, and I can see nothing. The clean side is turned toward the French, and I see clearly, as in broad daylight." Having said this, he was silent, and that troublemaker was left confounded.

Toward evening, Reverend Father Vimont, superior of the mission, caused the Iroquois to be brought to our house, where he presented them with some small gifts: some petun, or tobacco, and to each of them a handsome calumet, or pipe, with which to smoke it. Kiotseaeton thanked him very wittily: "When I left my country, I gave up my life and exposed myself to death, so I am indebted to you for still being alive. I thank you that I can still see the sun. I thank you for having received me well. I thank you for having treated me well. I thank you for all the good agreements that you have concluded, and all your words are very agreeable to us. I thank you for your presents. You have covered us from head to foot. Only our mouth remained free, and you have filled it with a fine calumet and have gladdened it with the flavor of an herb that is very pleasing to us. I therefore bid you adieu, but not for long. You will soon hear from us. Even if we are wrecked in the waters, even if our craft should sink, I think that the elements will in some way bear witness to our countrymen of your kind deeds, and I am convinced that some good spirit has gone before us so that our countrymen already have a foretaste of the good news that we are going to bring them."

On Saturday, the fifteenth, they started from Three Rivers. Monsieur the governor gave them two young French lads, both to help them to take back their canoes and their presents and to manifest the confidence that he had in those people.

Captain Kiotseaeton, seeing his people all embarked, raised his voice and said to the French and to the Indians who were on the banks of the great river: "Adieu, my brothers, I am one of your relatives. I am going to carry back good news to our country." Then, turning to Monsieur the governor, "Onontio, your name shall be great throughout the earth. I did not expect to return home with my head that I had risked. I did not think that it would go forth from your doors. But I am going back loaded with honor, with gifts, and with kindness. My brothers," he continued, speaking to the Indians, "obey Onontio and the French. Their hearts and their

thoughts are good. Remain united with them and accommodate yourselves to their customs. You will soon have news from us." The Indians
replied with a noble salvo of musketry, and the fort fired a cannon shot.
Thus ended their embassy. May God cause all this to succeed for his
greater glory.

IROQUOIS ATTACKS ON THE ALGONQUINS, 1647

*After a brief truce, war resumed in the spring of 1647. It began when a
Huron-French diplomatic mission to the Mohawk country was accused of
treachery and evil magic and the emissaries, including the Jesuit Isaac
Jogues, were killed. The Mohawks then launched raids into the St. Lawrence and Ottawa valleys, easily taking several unsuspecting Algonquin
bands. The raids followed the typical pattern of stealth and ambush. The
objective was to kill some of the enemy's warriors and, above all, to capture prisoners. The latter would be conducted to the attackers' home village
and then, in some cases, tortured and killed. Other prisoners — especially
women and children — would be ritually adopted, accepted as new family
members, and integrated into the captors' community. The following ex-
cerpt from the* Relation of 1647 *tells of the adventures of some Algonquin
captives taken in this way.*

JÉRÔME LALEMANT

Some Iroquois Surprised after Defeating the Algonquins; A Woman Kills an Iroquois and Escapes

1647

On the twenty-ninth of May [1647], a canoe paddled by three Indians
of the Petite Nation of the Algonquins[1] arrived at Montreal. These poor
people were much astonished upon learning of the defeat of the upper

---

[1] The Petite Nation was an Algonquin band whose territory lay on the Ottawa River,
above Montreal.

Algonquins, . . . even though they had had strong suspicions of the treachery of the Iroquois. "This winter, we noticed tracks of the enemy who had approached very close to us," they said. "What particularly surprised us was that one of them had encountered a bear trap which we had set, and, instead of awaiting us or seeking our trail, he dismantled the trap, scattering the pieces so that we could plainly see that no animal could have done this. Someone wished us to understand that we should be on our guard, for an enemy was not far away."

Such charity is not common among barbarians. They added that a certain disease had broken out among the caribou, which made them vomit blood from the mouth and remain quite still when pursued. They saw as many as five, six, or seven fall stone dead in a moment. This so terrified them that they resolved to leave their country in order to come and live with the French. From time to time, God draws people out from the remote interior, people who would otherwise be beyond our reach, in order to bring them to a knowledge of Him through proximity with those who are able to instruct them. These poor people, afraid of meeting the Iroquois on their return, begged Monsieur d'Ailleboust [2] to provide them with some weapons, for they were resolved to fight if they encountered any enemies. Monsieur d'Ailleboust believed that they ought not to be denied in a matter so important.

Being armed, they made a side trip to Three Rivers and from there set off for their own country, without finding any enemy. One of them, supposing that the river was quite free, embarked with his wife in order to journey as far as the island [3] and tell the Indians of that country that their relatives had been captured and massacred near Three Rivers, so that they should be on their guard. As he was proceeding along in his little bark gondola, he perceived an Iroquois canoe in the distance. Turning to his wife, who was steering the canoe, he asked: "Would you be brave enough to help me if I wished to go and attack that canoe?" There were perhaps seven or eight men in it and he was alone, but he was determined nevertheless. His wife answered him: "I would follow you anywhere, for I have no wish for life after your death." They plied their paddles, straining to overtake that little craft. Before being discovered, however, they saw that farther on there were four or five more canoes, all filled with men. That stopped them, for they could see that there was no need to fling themselves rashly against a waiting enemy.

[2] Louis d'Ailleboust de Coulonge et d'Argentenay was acting governor of Montreal from 1645 to 1647 and governor of New France from 1648 to 1651.
[3] Probably Allumette Island, an Algonquin meeting place on the upper Ottawa River.

What was this poor man to do? He was unwilling to flee, but he could not advance without dying. "I must find out what capture those people have made," said he to his wife, "for I can see by their bearing that they have been victorious. I am sure they have captured some of our compatriots." He put his wife ashore and then went to the other side of the river. Giving the impression that he had come from the country of the Iroquois, he fired a shot from his arquebus. The Iroquois, not seeing him clearly, and supposing perhaps that it was some troop of their own soldiers newly arrived in the area, gave forty shouts, drawing forty times this sound from the depths of their chests: *hee.* "That is sufficient," said that Algonquin. "I need nothing further to tell me what I wanted to know: Assuredly they hold forty of our people prisoners." He took his wife back on board, then made haste to paddle away in the direction of some men he had left behind. Relating to them what he had seen and heard, he called on them to go after the enemy. Seven young men volunteered. They got into two canoes and went quickly to the place where the enemy was.

There are no hunters so eager for game as the Indians are when hunting men; no cat could be more adroit in crouching, concealing itself, and then jumping upon a mouse than is an Indian in surprising and rushing upon his prey. They glide softly, track their enemies, and go reconnoitering as quietly as a wolf. In the darkness, they could see a cluster of five cabins. "Come," they said, "let us kill and die; let us sell our lives dearly." Each one of these cabins contained more warriors than all the attackers. The plan was that six of them should enter the three largest cabins, two into each, while the other two took the two smaller ones. There were two Christians in this little band, and they said their prayers, like persons going to their death. About midnight they went in, swords[4] in hand, and with amazing speed they ran through the unfortunate sleepers within. (They also accidentally killed a woman of their own nation recently captured by those barbarians.) In the end, they had taken the lives of ten Iroquois, wounded many others, and freed ten captives. The combat took place in strange confusion. "Who are you?" the Iroquois would say, only to be answered with the thrust of a sword. The darkness made this confusion all the more horrible. A tall Iroquois, pierced through by a sword, fell upon the man who had wounded him and broke the weapon in grappling with him. The Algonquin escaped from the other's grasp and pursued him with a volley of stones, but the Iroquois caught him

---

[4]The *Relation* uses the term *espée* (sword). It is possible that the Algonquins used this European weapon, but more likely they were armed with knives or spears.

once again and would have destroyed him had not his comrade arrived in time to strike the Iroquois a blow which felled him to the ground.

On being set free, the captive women cried to their liberators: "Flee! There are many Iroquois nearby; if daylight reveals you, you will be done for." At these words, they took the scalps from the dead and threw into the river great bundles of beaver skins taken from the Algonquins by those treacherous people. They could not carry away such a heavy burden, but they did not want their enemies to have the use of the pelts either. Finally, they took the persons they had delivered into their canoes and retired to a place of safety. It would not take many soldiers such as these to trouble the Iroquois greatly.

When they were entirely free of danger, the captives related how they were taken. "Many Indians of the upper countries," they said, "had come to the island, in order to join the Hurons who were to go down to the French. Thirty families had the intention of settling with those who teach the way to heaven. There was not an Indian who was not laden with pelts in order to buy his little necessaries at the stores of the country. A Huron who had been captured some years earlier by the Iroquois and who had been made a captain of these robbers led them to the place where we were, which was so much easier for him as he had a thorough knowledge of all those regions. Our people, who were not expecting them, were much astonished when they saw them, arms in hand. At first they offered some resistance, but seeing three of our men killed by arquebus shots at the outset, they took flight. Avarice prevented the Iroquois from pursuing them; their eyes were dazzled by the great number of beavers that we had, and they thought only of pillage. That saved the lives of many people, but those of us who had children were soon taken. This is how," they said, "our misfortune came to pass."

Besides these ten persons set at liberty by those eight Algonquins, one Amazon, who had been taken with the others, bravely escaped from the hands of those who held her captive. For ten days, the Iroquois had been dragging her along with the other prisoners. Though she was bound [at night] by the feet and the hands to four stakes, which held her in the shape of a Saint Andrew's cross, she nevertheless resolved to escape. Noticing that the bonds on one of her arms did not press her very tightly, she managed to free that arm. This free hand soon untied the cords which held the rest of her body. All the Iroquois were sleeping profoundly. She got to her feet and stepped over those great bodies still buried in sleep. Just as she was about to go out, she came across a hatchet. Seizing the weapon and impelled by some warlike fury, she brought it down with all her strength upon the head of an Iroquois lying at the entrance of the cabin. As this man thrashed about, the others were awakened. A bark torch was lit, and they saw the wretched man bathed in his own blood. They looked for the perpetrator of this murder, and they found the woman's place empty and the man's hatchet covered with blood. Everyone rushed out. The young men ran hither and thither, but that good woman had hidden in a hollow stump that she had noticed the day before. From her hiding place, she listened to their commotion, in great fear of being discovered. Finally, seeing that her pursuers had all gone one way, she left her den and ran in the opposite direction as fast as she could. When daybreak came, those barbarians circled the area looking for her tracks. These they found and set off in pursuit, following her for two whole days, at the end of which this poor creature heard them moving all around the place where she was. She believed that her life was at an end. But, by good fortune, she came upon a pond formed by beavers. She plunged in, breathing only from time to time and so adroitly that she was not perceived. Finally, the searchers tired of the pursuit and, giving up hope of finding her, returned to their own people.

Finding herself free, she set forth on her journey. She passed thirty-five days in the woods without a robe or any other clothing, having only a little piece of bark from a tree with which to hide herself from her own eyes. She found no hostelries or refreshments other than currant bushes and some small wild fruits and roots. She swam across the smaller rivers, but when she came to the broad St. Lawrence, she gathered logs, attaching and binding them stoutly with the bark of a tree which the Indians use for making cords. Now that she was in a safer place, she walked along the banks of the great river without knowing exactly where she was headed, for never had she been near any of the French settlements, nor, in all likelihood, had she ever seen a Frenchman — she only knew that people came to see them by water, and so she had no other guide than the course of that great river. The insects — mosquitoes, flies, and wasps — were devouring her, and she could not defend herself from them on account of her nakedness. At last, having found an old hatchet, she built herself a bark canoe in order to travel along with the current and to better scan the banks for houses. I leave you to imagine her anxiety, for she had no knowledge of the place which she sought and no idea where the great stream was taking her. It is so broad in several places, it spreads into such great expanses of water, that it is difficult from the middle to see a house on the shore.

Finally, having traversed Lake St. Pierre, which is near Three Rivers, she perceived a canoe of Hurons who were going fishing. She straightway fled into the woods, unable to recognize whether they were friends or enemies; in addition, modesty made her conceal herself; and so she proceeded on from there only by night. In fact, she resumed her journey about eight o'clock in the evening. She discovered the French fort, and at the same moment some Hurons noticed her. The latter advanced straight toward her, in order to find out who she was. Seeing them come, she left the shore of the river and retreated into the woods, shouting to them not to approach — that she was completely naked and that she had escaped from the hands of the enemy. One of those Hurons threw her a mantle and a sort of robe. Putting this on, she came out of the woods and accompanied them to the house of the French. Our fathers sent for her and questioned her about her journey. She related what I have just told, joyful as she was to see herself at liberty and wondering at the charity of those whom she had so long been searching for without knowing exactly where they dwelt. She arrived at Three Rivers on the twenty-sixth of July greatly exhausted and emaciated. O God, what sufferings! What a lover of life is man! If these crosses had been accepted for Jesus Christ, how precious they would be! She had no thought of suffering them for her God, for she had never heard of Him, since she had never been approached by those who distribute the bread of life to poor famished ones.

THE HURONS ANNIHILATED, 1649

While the Mohawks were raiding the canoe routes of the Ottawa and St. Lawrence rivers in the late 1640s, other Iroquois armies were stepping up attacks against the Huron country farther west. For reasons that are not entirely clear, Iroquois war aims shifted in a direction that boded ill for their enemies. Whereas traditionally they tried to inflict some damage while capturing booty and prisoners, they now seemed intent on destroying an entire people. Moreover, they were well equipped with guns purchased from the Dutch traders at Fort Orange (the French made only limited supplies of firearms available to their allies), and these weapons, together with the well-established military traditions of the Iroquois, terrified all their opponents.

Winter was just coming to an end in March 1649 when the Hurons were taken by surprise by a large Iroquois invasion months in advance of the summer season of travel, trade, and warfare. The attackers quickly destroyed two outlying villages, and although the heart of the Huron country was not directly affected, the Hurons were unnerved by this bold strike. Over the years, their military strength had been reduced by population loss caused by the devastating epidemics described in chapter 3. Even more fundamentally, according to some scholars, they had become dependent on trade with the French, and their social cohesion had been undermined by cultural and religious divisions. After years of largely fruitless efforts, the Jesuits had finally succeeded in converting many Hurons, and these Christians accordingly withdrew from many of the "pagan" ceremonies that had played such an important part in binding the community together. Weakened, divided, and demoralized, the Huron nations collapsed as a result of the Iroquois hammer blows of 1649. Many individuals and families surrendered to the enemy and became adopted Iroquois. Others merged with neighboring tribes and maintained a wandering existence in the Great Lakes region. One small band of Catholic Hurons followed the Jesuits down to Quebec City.

PAUL RAGUENEAU

Of the Capture of the Villages of the Mission of St. Ignace, in the Month of March of the Year 1649

1648–1649

The progress of the faith kept increasing from day to day, and the blessings of Heaven were flowing down in abundance upon these peoples, when God chose to exercise his divine providence to derive his glory from them in ways which are adorable, though unexpected and very severe for us.

The sixteenth day of March in the present year, 1649, marked the beginning of our misfortunes — if an event, which no doubt has been the salvation of many of God's elect, can be called a misfortune.

The Iroquois, enemies of the Hurons, arrived by night at the frontier of this country. They numbered about a thousand men, well furnished with weapons, most of them carrying firearms obtained from their allies, the Dutch. We had no knowledge of their approach, although they had started from their country in the autumn, hunting in the forests throughout the winter, and had made a difficult journey of nearly two hundred leagues over the snow in order to take us by surprise. By night, they reconnoitered the condition of the first place upon which they had designs. It was surrounded by a pine stockade fifteen or sixteen feet in height, and a deep ditch with which nature had strongly fortified this place on three sides. There remained only a small space that was weaker than the others.

It was at this weak point that the enemy made a breach at daybreak, but so secretly and promptly that he was master of the place before anyone could mount a defense. All were then sleeping deeply, and they had no time to recognize the danger. Thus this village was taken, almost without striking a blow and with only ten Iroquois killed. Part of the Hurons — men, women, and children — were massacred then and there, while the others were made captives and were reserved for cruelties more terrible than death.

Only three men escaped, running, almost naked, across the snows. They bore the alarm and spread the terror to a neighboring town about a league distant. This first town was the one which we called St. Ignace, which had been abandoned by the majority of its people at the beginning of the winter, the most apprehensive and most clear-sighted having withdrawn from it in view of the danger. Thus the loss was not so considerable and amounted only to about four hundred souls.

The enemy did not stop there, but followed up his victory, and before sunrise he appeared in arms to attack the town of St. Louis, which was fortified with a fairly good stockade. Most of the women and the children had just gone from it upon hearing the news which had arrived regarding the approach of the Iroquois. The people of greatest courage, about eighty persons, being resolved to defend themselves well, courageously repulsed the first and the second assaults, killing about thirty of the enemy's boldest men, in addition to many wounded. But finally, the larger number prevailed, as the Iroquois used their hatchets to undermine the palisade of stakes and opened a passage for themselves through some considerable breaches.

About nine o'clock in the morning, we perceived from our house at St. Marie the fire which was consuming the cabins of that town, where the enemy, after entering victoriously, had reduced everything to desolation. They cast into the flames the old, the sick, the children who had not been able to escape, and all those who, being too severely wounded, could not have followed them into captivity. At the sight of those flames, and by the color of the smoke which issued from them, we understood sufficiently what was happening, for this town of St. Louis was no more

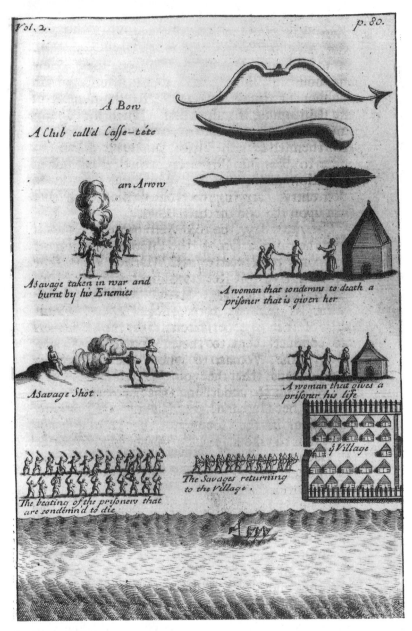

A Bow

A Club call'd Casse-tête

an Arrow

A savage taken in war and burnt by his Enemies

A woman that condemns to death a prisoner that is given her

A savage Shot.

A woman that gives a prisoner his life

ỹ Village

The beating of the prisoners that are condemn'd to die

The Savages returning to the Village.

La Guerre (War)

From the *Voyages of Baron Lahontan*. This picture was created in Europe on the basis of description rather than direct observation. At the bottom left, prisoners are seen running the gauntlet.

Courtesy of the Newberry Library, Chicago.

than a league distant from us. Two Christians who escaped the fire arrived about this time and confirmed this.

In this town of St. Louis were at that time two of our fathers, Father Jean de Brébeuf and Father Gabriel Lalemant, who had charge of a cluster of five towns. These formed but one of the eleven missions of which we have spoken above, and we call it the mission of St. Ignace.

Some Christians had begged the fathers to preserve their lives for the glory of God, which would have been as easy for them as for the more than five hundred persons who went away at the first alarm, for there was more than enough time to reach a place of safety. But their zeal could not permit such a thing, and the salvation of their flock was dearer to them than the love of their own lives. They employed the moments left to them as the most precious which they had ever had in the world, and through the heat of the battle their hearts were on fire for the salvation of souls. One was at the breach, baptizing the catechumens,[1] and the other was giving absolution to the neophytes.[2] Both of them urged the Christians to die in the sentiments of piety with which they consoled them in their miseries. Never was their faith more alive, nor their love for their good fathers and pastors more keenly felt.

An infidel, seeing the desperate situation, spoke of taking flight, but a Christian named Etienne Annaotaha, the most esteemed in the country for his courage and his exploits against the enemy, would never allow it. "What!" he said. "Could we ever abandon these two good fathers, who have exposed their lives for us? Their love for our salvation will be the cause of their death, for there is no longer time for them to flee across the snows. Let us then die with them, and we shall go together to heaven." This man had made a general confession a few days previously, having had a presentiment of the danger awaiting him and saying that he wished that death should find him disposed for Heaven. And indeed he, as well as many other Christians, had abandoned themselves to fervor in a manner so extraordinary that we shall never be sufficiently able to bless the guidance of God over so many predestinated souls. His divine providence continues lovingly to guide them in death as in life.

All of this band of Christians fell, mostly alive, into the hands of the enemy, and with them our two fathers, the pastors of that church. They were not killed on the spot, for God was reserving them for much nobler crowns, of which we will speak below.

---

[1] Native converts still learning the catechism and therefore not yet baptized.
[2] Recently baptized Christians (that is, native Catholics).

After the Iroquois had dealt their blow and burned down the town of St. Louis, they returned to St. Ignace, which they had left strongly garrisoned, so that it might serve them as a place of retreat in case of misfortune. The supply of food which they had found there would serve them as refreshments and provisions for their return trip.

On the evening of the same day, they sent scouts to reconnoiter the condition of our house at Ste. Marie.[3] After these men had reported to the council of war, they decided to attack us the next morning, and they promised themselves a victory which would be more glorious to them than all their previous military successes. We were in a good state of defense and found not one of our Frenchmen who was not resolved to sell his life very dear and to die in a cause which — being for the interests of the faith and for the preservation of Christianity in these countries — was more God's cause than ours. It was in Him that we placed our greatest confidence.

Meanwhile, one portion of the Hurons, who are called Attignawantans (that is, the nation of those who use the bear as their insignia), armed in haste and were on hand the next morning, the seventeenth of March, about three hundred strong. While awaiting more powerful forces, they concealed themselves along the approaches, intending to surprise some portion of the enemy.

About two hundred Iroquois, forming a detachment to lead the attack on our house, encountered some advance guards of that Huron troop. The latter quickly took flight after some skirmishing and were eagerly pursued until within sight of our fort, many of them having been killed while they were in disorder in the midst of the snows. But the more courageous of the Hurons stood firm against those who engaged them in combat and had the better of the fighting, forcing the Iroquois to take refuge behind the palisades of the town of St. Louis (the walls had not been burned, but only the cabins). These Iroquois were pressed into the palisade, and about thirty of them were taken captives.

The main body of the enemy, hearing of the defeat of their men, came to attack our people in the very midst of their victory. This was the elite from among the Christians of the town of La Conception and some others from the town of La Magdelaine. Their courage was unflagging, though they numbered only about one hundred and fifty. They said their prayers and then sustained the assault of a place which, having been so

---

[3] Ste. Marie was the fortified settlement the Jesuits had built in the heart of the Huron country.

recently captured and recaptured, was no longer adequate for defense. The clash was furious on both sides. Our people made many sallies, and in spite of their small numbers, they succeeded in making the enemy give way. But the combat continued far into the night until not more than a score of Christians were left, most of them wounded, and victory belonged entirely to the infidels. However, it had cost the Iroquois dearly, for their chief was seriously wounded and they lost nearly a hundred of their bravest men on the spot.

All night our French were in arms, expecting to see this victorious enemy at our gates. We redoubled our devotions, in which our strongest hopes were lodged, for help could come only from Heaven. Since it was the eve of the feast of the glorious Saint Joseph, patron of this country, we felt ourselves bound to have recourse to this powerful protector. We made a vow that each of us who were priests would say a Mass in his honor every month for a whole year. And all the people here added their own vows for various forms of penitence, in order to prepare us more holily for the accomplishment of God's will for us, whether for life or for death. We all regarded ourselves as so many victims consecrated to our Lord, who must await from his hand the hour when they should be sacrificed for His glory, without attempting to delay or wishing to hasten it.

The whole day passed in a profound silence on both sides, as the terrified country waited in expectation of some new misfortune.

On the nineteenth, the day of the great Saint Joseph, a sudden panic fell upon the enemy camp: Some withdrew in disorder, while others thought only of flight. Their captains were forced to yield to the terror which had seized them. They hurried their retreat, driving forth in haste a part of their captives, who, like packhorses burdened beyond their strength, bore the spoils which the victors were carrying off. They would not be put to death just yet.

The other captives who remained were those selected to die on the spot. The Iroquois attached them to stakes fastened in the earth, which they had placed in various cabins. On leaving the town, they set fire to these on all sides, listening with great enjoyment to the frightful cries uttered by these poor victims in the midst of the flames, where children were broiling beside their mothers, where a husband watched his wife roasting at his side, where cruelty itself would have felt compassion before a spectacle which had nothing human about it, except the innocence of those who were in torture, most of whom were Christians.

An old woman escaped from the midst of that fire and bore the news of it to the town of St. Michel, where there were about seven hundred men in arms, who set off in pursuit of the enemy. But they were unable to overtake him after two days' march. Furthermore, they lacked provisions, and they feared engaging in equal combat with an enemy flushed with victory and well supplied with firearms, of which our Hurons have very few. All these considerations obliged them to retrace their steps without having accomplished anything. By the trails, from time to time, they came upon various captives who, lacking the strength to keep up with the conqueror in his hurried retreat, had had their heads split by a hatchet blow, and still other [bodies] were fixed to posts, half-burned.

5

Writings on the Natural Environment

The *Jesuit Relations* contain many passages on the North American environment — its flora, fauna, and landscape. As with the ethnographic writings, these texts are intriguing both for what they tell us about nature at the time of contact and for what they reveal about seventeenth-century European attitudes and approaches to the subject. At the time of the early Jesuit missions, North America remained, for the French, a forbidding and mysterious region. The endless forests and the harsh climate of Canada sometimes suggested a literally God-forsaken quality, since in this period uncultivated nature was regarded as evil and ugly rather than picturesque. European observers began to consider the land attractive and benign when they saw (or imagined that they saw) settlers cutting down trees, building towns, and tilling the soil.

Looking up from the earth and its creatures, the Jesuits also commented on the stars above and on the appearance of unusual objects in the night sky. Scientific curiosity led them to observe and record the appearance of comets, eclipses, and other "celestial phenomena" for the benefit of researchers in Europe. Paradoxically, perhaps, they also tended to regard these events as signs from God, and they wondered whether they should interpret them as warnings of disaster or heralds of good fortune.

In addition to what they reveal about European views of nature, the *Relations* provide glimpses of native modes of thinking about the relationship between humans, animals, and the cosmos.

MONTAGNAIS EXPLANATIONS OF A SOLAR ECLIPSE

Whereas Europeans of the seventeenth century tried to understand the world around them in either natural or religious terms, Algonquian and Iroquoian peoples of the time were not so inclined to separate natural and supernatural frames of reference. They speculated about the causes of

*mysterious celestial phenomena such as thunder or eclipses through stories
featuring figures that combined human, animal, and magical/spiritual
qualities. A case in point is the pair of Montagnais tales about the eclipse
of the sun recounted here by Father Paul Le Jeune. Although Le Jeune seems
to have been a faithful recorder of oral legend, he was unable to resist the
temptation to editorialize about the "ridiculous fables." What appears to
bother the Jesuit, aside from the non-Christian content of the stories, is the
fluid and open-ended quality of Montagnais myth — the absence of dogma
and of absolute truth claims.*

PAUL LE JEUNE

Of Their Customs and Their Belief

1637

Here is an admirable explanation for an eclipse of the sun. They say
there is a certain being — partly human, partly nonhuman — who has a
great love for men. He is angry with a very wicked woman and at times
even conceives the desire to kill her. But he is deterred from it because
in killing her he would also kill the day and would bring eternal night
upon the earth. This wicked creature is the wife of the Manitou, and it is
she who makes the Indians die. The sun is her heart, and hence whoever
should slay her would kill the sun forever. Sometimes this man gets angry with her and threatens her with death, so that her heart trembles
and grows feeble, and it is at such times, according to them, that we see
the sun eclipsed. . . .

. . . They have so many different beliefs that you can never be sure exactly what they believe. Alas! How can certainty be found in the midst of
error?

They believe, according to what Makheabichtichiou[1] told me, that all
the people in the world will die, except for two persons, a man and a
woman. All the animals will die also, except for two of each kind, and the
world will be populated anew from these few that are to remain.

I have heard them tell a number of fables; at least I imagine the most

---

[1]Makheabichtichiou was a leading Montagnais who seriously considered converting
to Christianity. In 1637 he met frequently with Father Paul Le Jeune to discuss religion, but
he could never accept the conditions attached to baptism.

sensible among them regard these tales as fables. I will consider only one, which seems to me very ridiculous. They relate that a man and a woman were in the woods when a bear came and attacked the man, strangled him, and ate him. A hare of terrible proportions attacked the woman and devoured her. However, it did not touch the child that she still bore in her womb, of which she was about to be delivered. A woman, passing the place shortly after this carnage, was greatly astonished to see this living child. She took him, raised him as her son, but called him her little brother, giving him the name Tchakabech. This child did not grow in stature but remained always like a child in swaddling clothes, yet he attained a strength so formidable that he used the trees as arrows for his bow.

It would take too long to recount all the adventures of this man-child. He killed the bear that had devoured his father and found his [father's] hair still preserved in its stomach. He also put to death the great hare that had eaten his mother, whom he recognized from the bundle of hair that he found in its belly. This great hare was some sort of spirit of daylight, and they call one of these spirits, whom they consider a great talker, by the name of Michtabouchiou, meaning "Great Hare."

To cut the story short, this Tchakabech climbed a tree, for he wished to go to the sky. When he had almost reached the top, he blew against this tree, which grew tall and large at the breath of this little dwarf. As he climbed higher and higher, he continued to blow, and, accordingly, the tree grew taller and taller until it finally reached right to the sky. There he found the loveliest country in the world: Everything was delightful, the land was excellent, and the trees were beautiful.

After he had looked around, he returned to bring the news of all this to his sister, that he might induce her to mount to the sky and remain there forever. And so he climbed down, building cabins at intervals in the branches of the tree, where he would have his sister lodge while ascending. His sister at first would not consent, but he represented to her so strongly the beauty of that land that at last she decided to undertake this difficult journey. She took with her one of her little nephews and climbed the tree, Tchakabech going behind to catch them if they should fall. At every halt they found their cabin ready, which was a great comfort to them. Finally, they reached the sky, and to ensure that no one could follow them, this child broke off the top of the tree just enough so that no one could reach the sky from it.

After they had thoroughly admired the country, Tchakabech went to set snares, perhaps in the hope of trapping some animal. Arising in the night to go and look at his nets, he saw them all on fire and did not dare go near them. He returned to his sister and told her, "My sister, I do not know what there is in my nets. I saw only a great fire, which I did not dare approach." His sister, suspecting what it was, said to him, "Ah! My brother, what a misfortune! You have surely captured the sun in your snare. Go quickly and release it. Perhaps, while walking in the night, it accidentally fell into it."

The astonished Tchakabech went back to the snare. Looking closely, he found that he had indeed captured the sun. He tried to free it but could not get close enough. Luckily, he came upon a little mouse. He picked it up, blew upon it, and made it become big enough to use it to loosen his snares, thus releasing the sun. The sun, finding itself free, continued on its course. While it had been caught in these toils, there was no day on the earth below. How long this lasted, or what became of the child, they do not say and have no way of knowing.

THE MORAL QUALITIES OF ANIMALS

The Relations *contain numerous anecdotes about the wild animals of North America, and frequently these are presented as the embodiment of vices and virtues. The "industrious" beaver was a figure of endless fascination, and so too were creatures that displayed aggressive qualities valued in men as properly masculine. Human characters make their appearance in the following portraits from nature, and even though they win in the end, they are not the real heroes of the stories.*

JÉRÔME LALEMANT

Various Matters

1647–1648

What the poets have invented about the abduction of Ganymede[1] has a basis in the boldness of eagles. Not long ago, one of those great birds swooped down on a little nine-year-old boy. It placed one of its feet on his shoulder and seized him by the opposite ear with the talons of the other. When the poor child began to cry out, his little three-year-old brother

---

[1] Ganymede was a beautiful Trojan youth. Zeus caused an eagle to carry him off to heaven, where he served as the god's cupbearer.

---

took a stick and tried to strike the eagle, but it would not let go. Still, this did perhaps prevent it from tearing the child's eyes and face with its beak and gave the father time to come to his assistance. When the bird heard the noise of human voices, it appeared somewhat surprised but did not release its prey. The father came running and had to break its thigh. Fortunately, he had a sickle in his hand, so that when the eagle felt itself wounded and tried to fly away, he was able to cut off its head. The Indians say that eagles quite often attack men and that they sometimes carry off beavers and sturgeons heavier than a sheep. This seems to me unlikely. Some say that these are griffins and claim that the latter have been seen in these countries. I merely relate what I have heard.

I do not remember whether I have already mentioned that a Frenchman fired an arquebus at a crane and broke its wing, whereupon the bird ran straight at him on its long legs, thrusting its beak at his face like a lance, and with such impetuosity that the hunter had to leave the battlefield to his enemy. He finally overcame it by ruse. Concealing himself in the woods, he reloaded the arquebus and then put an end not only to [the Crane's] flying but also to its running.

God has given anger to all animals so that they may repel what is hostile to them. Even turtles revenge themselves on their enemies. There are several kinds of turtles and tortoises here: Some have a thick and strong shell, others a thinner and more delicate one. The second kind, which are not so well provided with defensive armor, are bolder. A Frenchman caught one of considerable size, which he thought he had killed with a club. He tied a string to its tail and threw it over his shoulder. When the animal, which is rather tenacious of life, recovered from the stupor caused by the blows to its head, it seized its foe by the back with its small jaws and bit him so hard that he yelled with pain. He dropped the cord to allow the tortoise to fall, but it would not loosen its hold and remained suspended by its teeth, biting harder and harder and refusing to let go. Its anger could not be calmed until, finally, its head was cut off.

EARTHQUAKES, COMETS, AND OTHER PROPHETIC SIGNS

In 1663 nature went insane in New France: Various strange apparitions appeared in the sky, and then a violent earthquake struck, with aftershocks occurring over a six-month period. The fact that these frightening and unusual phenomena occurred at a time of grave crisis in the war against the

Iroquois convinced many French and natives that God intended them as signs. Whether they were portents of doom or heralds of deliverance was not entirely clear, but in either case the Jesuits recommended prayer and repentance as the best response.

The Relations *speak first of phenomena that are not really so unusual in northern latitudes: the aurora borealis (northern lights) and sun dogs (a rainbow effect caused by ice crystals in the atmosphere). The "ball of fire" described in this text may have been a meteor. A more genuine "prodigy" was the earthquake that began on February 5, causing landslides and other alterations to the landscape that can still be seen in the Quebec City region. It was indeed something of a miracle that no one was injured. Throughout the long passage devoted to the earthquake, one is struck by the consistent tone of awe and wonder at the powerful forces set loose upon the land.*

In these texts, and in the one that follows on a comet observed in 1664, passages of precise, firsthand observation remind us that the scientific revolution was then under way in Europe and the Jesuits were beginning to win fame for their achievements in astronomy. However, careful research alternates with improbable hearsay reports and prophetic visions. The juxtaposition may seem strange if we expect figures in the past to sort themselves into the "modern" and the "traditional," but it is characteristic of the Jesuits. Thoroughly up-to-date in matters of scientific knowledge and methodology, they were nevertheless inclined to see signs of heavenly communication in the wonders of nature.

JÉRÔME LALEMANT

Three Suns and Other Aerial Phenomena Which Appeared in New France

1662–1663

Heaven and earth have spoken to us many times during the past year, and in a loving and unknown language which moved us to both fear and admiration. The heavens began with phenomena of great beauty, and the earth followed with violent upheavals, which made it very evident to us that these mute and brilliant voices in the air were more than mere vapor, since they presaged convulsions that were to make the earth tremble and, in so doing, to make us tremble as well.

JR 48:36–39, Jérôme Lalemant, *Relation of 1662–63.*

Beginning last autumn, we saw fiery serpents flying through the air, intertwined in the form of the caduceus,[1] borne on wings of flame. Over Quebec we saw a great ball of fire which illuminated the night almost with the splendor of day, though our pleasure in beholding it was mingled with fear because of the sparks which shot out in all directions. This same meteor appeared over Montreal but seemed to issue from the moon, and with a noise like cannon fire or thunder. It traveled through the air for three leagues before it finally vanished behind the great mountain whose name that island bears.

But what seemed to us most extraordinary was the appearance of three suns. Toward eight o'clock in the morning on a beautiful day last winter, a light and almost imperceptible mist arose from our great river. When struck by the sun's first rays, it became transparent, though it had sufficient substance to bear the two images cast upon it by that heavenly body. These three suns were almost in a straight line, appearing to be offset by a few yards, with the real one in the middle and the two others on either side. Each of the three was crowned by a rainbow of shifting colors; sometimes it appeared iris-hued, and sometimes it was a luminous white, as if an exceedingly strong light were just beneath it.

This spectacle lasted almost two hours upon its first appearance, on the seventh of January, 1663, while upon its second, on the fourteenth of the same month, it did not last so long, but only until the iris hues gradually faded and the two suns at the sides also vanished, leaving the central one victorious.

We may here record the solar eclipse which occurred at Quebec on the first day of September, 1663, and which was observed and measured, with great precision, at exactly eleven digits. It made our forests pale, somber, and gloomy. Its beginning was at one hour, twenty-four minutes, and forty-two seconds past noon, and it ended at fifty-two minutes and forty-four seconds past three.

---

[1] The caduceus was the wand of Mercury and other mythical heralds of ancient times. It is usually depicted with two serpents twined around it.

JÉRÔME LALEMANT

Universal Earthquake in Canada and Its Marvelous Effects

1662–1663

On the fifth of February, 1663, about half past five in the evening, a loud roaring was heard at the same time throughout the length and breadth of Canada. This noise, which sounded as if the houses were on fire, made everyone rush outdoors to escape so unexpected a conflagration, but instead of smoke and flames, people were much surprised to see the walls swaying and all the stones in motion, as if they had been detached. Roofs seemed to bend down in one direction and then back again in the other; bells rang of their own accord; beams, joists, and boards creaked; and the ground leaped, making the palisade stakes dance in a way that would not have seemed possible had we not witnessed it in different places.

Then all left their houses: Animals took flight; children cried in the streets; men and women, seized with terror, knew not where to take refuge, as they expected at any moment to be either overwhelmed under the ruins of the houses or swallowed up in some abyss that would open beneath their feet. Some knelt in the snow and cried for mercy, while others passed the rest of the night in prayer, for the earthquake still continued, maintaining a certain swaying motion much like that of ships at sea, so that some experienced from this tossing the same heaving of the stomach that one suffers on the water. The disturbance was much greater in the forests. There seemed to be a battle between the trees as they crashed against one another — and not merely with their branches; it seemed that even the trunks were being torn out to leap one upon another, with a din and confusion that made our Indians say that all the woods were drunken.

War seemed to have pitted even the mountains against one another, some of them being uprooted and hurled against the others, leaving yawning chasms in the places from which they had sprung. At times, too, they buried the trees that covered them deep in the ground up to their topmost branches, and at other times they would thrust them into the ground, branches downward in place of the roots, leaving only a forest of upturned trunks.

JR 48:40–57, Jérôme Lalemant, *Relation of 1662–63.*

During this general wreck on land, ice of five and six feet in thickness burst into fragments, and as it split open in various places, great clouds of smoke or jets of mud and sand issued forth and ascended high in the air. Our springs either ceased to flow or gave forth only sulfurous waters; rivers either disappeared entirely or were thoroughly defiled, the waters of some turning yellow while others went red. And our great river St. Lawrence appeared all whitish almost as far as Tadoussac, a prodigy truly astonishing to those who know the volume of water carried by this broad river below the Ile d'Orléans and how much matter it must have taken to whiten it.

The air was not exempt from the disturbances affecting the waters and the earth. Besides the roaring that constantly preceded and accompanied the earthquake, specters were seen, as well as fiery phantoms bearing torches in their hands. Pikes and lances of fire were seen, waving in the air, and burning torches gliding over our houses — without, however, doing further injury than to spread alarm wherever they were seen. There was even heard, during the silence of the night, what sounded like plaintive and feeble voices in lamentation, while white porpoises [belugas] were heard crying aloud before the town of Three Rivers — a very unusual occurrence — filling the air with a pitiful bellowing. . . .

Word comes from Montreal that during the earthquake fence stakes were plainly seen to jump up and down as if in a dance; of two doors in the same room, one closed itself and the other opened of its own accord; chimneys and housetops bent like tree branches shaken by the wind; on raising the foot in walking, one felt the ground coming up after him and rising in proportion to the height to which he lifted his foot, sometimes giving the sole a quite smart rap; and other similarly surprising things.

From Three Rivers they write as follows:

> The first and severest of all the shocks began with a rumbling like thunder, and the houses were shaken like treetops during a storm, amid a noise that made people think there was a fire crackling in their attics.
>
> This first shock continued half an hour, although its full force really lasted only a scant quarter of an hour. There was not a person who did not think the earth was about to split open. We further observed that, while this earthquake was almost continuous, still it was not of the same intensity, sometimes resembling the rocking of a great vessel riding gently at anchor, a motion which caused giddiness in many. Sometimes the disturbance was irregular and precipitated by various sharp movements and sometimes of considerable severity. At other

times it was more moderate, but most commonly consisting of a slight quivering motion, which was perceptible during intervals of quiet. According to the report of many of our Frenchmen and our Indians who witnessed the quake five or six leagues up our river [the St. Maurice], the banks on either side of the river, which used to rise to a prodigious height, are now flat, having been shaken from their foundations and reduced to the level of the water. These two mountains with all their forest cover fell into the river and formed there a mighty dike that forced that stream to change its course and to spread over the flats that had been created. Here it carved a new channel, picking up earth and mingling it with the waters, which became so thick and turbid as to change the color of the great St. Lawrence River.

You can imagine how much soil it must take to keep these waters flowing constantly full of mire every day for nearly three months. New lakes are seen where there were none before; some mountains have disappeared, having been swallowed up; a number of rapids have been leveled; a number of rivers have disappeared; the earth was rent in many places, and it has opened chasms whose depths cannot be sounded. In sum, such confusion has been wrought, of woods overturned and swallowed up, that we now see fields of more than a thousand acres utterly bare, and as if newly plowed, where a short time ago there were only forests.

We learn from the Tadoussac area that the earthquake was no less severe there than elsewhere, that a shower of ashes was seen crossing the river like a great storm, and that anyone following the coast from there to Cap de Tourmente would see its prodigious effects. Near Baie St. Paul, on the edge of the river, a small mountain about a quarter of a league in circumference sank into the water; but as though merely diving, it rose again from the depths to become an island, changing a dangerous stretch of water into a haven of safety against the winds. And farther down, near Pointe aux Allouettes, a whole forest broke away from the mainland and slid into the river, so that now green, living trees can be seen growing straight up out of the water.

All in all, three circumstances make this a most remarkable earthquake. The first is its duration, for it continued into the month of August, that is, for more than six months. Admittedly, the shocks were not always equally severe in all places. . . . The second circumstance concerns the extent of this earthquake, which we believe to have affected all of New France, for we learn that it was felt from the Ile Percé and Gaspé, which are at the mouth of our river, up to Montreal and beyond, as well as in New England, Acadia, and other far distant regions. Thus, as far as we can tell, the earthquake occurred over a tract two hundred leagues in length by one hundred in width, or an area of twenty thousand square leagues, all of which was shaken at once, at the same minute of the same day.

The third circumstance concerns God's special protection over our settlements. Right nearby we see great clefts that were formed and a prodigious extent of country utterly wrecked, yet we have not lost a single child, nor even a hair from our heads. All around us is upheaval and ruin, and yet we had only some chimneys destroyed, even as the surrounding mountains were swallowed up.

We have all the more reason to thank Heaven for this most loving protection, inasmuch as a person of probity and of irreproachable life felt presentiments of what afterward occurred and declared them to [her confessor].[1] On the very evening that this earthquake began, she had a vision of four frightful specters occupying the four quarters of the lands surrounding Quebec and shaking them violently, as if bent on overturning everything. They would undoubtedly have succeeded, had not a higher Power of venerable majesty, the ultimate source of all the disturbance and movement, opposed their efforts and prevented them from harming those whom God wished, for the sake of their own salvation, to frighten but not to destroy.

The Indians, as well as the French, had had presentiments of this fearful earthquake. A young Algonquin girl, sixteen or seventeen years of age, named Catherine (who has always lived a very innocent life, and who, indeed, owing to her extraordinary trust in the cross of the Son of God, had been cured, as if by a miracle, of an illness from which she had been suffering for an entire winter without any hopes of recovery), testified in all sincerity that on the night preceding the earthquake she saw herself with two other girls of her age and nation mounting a great stairway. At the top was a beautiful church, where the Blessed Virgin appeared with her son, predicting to them that the earth would soon be shaken, trees would strike against one another, and rocks would be shattered, to the general consternation of all the people. This poor girl, much surprised at this news, was afraid that it was some illusion of the Devil and determined to reveal everything as soon as possible to the father in charge of the Algonquin church. On the evening of the same day, a short time before the earthquake began, she shouted in a transport of

---

[1] The identity of this mysterious individual was revealed only after her death five years later. It was the Quebec hospital nun Catherine de St. Augustin, a mystic ascetic who told her Jesuit confessor of her extraordinary visions and experiences. The confessor, Paul Ragueneau, later published her life story, and the episode featuring the demons shaking the earth made a special impression on readers.

excitement and as if wrought upon by a powerful influence, saying to her parents, "It is coming soon; it is coming soon." And she afterward had the same presentiments before each tremor.

We add a second deposition, of much greater detail, which we took from another Algonquin woman — twenty-six years of age and very innocent, simple, and sincere — who was questioned by two of our fathers concerning her experiences and answered them in all frankness. Her replies were confirmed by her husband, her father, and her mother, who saw with their own eyes and heard with their own ears what follows. Her deposition runs thus:

> On the night of the fourth of February, 1663, being fully awake, sitting up in bed, and in full possession of my senses, I heard a voice, distinct and intelligible, which said to me: "Strange things are to happen today; the earth will tremble." Thereupon I was seized with great fear, seeing no one from whom those words could have come. Filled with alarm, I endeavored, with considerable difficulty, to go to sleep, and when day broke, I spoke quietly to my husband, Joseph Onnentakité, and told him what had happened to me. However, he rebuffed me, saying that I was lying and wished to fool him, and so I said nothing further. At about nine or ten o'clock on the same day, on my way to the woods to gather firewood, I was just entering the forest when the same voice was heard, saying the same thing to me and in the same manner as on the night before. My alarm was much greater, as I was entirely alone. I looked all around to see if I could catch sight of anyone, but there was nothing. Accordingly, I cut a load of wood and went home, meeting my sister on the way, as she was coming to help me. I told her what had just occurred. She went ahead and, entering the cabin before me, recounted my experience to my father and mother, but, as it was all very extraordinary, they merely listened without giving it any special thought. There the matter rested until five or six o'clock in the evening of the same day, when an earthquake occurred, and they realized that what they had heard me say in the forenoon was only too true.

FRANÇOIS LE MERCIER

Of the Comets and Extraordinary Signs That Have Appeared at Quebec and in Its Vicinity

1664–1665

We do not pretend to give an exact account here of all the unusual comets that have appeared to us this year. Our design is merely to report some observations, which may perhaps serve as a basis from which the curious may obtain some further information.

It was the twenty-ninth of November of the year 1664 that the first comet began to be noticed at Quebec, though some claim to have seen it about the fifteenth and others insist that it appeared even before All Saints' Day [November 1]. . . .[1]

On the twenty-first day of December, at half past four in the morning, the altitude of the comet was 20 degrees, 8 minutes; that of Arcturus,[2] 44 degrees, 45 minutes; the azimuth[3] from the latter to the comet, 69 degrees, 20 minutes. The comet was then at 164 degrees, 58 minutes [right ascension], and 23 degrees, 8 minutes southern declination.

On the following day, December twenty-second, at quarter past four in the morning, the comet's altitude was 15 degrees, 15 minutes; that of Spica,[4] 21 degrees, 54 minutes; and the azimuth between the comet and Spica, 38 degrees, 22 minutes. The star was east of the comet, and consequently the latter's southern declination was 27 degrees, 31 minutes, and its right ascension 162 degrees, 51 minutes.

On the twenty-third, at half past one in the morning, the comet's altitude was 6 degrees, 36 minutes; that of Keleb Alased,[5] or the lion's heart, 47 degrees, 15 minutes; and the azimuth between the two, 20 degrees, 10 minutes. By calculation the right ascension of the comet is found to be 150 degrees, 15 minutes, and its southern declination 30 degrees, 27 minutes. . . .

---

[1] This comet, officially named C/1664 W1, was first sighted on November 17, 1664, by Chinese astronomers. It was also observed in Europe, Japan, South Africa, and British America. Gary W. Kronk, personal communication.

[2] A star.

[3] The azimuth is the horizontal angle between a given heavenly body and a point south of the observer.

[4] A star.

[5] A star.

JR 50:68–71, François Le Mercier, *Relation of 1664–65.*

NATURE AS A STOREHOUSE OF RESOURCES

A source of awe, the haunt of animals evil and valorous, the object of measurement and analysis, a medium of divine communication: The North American environment appeared in all these guises in the pages of the Jesuit Relations. But it was also a treasure trove of resources that, if put to good use by the French colonists, could provide material benefit for them and revenue for their king. Following is a report on the various development projects afoot in New France in the mid-1660s, with glowing predictions of future prosperity through the exploitation of the forests, the waters, and the soil.

The author, Father François Le Mercier, attributes Canada's economic boom to the altered military situation, and that was certainly a large part of the story. In 1665 young Louis XIV had sent twelve hundred soldiers of the Carignan Salières regiment to the colony, and they had defeated the Mohawks, with the result that all the Iroquois made peace with France and France's native allies. Secure now from raids, the settlements of the St. Lawrence Valley grew and prospered. The boom was also due to massive government expenditures aimed at stimulating immigration, trade, industry, and agriculture. In trumpeting the colony's sunny prospects, the ever-politic Jesuits were taking their cue from the royal administration.

FRANÇOIS LE MERCIER

Of the Condition of Canada over the Last Two Years

1666–1667

Since the king has had the kindness to extend his protection over this country by sending the Carignan Salières regiment here, we have seen Canada transformed. We can state that it is no longer that forbidding and frost-bound land which was formerly painted in such unfavorable colors, but a veritable new France — not only in the healthiness of its climate and fertility of its soil, but in the other conveniences of life, which are being revealed more and more with each passing day.

The Iroquois used to keep us so closely confined that we did not even dare till the lands that were under the cannons of the forts, much less go any distance to discover all the bounties of a soil which is hardly different from that of France. But now the terror of His Majesty's arms has filled these barbarians with fear and compelled them to seek our friendship, instead of constantly molesting us in bloody war. Thanks to the ensuing calm, we are exploring the riches of this country and finding how much promise it holds for the future.

Monsieur de Tracy[1] has gone to carry the good tidings to the king, after having made both peace and war at the same time, while opening for the gospel the door to the Iroquois nations. He went away from us much to the regret of all these peoples, leaving the country in the charge of Monsieur de Courcelles,[2] whose courage has already contributed greatly to the happiness we now enjoy and continues with the same zeal to secure us in its possession. Having made himself feared by the Iroquois, through the expeditions which he has led into their country, he will hold those barbarians — whether with their consent or by force — to the terms of the peace agreement which they came here to obtain. Already he is giving us an advance taste of the resultant blessings, which we had never before experienced.

Peace was indeed concluded with all the Iroquois nations after the king acceded to the pressing request of their ambassadors. The latter took three Jesuits back to preach the holy gospel and maintain this peace among the lower nations.[3] The settlers of the colonies then saw that they could spread abroad and till their lands in perfect quiet and great safety, not only on account of this peace but also because care is taken to maintain and enlarge the frontier forts and to provide them with all necessary supplies for the soldiers who defend them.

With this in mind, Monsieur Talon,[4] intendant for the king in this country, made it his first priority to do everything possible to find the means of making this country prosperous. He makes trials to find out what the land can produce, and he establishes all possible business and commercial connections, not only with France but also with the West Indies, Madeira, and other countries in Europe as well as in America.

[1] Alexandre de Prouville de Tracy, marquis and lieutenant general for French America from 1663 to 1667. Under Louis XIV, he strengthened France's military position in the West Indies and Canada.

[2] Daniel de Rémy de Courcelles was governor of New France from 1665 to 1672.

[3] The "lower nations" Le Mercier refers to were the Mohawks and Oneidas, dedicated enemies of the French and the last Iroquois tribes to make peace with the latter.

[4] Jean Talon was the first intendant of Canada, serving from 1665 to 1668 and again from 1670 to 1672. His position entailed responsibility for legal, financial, and economic affairs in the colony.

He has been so successful in this that fisheries of all kinds are in operation, the rivers being very rich in fish such as salmon, brill, perch, sturgeons, and even herring and cod, which can be caught without leaving the St. Lawrence and which, wet-salted or dried, can be sold in France at a great profit. This year, these fisheries have been carried out in shallops on a trial basis, and this has turned out to be very productive.

Similarly, the seal fishery furnishes the whole country with oil and yields a great surplus that is sent to France and to the West Indies. This fishery was tried during the past year, and in three weeks' time it netted Sieur l'Espine, over and above all expenses, nearly eight hundred livres for his share alone. The white whale [beluga] fishery, which they hope to operate without great expense, will yield even more oil and of a higher grade for manufacturing purposes.

The trade which Monsieur Talon proposes to carry on with the islands of the West Indies will not be the least of this country's resources, and already, to ascertain its value, he is this year shipping to those islands wet- and dry-salted cod; salted salmon; eels; peas, both green and white; fish oil; staves; and boards — all the produce of this country.

But as colonial fisheries are the soul and basis of this commerce, he intends to establish them as soon as possible. To that end, he proposes to form a company to establish the facilities and to bear the initial expense. In a year or two they will yield marvelous profits.

With assiduous devotion, he busies himself investigating all possible sources of profit that the St. Lawrence and other rivers of this country might produce, yet this does not stop him from turning his attention also to the gain that may be derived from Canada's bountiful land.

Consequently, he is directing a careful search for mines and minerals, which appear to be numerous and rich, and he orders the cutting of all kinds of timber, which is found everywhere in Canada and which provides building materials for the French and others who need to provide themselves with shelter when they arrive here. He has started the manufacture of staves, for export to France and to the West Indies, and of masts, samples of which he is sending this year to La Rochelle[5] for the use of the navy. He is also interested in lumber for shipbuilding, which was tried in this country. A bark[6] was constructed here and proved to be very serviceable, and a large vessel is now ready to be launched.

Besides the ordinary grains that have up to now been harvested, he has initiated the planting of hemp. Hemp growing will increase until the

[5] A seaport in southwestern France.
[6] A bark was a substantial sailing ship with three or more masts.

country is filled with it, so that it will be able not only to supply its own needs but also to furnish large quantities to France. As for flax, experiments with this crop over the past year showed that it thrives and produces a very good yield.

Even the French ewes commonly bear two lambs after their first year feeding in this country.

I do not speak here of what may be hoped for from the more southern districts of Canada;[7] there it has been observed that the soil produces naturally the same kinds of trees and fruits as does Provence. It is at about the same latitude and has a climate of nearly the same atmospheric temperature. . . .

[7] By "the more southern districts of Canada," the author presumably means territories then claimed by France, now parts of New York and the midwestern states.

6

Missions to the Iroquois

To convert the Iroquois — for so long the deadly enemies of France and, the *Relations* often suggested, of God himself — was one of the great ambitions of the Jesuits. Some abortive attempts were made in the 1650s during pauses in the fighting, but success came only after 1667, when a comprehensive and lasting peace was established. Many factors had conspired to change the situation around that time. The English had taken over the Hudson Valley from the Dutch; European trade, technology, and other influences were having their usual disturbing effects; epidemics were taking a severe toll; and imported alcohol was devastating the natives. With the Mahicans and other enemies pressing them from the south and east, the Iroquois were anxious to end the costly conflict with their northern neighbors. The arrival of a large French military force in Canada only added to the urgency. Two French invasions, which left the Mohawks' fields devastated and their villages in smoldering ruins, convinced them to come to terms with the French, even though they were never actually defeated in battle.

The Jesuits worked among the Five Nations of the Iroquois League until 1684, when war resumed and the French missionaries were expelled. Meanwhile, a decade and a half of favorable conditions had netted a substantial number of converts, many of whom migrated north to live near the French settlements along the St. Lawrence. Ironically, given their record as the most determined enemy of the French, it was the Mohawks who came to predominate among these "mission Indians." While the non-Catholics of the original Iroquois nations then went on to pursue their historical destinies beyond the influence of the Society of Jesus, the Iroquois converts of Canada developed their own distinct way of life as allies of the king of France and autonomous residents of the St. Lawrence Valley.

MISSION TO THE MOHAWK COUNTRY, 1667

By the terms of their treaty with the French, the Iroquois had to admit Christian missionaries into their midst. This was a standard feature of the French alliance system, and it fit with native expectations that former enemies, who had since become friends, would send emissaries as a human embodiment of the new relationship. The text that follows recounts the experiences of three Jesuits — Jacques Fremin, Jean Pierron, and Jacques Bruyas — as they made their way to the land of the Mohawks in 1667 and established their headquarters at the rebuilt town of Gandaouagué. Iroquois success in decades of warfare and the resulting stream of captives brought to their towns had produced a population with a substantial percentage of people who were born Hurons, Montagnais, and Algonquins and who, in many cases, had been exposed to Christianity. It was to these "old Christians" that the missionaries first directed their efforts, while other Mohawks were drawn in later.

FRANÇOIS LE MERCIER

Of the Mission of Ste. Marie among the Mohawk Iroquois

1667–1668

Fathers Fremin, Pierron, and Bruyas set out in July of the year 1667 for the land of the lower Iroquois in order to reestablish the missions there which had been interrupted by the wars. They were detained a long time ago at Fort Ste. Anne, at the entrance to Lake Champlain, out of fear of a band of Mahican Indians (we call them Wolves), who are enemies of the Iroquois. However, they left that fort at last, resolved to run the same risks and pass through the same dangers as the Iroquois ambassadors with whom they were traveling to their country. We can give no better account of their voyage, their arrival and welcome, and the fruits of their efforts to plant the faith in these wild and barbarous regions than in quoting from the journal they kept. . . .

"Arriving within three-quarters of a league of the falls by which Lake St. Sacrement [Lake George] discharges, we all halted without knowing why until we saw our Indians at the waterside gathering up flints, which were almost all cut into shape. We did not give this much thought at the time, but have since then learned the meaning of the mystery. Our Iroquois tell us that they never fail to stop at this spot and pay homage to a race of invisible men who dwell there at the bottom of the lake and who devote themselves to preparing cut flints for those who pass that way. The latter must, however, pay their respects by presenting them with tobacco, and the more they give, the more the supply of these stones is likely to remain plentiful. These men of the water travel in canoes, as do the Iroquois. When their great captain dives into the water to enter his palace, he makes such a loud noise as to terrify anyone who does not know about this great spirit and his little men. When our Iroquois, in all seriousness, recited this fable to us, we asked them if they did not also offer tobacco to the great spirit of Heaven and to those who dwell there with him. They replied that the spirits of the sky do not need it as do those of the earth. The occasion of this ridiculous story is the fact that the lake is indeed subject to terrible storms with pounding waves . . . and when the wind blows onshore, it drives onto this beach hard stones which are good for striking fire. . . .

"[Later in the voyage] . . . our mariners landed at the end of Lake St. Sacrement and made ready for the portage, barely half a league long through the woods. Everyone took some of the baggage or the canoes. We reembarked and then, after a few strokes of the paddle, we at last forsook those canoes, happy to have arrived safely at the end of the lake. From there, we had only thirty leagues of overland travel to reach our long-sought destination.

"Since the whole country of the Iroquois was at that time greatly in fear of a renewed French invasion, fourteen warriors had been at the entrance to this lake for several days, constantly on the lookout for an army on the march, so that they could quickly spread the word to the entire nation. Their plan was to lay ambushes in the woods, in order to attack advantageously and harass the invaders along the line of march. Accordingly, a third [sic] band was posted there, for reconnaissance purposes. But, by great good fortune for them and for us, we came to them not as enemies, but as angels of peace. They, for their part, ceased to be lions and became our servants, making themselves very useful as porters: Providence placed them there to take our baggage, which would otherwise have been very troublesome to transport over land to their country.

"And so we proceeded in company and, by short marches, came to within three-quarters of a league of their principal town, called Gandaouagué. It was here that the late Father Jogues watered the earth with his blood and where he was so badly treated during eighteen months of captivity [see the selection on page 157]. We were received there with the customary ceremonies and with all possible honors. We were conducted to the cabin of the foremost captain, where all the people crowded in to look at us, quite delighted to see among them such peaceable Frenchmen, when the French had appeared there not long before as though in a fury, putting everything to the torch.

"The first care of Father Fremin was to go through the cabins looking for Huron and Algonquin captives, who alone constitute two-thirds of the town. He baptized at once ten of their children, presenting to God these blessed first fruits of the new mission. . . .

"Our chapel was built by the efforts of the Iroquois themselves, who applied themselves to the task with incredible ardor. We opened it, and our old Christians, who had formerly been instructed in their own Huron country by our fathers, could once again hear the holy Mass. Here it must be confessed that we could not help shedding tears of joy at seeing these poor captives so fervent in their devotions and so constant in their faith after all the years they had been deprived of all instruction. Such is the reward that God gives us in advance for the little labors which this barbarous life imposes on us for love of Him. The days slip by more quickly than we realize, and we are obliged to spend eight hours at a stretch directing the prayers of people who come to the chapel, while the rest of the time passes rapidly in other apostolic functions.

"The mothers bring us their little children, that we may make the sign of the cross on their foreheads, and they themselves adopt the habit of doing the same thing before putting them to bed. Their ordinary conversation in the cabins is about hell and paradise, subjects on which we often speak to them.

"The same custom is followed in the other towns, in imitation of this one, and we are from time to time invited to go and administer the sacraments to them and establish infant churches insofar as the state of barbarism allows.

"At the very first visit made by Father Fremin to one of these villages, he found forty-five old Christians, who gave him, and who themselves received in return, much consolation. He felt moved to bear witness to the truth, declaring that he would never have believed, until he saw and experienced it, how firmly rooted piety is in the souls of these poor captives, for their devotion greatly surpasses that of the common run of Christians, even though they were deprived for so long a time of any help from their pastors. They came forward for the sacrament, they had their children baptized, and they showed the spot where they assemble every evening, without fail, to maintain their fervor by the public prayers which they offer together. There some Iroquois joined them, attracted by the odor of this good example and persuaded, by this noble constancy, of the truth of our holy faith. . . .

"There are many obstacles to the establishment of the faith among these peoples which have been amply discussed in earlier *Relations,* but one of the greatest has not yet been mentioned. Drunkenness, caused by the brandy that the Europeans of these coasts began to sell to the natives some years ago, has proven very useful to the Devil.

"It is so common here, and causes such disorders, that it seems sometimes as if all the people of the town have gone crazy, so great is the license they allow themselves when they are under the influence of liquor. Firebrands have been thrown at our heads and our papers set on fire; our chapel has been broken into, and we have been often threatened with death. During the three or four days these disorders last — and they are quite frequent — we are made to suffer a thousand insults without complaint. We cannot eat, nor can we rest. . . .

"When the storm has passed, however, we return to our functions peaceably. For example, we celebrated the festival of Christmas with all the devotion imaginable on the part of our neophytes, several of whom attended six consecutive Masses. Thus, God does not leave us in perpetual bitterness.

We have forty Hurons who make public profession of Christianity, and for the most part, they are making very good progress and are very zealous. During the first three months we baptized fifty persons; of these, two Iroquois women and two Algonquin women are in the way of salvation, as we have reason to believe, in view of the pious sentiments in which they died. Since then, we have baptized fifty more and, of all these, thirty children are certainly in Heaven."

―――――

THE MOHAWKS CONVERTED

The following Relation *was written by Father Jean Pierron two years after the initial report on the Mohawk mission, which appears in the previous section. The missionary's high-handed approach and arrogant tone is quite striking, and it is in marked contrast to the more delicate methods of an earlier generation of Jesuits who ministered to the Hurons. Pierron appears to have deliberately provoked a crisis in relations with leading figures in the main Mohawk town of Gandaouagué. In talking of returning to Quebec, the missionary was clearly threatening a breach with France and a possible armed invasion of the country. Feeling especially vulnerable at the time, the Mohawks went to desperate lengths in an attempt to propitiate him, promising to "overthrow the country" and accept the ceremonies and rules of conduct of Christianity.*

Subsequent events suggest that Pierron negotiated not with the entire Mohawk nation, as implied here, but with a pro-French faction, one largely based, it would seem, in the foreign-born population. In the aftermath of the meeting described here, many, but by no means all, of the people of Gandaouagué did their best to integrate the Catholic religion into their Iroquoian way of life. Those who were most strongly committed to the French alliance and its Christian corollary eventually moved to live close by the French-Canadian settlements of the St. Lawrence. The resulting Christian Mohawk community of Sault St. Louis/Kahnawake is described in the next section.

JEAN PIERRON

Of the Mission of the Martyrs in the Country of the Mohawks, or the Lower Iroquois

1669–1670

In eight months I have baptized only fifty-three persons, nearly all of whom have gone to Heaven. If I have contributed to the salvation of even one soul, I should consider myself more than adequately recompensed for all my efforts, for Christ gave his blood for that soul. . . .

I have made use of every device that God has suggested to me to make them give up their bad habits, for to convert these peoples, you must begin by touching their hearts before you can convince their minds. It is with this in mind that I painted some spiritual and devout pictures that have been of powerful assistance in teaching them. I do the catechism twice a day, with all the success that could be expected of these poor Indians, though I was often surprised at the quite extraordinary impression that the word of God made on their souls.

I have attacked drunkenness and debauchery, which are, as it were, the divinities of this country, for these peoples are madly attached to them. These vices I have combated by invoking the fear of God's judgment and, along with that, the dread of the armed might of a great king, whose name alone is enough to hold them to their duty. I have tried to win them over with the greatest possible gentleness and intimacy. . . .

At first I had thought that, in order to establish Christianity on a solid basis among these peoples, it was necessary to make use of reading and writing, two things of which the Indians have no knowledge. Accordingly, I spent a month teaching both to our Iroquois children and, as a result, some of them did learn to read and write fairly well. But I did not have a sufficient supply of the little rewards that one needs to keep children interested in this pursuit, and, moreover, I was left with too little time for the essential duties of my mission. And so I had to find some other expedient which would be just as effective but would leave me more time for the responsibilities of my ministry.

Some days later, God inspired me with an idea which is much easier and which produces great results among these peoples. It is a game designed to capture our Indians by means of what they most love, for gaming constitutes their principal activity when they are not at war. Thus I hope to bring them to their salvation through the very thing that so often brought about their ruin.

Through this means, I intend to do away with the peculiar ignorance in which they live, touching all that concerns their salvation, and to compensate for their imperfect memory. This game communicates its message through pictures and provides sound instruction by means of the emblems with which it is filled. Those who wish to amuse themselves with it have only to look at it to learn all that they have to do to live a Christian life. They will remember all that they have learned and never be able to forget it. . . .

It is thus that our Indians learn as they play to effect their salvation. I have tried to join what they love so passionately to that which they ought to love even more so that they might receive instruction without any unpleasantness. . . .

[Father Pierron describes a sacred Feast of the Dead (see page 61 for a Huron version of this ceremony) that he attended, only to denounce Mohawk customs, calling on those present to convert to Christianity and quarreling with a Mohawk chief who had made a great effort to accommodate the Jesuits. He goes on to recount another occasion when he provoked a dispute with this leader.]

The same captain gave me still another occasion to speak to him a little severely when he told me, rather rudely, that I must withdraw from their company because they were going to sing according to their custom. It is true, I did not understand a word of their song and did not wish to take part in it; nevertheless, as I was not one to disturb their music, I thought he was wrong to make me leave. Moreover, since one must not pardon any offense in this kind of people, when they commit faults which they themselves ought to reckon as such, I told them that I would not disturb the feast by remaining quietly where I was. Besides, I said, it was not fitting for me to leave the circle of men and join the women or go among other persons whom I did not know. However, as I saw they were very urgent that I should withdraw, I did so, for fear of offending them, and retired to the quarters of the Onondagas, declaring my displeasure to their captain, who considered it perfectly justified.

After the ceremony, which lasted five hours, I returned to the town without waiting for the rest of that solemnity which was to be concluded by our Mohawks. They were aware of my resentment, and they believed it was to be feared, all the more so because some time before I had spread a rumor that I intended to go to Quebec. The whole body of Mohawks blamed the imprudence of the captain who had offended me and were extremely sorry for the affront that he had offered me. He himself soon recognized his mistake and hastened to come and apologize. . . .

"My brother," he said, "I cannot believe, even though everyone asserts it, that you are irritated in spirit and your heart [is] filled with bitterness toward me. . . . They say that you are going to Quebec and that you no longer wish to live with us. However that may be, I beseech you not to get us into trouble with Onontio, for this would cause problems for you, if so many old and young people, people who love and honor you greatly, were to come to harm on your account." . . .

[In response, Pierron reiterates his complaints about being snubbed and excluded.]

. . . After giving me a patient hearing, this captain replied with great sincerity: "My brother, I see clearly what lies at the bottom of this quarrel: It is that we are not yet Christians. But if you will entrust this important matter to me, I promise you a favorable result. Here is how you must proceed. First, you must gather everyone together, and then, presenting three fathoms of wampum, one for each of our families [clans], you will tell us with each of these presents what is in your heart. After that, leave it to me, and I will take care of the rest. I hope that all goes well." . . .

This captain, who had great authority with the Indians and possessed great adroitness in managing important affairs, threw himself into the task, personally visiting all the most influential men of the country to discuss this great project with them. . . .

He brought all the most significant persons from the villages of the Mohawks and assembled them in my cabin. I then began to deliver them a speech that I made as emphatic as I could, upon their false divinities, their sorcerers, and all their superstitions. "My brothers," I said to them, "I am filled with joy to see you all assembled here. You heard that I was going away to Quebec, and it is true. But I will not deprive you of my bodily presence by departing without your knowledge, or of my spiritual being by concealing my thoughts from you. I will open my heart to you without reserve. I am not unaware that you fear lest I shall not return to you again and that you greatly desire to have me remain here, to maintain the peace that you enjoy with the French. I have come here only to die here, and you know that in the three years that we have lived together, free from the disturbances of war, I have spared neither my exertions, my health, nor my life to assure you an eternal happiness. . . .

"You wish me to remain here with you, in order to maintain the peace, and to keep me, you often allege to me that you are now one, in body and in soul, with the governor of the French and with me. Have you any reason to say this, you who have neither the same sentiments, the same inclinations, nor the same behavior as us? How could my soul be yours, when I am convinced that mine is a pure spirit, immortal, and like to the master of your lives, while you believe that yours is either a bear, a wolf, a serpent, a fish, a bird, or some other kind of animal that you have seen in a dream? Moreover, your soul and mine have very opposite sentiments. You think that the master of life is a demon, whom you call Agreskoué, whereas I say that your Agreskoué is a slave whom God, who is the master of our lives, keeps chained in Hell as a proud and wicked spirit. You believe in an infinite number of fables as so many truths, and I regard them as so many lies. If, then, our souls have such opposite tendencies, how can there be any firm and true peace between the soul of the French and the soul of the Mohawks?

"The French, seeing that you do not believe what they believe, will have every reason to mistrust you and to think that the Mohawk is a deceiver and a perfidious person, since he does not believe himself to be bound by the same obligations to be honest and since he has no law that prevents him from breaking the peace with the same lack of faith with which he broke it before. If you have no fidelity toward God, the master of our lives, how will you have any toward men? Be assured that we shall never believe that you wish to live on good terms with us until you serve the same Master that we serve. As long as your minds do not embrace all our ideas concerning virtue and heaven, our hearts cannot be united.

"So, my brothers, in order to have a firm and unshakable peace of the sort you desire, you must be like me and believe what I believe. Then Onontio will say: 'Now I believe the Mohawk to be sincere and faithful, and now I love him as one of my children.' All the French will rejoice to know that you are their brothers, and wherever they meet with you, they will bestow on you a thousand acts of friendship and a thousand endearments. All of France will take an interest in your good fortune, all the world will know of it, and all of Heaven will be filled with joy. God himself — yea, that great master of our lives, who has his palace in Heaven — will not fail to prepare for the Mohawk, if he becomes Christian, a happiness without end."

After this speech, I threw down a fathom of wampum, saying: "Mohawk, my brother, if it is true that you wish to hear me, there is my voice, which at once warns you and begs you to renounce Agreskoué and never speak of him again, but instead adore the true God and observe the law." This first speech was received with a great cry of approval, and it seemed to me that those Indians were moved by my speech.

Then I threw down another fathom of wampum to oblige the shamans to stop invoking demons for the cure of their sick, but instead to make use of natural remedies, whose power and usefulness I had often shown them. I dwelled on this point at length because it is one of the superstitions to which they give most credence. Thereupon I heard a second cry of joy, with which all those assembled, including even the shamans who were present, testified to me their disposition to do all in this matter that I should wish.

The last present that I made, to do away with the superstition of dances, was received with the same acclamation.

After this I was told, in a few words, that an answer would be given me in a council. Thus passed off that first interview, which gave us great hopes for the conversion of this people. . . .

[The Mohawk council replies favorably, signifying a desire to accede to the missionary's demands.]

Some days later, I saw that the sorcerers of this town were throwing into the fire their tortoiseshells and the other instruments of their calling, that the women did not summon the shamans anymore in their illnesses, that no dance was any longer allowed except that which I approved, and that all the Indians of this country declared themselves openly for the faith. The elders prompted the youth to come for instruction, to have recourse to prayer, and to make a public profession of the

Christian religion. Leading by their example, the elders crowded into the chapel and devoted themselves to prayer. One could not ask for a greater inclination for the faith than that which appears in our Indians, and although their natural inconstancy still divides my heart between fear and joy, I yet hope that God will have the goodness to finish the work that he has begun.

THE IROQUOIS MISSION OF SAULT ST. LOUIS/KAHNAWAKE

Historians of the Iroquois suggest that in the difficult years following 1667, one portion of Mohawk society sought security through forging links with the English, newly installed in New York, while another opted for close affiliation with the French. This second party, in which assimilated captives may have predominated, accepted Christianity and even opted to migrate to the French settlements, since conflict with the Traditionalist-English alliance party made life in the Mohawk towns intolerable. Accordingly, large numbers of Mohawks and other Iroquois made their way to the Montreal area in the late 1660s and early 1670s. The Jesuits tended to interpret this move as an expression of religious idealism and submission to the French, but the Iroquois involved must have had a different view of the situation, for they remained fiercely jealous of their independence and determined to preserve their culture, even as they deferred to missionary authority in certain strictly religious matters.

The majority of Mohawk migrants settled across the St. Lawrence from Montreal, at a spot the French called Sault St. Louis. There they built a traditional Iroquoian village, which they named Kahnawake (sometimes spelled "Caughnawaga"), where they pursued a traditional mode of existence centered on the cultivation of corn and supplemented by winter hunting expeditions. Kahnawake was a hybrid, however, shaped by Christianity in important respects, especially with regard to the regulation of sexuality and marital practices and to the ceremonial life of the community, and yet remaining profoundly Iroquoian in its language and culture.

The Jesuit Relations, *as an annual publication, ended with the 1673 edition, at a time when the Kahnawake mission was just getting established. However, we have a letter dated 1682, from Father Claude Chauchetière, one of the resident missionaries, who describes a period of exceptionally intense religious activity that swept the community from 1676 to the early 1680s. Chauchetière was especially excited about the activities of a group of women (mostly young women) who renounced marriage and devoted themselves to a life of charity, prayer, and "mortification of the flesh." The ascetic practices of self-torture recounted below can be difficult for modern readers to understand without falling back on simplistic and ahistorical psychological explanations. In the European context of seventeenth-century Catholicism, it was seen as meritorious to inflict pain on one's body as a means of atoning for sins and imitating the lives of the saints and the Passion of Jesus. Obviously, missionaries communicated this ascetic ideal to the Indian converts of New France. And yet it will be apparent that the devout women of Kahnawake also drew on their Iroquoian culture in developing their special brand of religious devotion. Worth noting also is the undercurrent of tension between the "sisters" and their priests, which runs just below the surface of Chauchetière's enthusiastic account.*

CLAUDE CHAUCHETIÈRE

Letter of October 14, 1682

1682

. . . We are located sixty leagues from Quebec at a beautiful spot with a fine view called the Iroquois mission. It is the finest mission in Canada, and it resembles one of the best churches in France as far as piety and devotion are concerned. . . .

We have here a large farm where we keep oxen, cows, and poultry and harvest wheat for our subsistence. It is sometimes necessary to take charge of all temporal as well as spiritual matters, now that Father Fremin, as well as Father Cholenec, have gone down to Quebec due to illness. Some Indians plow their land and harvest French wheat instead of Indian corn. It is impossible to describe their joy when they can harvest twenty or thirty *minots*[1] of French wheat, enabling them to eat bread from time to time. But growing this kind of grain requires too much labor, and so they usually cultivate the soil in order to plant Indian corn. The men go hunting to procure a provision of meat, while the women go to the forests in search of firewood. If the Indians were given food, they

[1] A *minot* was a French measure, roughly equivalent to a bushel.

JR 62:166–87, Letter of Father Claude Chauchetière, October 14, 1682.

on donne la confirmation la 1re fois

Confirmation in the Faith

Bishop St. Vallier administers confirmation to Iroquois converts at the mission settlement of Sault St. Louis/Kahnawake, near Montreal. This pen-and-ink drawing is by Father Claude Chauchetière, one of the Jesuit missionaries, and dates from 1686.

Archives départementales de la Gironde.

would work much more than they do. Our village grows larger every year, while the Lorette Mission,[2] where Father Chaumonot is, steadily diminishes. That of the Mountain[3] neither decreases nor increases greatly, whereas ours grows continually. It is expected that all the Mohawks will reside here within two or three years. More than eighty have settled here recently. We have a chapel twenty-five feet wide and nearly sixty feet long. We have three bells, with which we produce a very agreeable carillon; and soon the Indians will have another bell, weighing two hundred pounds, to complete the harmony.

The usual exercises of our mission are as follows: We ring the bell at four o'clock in the morning, which is the hour at which we rise, as in our houses in France. Many of our Indians, through a spirit of devotion, come at once to the church to adore the Blessed Sacrament, and they remain there until the first Mass, which is said in winter at quarter to seven and in midsummer at five o'clock. While they are saying their prayers, I withdraw to my chamber, which is six feet long and five feet wide, to say my orison. After this, I say the first Mass, at which many are present even though the bell is not rung for it. The second, which is the Mass for the Indians, is said at half past five. I am present at it, as is everyone in the village — they attend every day, without a single person being absent. The prayers are said aloud. Afterward, a third Mass is held for the children, with me present. They pray in unison, and then I give them a brief catechism class. Such is my daily routine.

In addition to this, the Indians come frequently during the day to visit the Blessed Sacrament, especially on their way to the fields and when they are returning home. From eight o'clock until eleven, when we take our midday meal, I am busy visiting the Indians or working on books for them. For they are inconstant by nature — as they themselves will admit — and so it is necessary to visit them frequently, to encourage them, to settle their disputes, and to prepare newcomers for receiving the sacraments. There are 60 cabins, or in other words, 120 to 150 families, with at least 2 families to a cabin. To perform these visits properly would require all the time of one missionary, with another for the children, and a third for the more advanced who need instruction on virtue.

[2]The Jesuit mission of Lorette was located near Quebec City. It consisted mainly of Christian Hurons, survivors of the Iroquois attacks of the 1640s.

[3]Adjacent to Montreal, the mission of La Montagne (the Mountain) was maintained by priests of the Sulpician order. Iroquois and other native converts lived there. In the eighteenth century, the mission moved northwest of Montreal to Oka.

One thing that helps me in my work is the drawings that I make to illustrate the truths of the gospel and the ways of virtue, following the model devised by Monsieur de Nobletz.[4] I have one book containing colored pictures of the ceremonies of the Mass as connected with the Passion of our Lord, another with illustrations of the torments of Hell, and still another on the creation of the world. The Indians read these with pleasure and profit; these books are their silent teachers. One of our catechists,[5] aided by these books, preaches long sermons. I was pleased yesterday to find a group of Indians, at the door of a cabin, learning to read with books of this kind.

To return to our schedule and our usual occupations: The bell rings at eleven o'clock for our examination of conscience, and at the same time, the Angelus[6] is rung, which the Indians recite with great devotion. Our afternoon is spent giving instruction in the cabins. In my case, I visit the sick, a duty that, by itself, would be enough to keep one man occupied. I also have responsibility for a parish of one hundred French households. Father Bruyas, the superior of the mission, takes care of the temporal and spiritual needs of the Indians and acts as a father to them for the things of the body and of the soul. All last year, the two of us were the only priests here.

You will be pleased to hear about the austerities practiced by certain Indian women. Although there may be some indiscretion in their behavior, it will show you their fervor. More than five years ago some of them learned, I know not how, of the pious practices followed by the nuns of the Montreal hospital. They heard of disciplines, of iron girdles, and of hair shirts.[7] The religious life appealed to them, and so three of them formed an association in order to set up some sort of convent, but we stopped them, because we did not think that the time had yet come for this. However, though they were not cloistered, they at least observed the rule of chastity, and one of them died with the reputation of

[4] Father Michel Le Nobletz was famous for the internal missions he led into the heart of darkest France. In the early seventeenth century, he developed a series of allegorical pictures to communicate his message to the illiterate peasants of Brittany.

[5] A catechist was a layperson who taught the fundamentals of Catholicism to children and converts. At Sault St. Louis, the catechists were natives and, in most cases, women.

[6] The angelus is a prayer in honor of the Incarnation, recited at a time signaled by the ringing of a church bell.

[7] The reference here is to various devices used by Counter Reformation ascetics to "mortify the flesh" and elevate the spirit. Chauchetière mentions "disciplines," meaning self-flagellation; "iron girdles" *(ceintures de fer)*, which were belts, worn under the clothes, with sharp points on the inside, where they scratched the wearer's skin; and "hair shirts" *(haires)*, rough undergarments designed to be uncomfortable and irritating.

sanctity three years ago this spring.[8] They, and some others who followed their example, would be admired in France if what they do were known there.

The one who first initiated [these ascetic practices] began around Christmas of the year 1676, when she went to the foot of a large cross that stands beside our cemetery, took off her clothes, and exposed herself to the air. This was during a snowstorm, and she was pregnant at the time; and the snow falling on her back caused her so much suffering that she nearly died from it, along with her child, who was thoroughly chilled inside the mother's womb. It was her own idea to do this, and she said it was to do penance for her sins. She has since then acquired four companions who imitate her in her fervor. In the depth of winter, two of them made a hole in the ice and threw themselves into the water, where they remained during the time that it would take to say the rosary slowly and deliberately. One of the two, returning to her cabin and fearing that she would be found out, did not venture to warm herself at the fire, and so she lay down for the night with the ice still adhering to her shoulders. The men and women have invented several other such means of mortification by which to torment themselves as part of their habitual penance, but we have made them give up any excessive mortification.

During the past two years, they have greatly increased their fervor. This has occurred ever since God removed from this world one of these devout Indian women who live like nuns, the one who died with the reputation of sanctity. We cease not to say Masses to thank God for the graces that we believe we receive on a daily basis through her intercession. Journeys are continually made to her tomb, and the Indians, following her example, have become better Christians. Every day we see wonders worked through her intercession. Her name was Catherine Tegahkouita. During her lifetime, she had made an agreement with a friend to make each other suffer, because she was too weak to do so by herself, owing to her continual illnesses. She had begged her companion to do her the charity of severely chastising her with blows from a whip. This they did for a year, without anyone knowing it, and for that purpose they went every Sunday to a secluded cabin in the middle of the cemetery. There they took up their willow switches and mingled prayers with penance. Finally, after a year had passed, one of them saw that her companion had fallen sick, and her scruples led her to reveal their

---

[8]Chauchetière refers here to Catherine Tegahkouita, the subject of a selection on pages 171–85 of this book.

practices [to her confessor] and to ask whether there was any sinfulness
in them.

At that time, they were only using willow switches and thorns (which
grow very long here), but since they heard of disciplines, iron girdles,
and other such instruments of penance, the use of these has grown
every day. Since the men discovered that the women have been using
them, and not wishing to be outdone, they ask us for permission to use
these on a daily basis, but we are reluctant to allow it. The women, to the
number of eight or ten, began the practice, and the wife of the *dogique*—
that is, the man who leads the singing and the prayers — is among them.
In her husband's absence, she takes his place in leading public prayers
and singing, and in this capacity she convenes the devout women of
whom we have spoken, who call themselves sisters. They tell one another their faults, and they deliberate together upon what must be done
for the relief of the poor of the village, whose number is so great that
there are almost as many poor as there are Indians. The sort of monas-
tery that they maintain here has its rules. They have promised God never
to put on their fancy attire (for the Indian women have considerable
charm and take pride in adorning themselves with beaded necklaces,
and with vermilion, which they apply to their cheeks, and with earrings
and bracelets). They assist one another in the fields, and they meet together to incite one another to virtue. One of them has been received as
a nun in the hospital of Montreal.

There are married people here who have for a long time lived together as brother and sister. There are aged women, veterans in the
faith, who instruct the others as missionaries would do. God thereby as-
sists us in our need. There are women who have shared their fields, thus
taking the bread from their very mouths, as it were, to give it to new ar-
rivals in the village — people who are not yet in a position to do anything
for them in return — in order to win them for God. When there are wid-
ows or sick persons, the captains put their families [clans] to work, for
the love of God, at building cabins for those who have none. Some live in
the woods [on winter hunting expeditions] in the same state of innocence as do those in the village, and they return with consciences as
pure as when they went away. I may state, without exaggeration, that
when they return, we do not find in many of them matter for absolution,
and yet they are sufficiently enlightened to make confession of the least
imperfections, such as slight distractions during their prayers, petty acts
of impatience, forgetfulness, and things which are actually virtues rather
than vices. Modesty is natural to them. When they pray or sing in the

church, they do so with so much devotion that all the French settlers here who see them are impressed by it and say that they are more devout than we allege. I forgot to mention that when they are in the woods, they keep track of the Sundays and holidays by marking small lines to the number of seven, one for each day of the week. We put crosses on the lines that indicate the feast days and the Sundays, and they observe these exactly. . . .

. . . Thus have these man-eaters, which they were in the past, become lambs through the grace of Jesus Christ, to such a degree that they are now exemplars of virtue and of religion for all of Canada.

We have here no other demon to contend against than liquor and drunkenness, which make a hell of all the Iroquois villages, where life is continual suffering. It is the French who cause so much trouble in this connection, for in order to get from the Indians everything they own, down to their very shirts, they follow them everywhere, trying to make them drink and become intoxicated.

It is amazing to see how some of our Christian Indians distinguish themselves in repressing this evil. With incredible courage, they spill the liquor and they break the bottles, exposing themselves to insults and to blows of which some still bear the marks. And in spite of all this, they do not lose heart. I know three or four who would endure martyrdom to prevent offenses to God. They no longer follow the example of the French. In the past they had considered the latter to be good Christians, but they now see plainly that they are not.

When they return from the land of the Dutch, they relate to us with much pleasure their success in the disputes that they have had with the Dutch on points of religion, to the shame and confusion of those heretics. . . .

If you wish me to tell you something about the manner in which the Indians dress (if I had time, I would have painted some for you), you should know that it is not lacking in taste, especially on feast days. The women have no other headdress than their hair, which they part over the middle of the head and then tie behind with a sort of ribbon, which they make out of eel skin painted a bright red. I myself have often been deceived and have taken it for a real ribbon. They grease their hair, which thereby becomes as black as jet. As for the men, they are ridiculous in dressing their hair, and there is not one who does not do it up in some unique way. On Sundays and feast days, the men and women wear fine white shirts, and the women take wonderful care to clothe themselves so modestly that there is nothing indecorous or uncovered about them.

They closely fasten the shirt and let it hang down over a petticoat, consisting of a blue or red blanket, a fathom or more square, which they fold in two and fasten simply around the waist. The shirt, which falls over this sort of petticoat, reaches only to the knees. The Indians have often asked us if there were any vanity in their dress. They only dress this way when they go to church, on Communion, and on feast days. On the other days they are poorly but modestly clad. . . .

7

Martyrs and Mystics

Although the *Jesuit Relations* have much to say about the customs of the Indians and the history of the French colony, they are, to a significant extent, a collection of religious life stories. Like other writers of the period, the Jesuits loved to recount the heroic deeds of exemplary figures, but their biographical sketches tended to be fashioned on the pattern of the saint's life. Hagiography, or sacred biography, is a notable feature of many of the Jesuit chronicles of New France. Missionaries who died for the faith were revered as martyrs, while mystical women — such as the hospital nun Catherine de St. Augustin and the Ursuline Marie de St. Joseph — were held up for admiration because of their ascetic practices (they deprived themselves of food and comfort and deliberately inflicted pain on their bodies) and their religious visions. Recognizing the hagiographic element in the *Jesuit Relations* helps us to gain a better understanding of the outlook and motivations of the missionaries themselves — something that is valuable in and of itself but is also a part of the process of coming to terms with the textual practices that shaped Jesuit historical and ethnographic writings.

THE ORDEAL OF ISAAC JOGUES

Saint Isaac Jogues was the first of the Jesuit martyrs of New France. His ordeal took place in two stages separated by a four-year period in which he had the opportunity, rare among martyrs, to write his own obituary. The story of his sufferings as recounted shortly after his death in the pages of the Jesuit Relations *includes long passages from the memoirs he left behind, along with background information sketched in by the Jesuit superior, Jérôme Lalemant. Note that the consequent shift of the narrative voice from the third person to the first person and back again can be confusing at times. Father Lalemant begins the narrative and, after speaking of himself in the third person, recounts the story of Father Jogues.*

The passage reproduced here tells of Jogues's capture by a Mohawk raiding party in 1642, his harrowing journey to the town of Gandaouagué, the tortures he suffered there, and the many months he spent in captivity, never knowing when he might be executed. After the end of the period covered by this part of the text, the Jesuit did manage to escape to the Dutch settlements on the Hudson River, and, after further adventures, he made his way to Europe. Amazingly, he chose to return to New France. Not long after his return, a truce was concluded in the war between the Mohawks and the French (see chapter 4). Because of his knowledge of the Iroquois language, Jogues was dispatched on two successive diplomatic missions to the scene of his ordeal. On the second of these, in 1646, the war party in Gandaouagué accused the Jesuit of sorcery and killed him with a sudden blow.

Although the Relation *concentrates on Jogues, it also tells us something about how prisoners of war were treated in Iroquoian societies of the time. In addition, it sheds some light on the conflict of competing Mohawk factions — one favoring accommodation with the French, the other wishing to prosecute war. As a captive who had not been adopted into an Iroquois clan, Jogues's life depended on the relative strength of the two factions. When he was killed on his second return visit, it was because the anti-French (and anti-Algonquin) party had gained the upper hand; indeed his murder may have been deliberately planned to plunge the Mohawks back into war. The 1646 offensive against the Algonquins of the St. Lawrence Valley was the immediate result.*

All these diplomatic, political, and military events — important though they may be for modern researchers — appear as mere "background noise" in the pages of the Jesuit Relations *dedicated to Isaac Jogues. What matters here is the religious meaning of the priest's bodily suffering, spiritual anguish, and preordained death. The threads of these experiences are woven together to create a story patterned on the sacrifices of the early Christian martyrs and on the Passion of Jesus Christ.*

JÉRÔME LALEMANT

How Father Isaac Jogues Was Taken by the Iroquois, and What He Suffered on His First Entrance into Their Country

1647

Father Isaac Jogues was born to a worthy family of the city of Orléans. After he gave some evidence of his virtue in our society, he was sent to New France in the year 1636. In that very year, he went up to the Huron country, where he remained until the thirteenth of June in the year 1642, when he was sent to Quebec upon the affairs of that important and arduous mission.

From that time until his death, there occurred many remarkable things, of which one cannot without guilt deprive the public since they are honorable to God and full of consolation for souls who love to suffer for Jesus Christ. What has been said of his labors in the earlier *Relations* came, for the most part, from some Indians who had been companions in his sufferings. But what I am about to set down issued forth from his own pen and his own lips: It was necessary to use a superior's authority, along with gentle persuasion in our personal conversations, in order to discover that which the very low esteem in which he held himself kept concealed in a profound silence.

Sometime before his departure from the Hurons in order to come to Quebec, finding himself alone before the Blessed Sacrament, he prostrated himself to the ground, beseeching our Lord to grant him the favor and grace of suffering for His glory. This answer was engraved in the depth of his soul, with a certainty similar to that which faith gives us: *Exaudita est oratio tua; fiet tibi sicut à me petisti. Confortare et esto robustus,* "Thy prayer is heard; what thou hast asked of me is granted thee. Be courageous and steadfast." The effects which followed have shown that these words, which were always present for him in all his sufferings, were genuinely substantial, words which issued from the lips of Him for whom saying and doing are one and the same thing.

Reverend Father Jérôme Lalemant, at that time superior of the mission among the Hurons, knowing nothing of this, sent for him and proposed to him the journey to Quebec. This would be a frightful voyage on

---

account of the difficulty of the route, and very dangerous because of the ambushes of the Iroquois, who every year massacred a considerable number of the Indians allied to the French. Let us hear him [Father Jogues] speak upon this subject and upon the outcome of his journey.

"Authority having made me a simple proposition, and not a command, to go down to Quebec, I offered myself with all my heart. I was all the more willing, since otherwise some of our fathers who were much better than I might have been exposed to the perils and hazards that we all anticipate. And so we set out, in danger from the moment of our departure. We were obliged to disembark forty times, and forty times to carry our boats and all our baggage amid the rapids and waterfalls that one encounters on this journey of about three hundred leagues. Although the Indians who were conducting us were very skillful, we nevertheless incurred some disasters, to the great peril of our lives and with some loss of our small baggage. At last, thirty-five days after our departure from the Huron country, we arrived much fatigued at Three Rivers, and from there we descended to Quebec. We blessed God throughout for His goodness in preserving us. Our business being finished in fifteen days, we observed the Feast of Saint Ignace, and the next day, the first of August of the same year, 1642, we left Three Rivers to return to the country whence we had come.

"The first day was favorable to us, but the second caused us to fall into the hands of the Iroquois. We were forty persons, distributed in several canoes. The one that kept the vanguard discovered on the banks of the great river some tracks of men, recently imprinted on the sand and clay, and gave us warning. We put to shore. Some said that these were enemy tracks; others were sure that they were footprints of the Algonquins, our allies. In the midst of this argument, Eustache Ahatsistari, to whom all the others deferred on account of his exploits in arms and his virtue, exclaimed: 'Be they friends or enemies, it matters not. I notice by their tracks that they are not in greater number than we, so let us then advance without fear.' We had made less than half a league when the enemy, concealed among the grass and bushes, rose with a great outcry and discharged a volley of shots at our canoes. The noise of their arquebuses so greatly frightened some of our Hurons that they abandoned their canoes and weapons and all their supplies to flee into the woods. This discharge had done us no great harm: No lives were lost, and only one Huron was shot through the hand. Our canoes, however, were broken in several places. We were four French, one of whom was in the rear and escaped with the Hurons, who abandoned him before approaching the enemy.[1] Eight or ten [Hurons], both Christians and catechumens, joined us. We led them in a short prayer as they bravely faced the enemy, and though it was thirty men against twelve or fourteen, our people held on valiantly. But when they saw another band of forty Iroquois, who had been in ambush on the opposite shore of the river, coming to attack them, they lost courage, and those who were not then caught up in the fighting abandoned their comrades and took to their heels. No longer sustained by those who followed him, a Frenchman named René Goupil (whose death is precious before God) was surrounded and captured, along with some of the most courageous Hurons.

"I was watching this disaster," says the father, "from a place very favorable for concealing me from the sight of the enemy, being able to hide myself in thickets and among very tall and dense reeds; but this thought could never enter my mind. 'Could I really,' I said to myself, 'abandon our French and leave those good neophytes and those poor catechumens, without giving them the succor that the church of my God has entrusted to me?' Flight seemed horrible to me. 'It must be,' I said in my heart, 'that my body suffer the fire of earth in order to deliver these poor souls from the flames of Hell. It must die a transient death, in order to procure for them an eternal life.' Having reached a decision without great opposition from my mind, I called one of the Iroquois who had remained to guard the prisoners. This man perceived me but hesitated to approach, for fear of some ambush. 'Come,' I said, 'be not afraid. Take me to the Frenchman and the Hurons whom you hold captive.' He advanced, seized me, and placed me in the number of those whom the world calls miserable. Tenderly embracing the Frenchman, I said to him: 'My dear brother, God treats us in a strange manner, but He is the master and he has done what has seemed best in his sight; he has followed his good pleasure. May His holy name be blessed forever.' This good young man at once made his confession, and I gave him absolution. I then approached the Hurons to instruct and baptize them. As more fugitives were being brought in by their pursuers every minute, I heard these too in confession, making Christians of those who had not been baptized. Finally, they brought that worthy Christian captain Eustache, who, on seeing me, exclaimed: 'Ah! My father, I swore and promised to you that I would live or die with you.' The sight of him pierced my heart. I do not remember what words I said to him.

[1] This phrase is obscure in the original French: ". . . se sauva avec les Hurons qui labandonnerent devant que d'approcher l'ennemy." The intended meaning may have been "escaped with the Hurons, who abandoned him before the enemy's approach."

"Another Frenchman, named Guillaume Couture, seeing that the Hurons were giving way, escaped like them into those great forests, and, as he was agile, he was soon out of the enemy's grasp. But he was seized with remorse because he had forsaken his father and his comrade. He stopped quite short, deliberating whether he should go on or retrace his steps. The fear of being regarded as treacherous made him turn around, and there he found himself facing five big Iroquois, one of whom was aiming a gun at him. The arquebus misfired, but the Frenchman did not fail to find his own mark and shot him dead on the spot. His shot spent, the four other Iroquois fell upon him like enraged lions, or rather like demons. They stripped him naked, beat him black-and-blue with clubs, and tore out his fingernails with their teeth, crushing the bleeding ends to cause him more pain. Finally, they pierced through one of his hands with a knife and led him, tied and bound in this sad plight, to the place where we were. When I recognized him, I broke away from my guards and embraced him. 'Courage, my dear brother and friend,' I urged him. 'Offer your pains and anguish to God on behalf of these men who torment you. We must not shrink back. Let us instead suffer bravely for His holy name. His glory was our only object in this journey.' The Iroquois were at first quite bewildered before these endearments, then, imagining perhaps that I was applauding this young man for killing one of their captains, they fell upon me with a mad fury. They stabbed at me and beat me and overwhelmed me with blows from their war clubs, flinging me to the ground, half-dead. When I began to catch my breath, the men who had not participated in the beating came up and used their teeth to tear out my fingernails. Then they took turns biting the ends of my two index fingers, and with the nails gone, this caused me excruciating pain, as if they were being ground and crushed between two stones until small bone splinters began to protrude. The good René Goupil was given the same treatment, though they did not at that point do any harm to the Hurons. They were angry with the French because of the latter's unwillingness the year before to accept the peace conditions they had been willing to offer.

"When the hunters had returned from their chase after a human quarry and the party had reassembled, these barbarians divided up their booty among themselves, rejoicing in their prey with great shouts of joy. As I saw them engrossed in examining and distributing our spoils, I sought also for my share. I went round to all the captives, baptizing those who were not yet baptized, encouraging these poor wretches to suffer steadfastly, in the assurance that their reward would far exceed the severity of their torments. I ascertained, on this round of visits, that we

Scenes of Jesuit Martyrdom

A famous and widely reproduced tableau depicts several separate scenes of torture and death as though they took place simultaneously. In the foreground, Isaac Jogues is seen kneeling, awaiting execution, his fingers mutilated from an earlier period of captivity. Gabriel Lalemant is being burned alive in the center, while to the right, Jean de Brébeuf stands with red-hot axe blades searing his chest.

Courtesy of the University of Western Ontario.

were twenty-two captives, not counting three Hurons killed on the spot. An old man, aged eighty years, having just received holy baptism, said to the Iroquois who were commanding him to embark: 'It is too late for an old man like me to go visiting foreign countries. I can find death here if you refuse me life.' These words were hardly out of his mouth before they felled him.

"And so we set out, led off to a country truly foreign, where our Lord favored us with a share of His cross. During the thirteen days that we spent on that journey, I suffered bodily torments almost unendurable and, in the soul, mortal anguish: hunger, the fiercely burning sun, the threats and hatred of those leopards, and the pain of our wounds, which, in the absence of any dressing, became putrid and worm infested. All this certainly caused us much distress. But these things seemed light to me in comparison with an inward sadness that I felt at the sight of our first and most ardent Huron Christians. I had expected them to be the pillars of that rising church, and I saw them become the victims of death. Seeing the path to salvation closed for such a long time to so many nations, people who perish every day for want of succor, made me die every hour in the depth of my soul. It is a very hard thing, a cruel thing, to see the triumph of the devils over whole nations redeemed with so much love and ransomed in the currency of a blood so adorable.

"Eight days after we left the shores of the great river St. Lawrence, we met two hundred Iroquois, who were coming to hunt for French and for our Indian allies, and this encounter brought down on us another attack. It is a belief among those barbarians that those who go to war are fortunate in proportion to their cruelty toward their enemies, and I can assure you that they made us thoroughly feel the force of that wretched belief.

"Once they perceived us, they began by thanking the sun for causing us to fall into the hands of their fellow countrymen. They next fired an arquebus volley to salute their victory. That done, they set up a theater on the hill and went into the woods in search of sticks or thorns, whatever they fancied. Thus armed, they formed two lines, a hundred on one side and a hundred on the other, and forced us, all naked as we were, to pass in between along that path of fury and anguish. There was rivalry among them to see who could land the most blows and the heaviest. They made me go last, that I might be more exposed to their rage. I had not gone halfway before I fell to the ground under that hail of redoubled blows. I made no effort to raise myself up, in part because of my weakened state, in part because I was ready to make of that place my sepulchre. Seeing me prostrate, they rushed upon me. God alone knows for how long a time and how many were the blows that landed on my body, but the sufferings undertaken for His love and His glory are filled with joy and honor.

"Seeing that I had not fallen by accident and that I did not rise again because I was too close to death, they adopted a cruel compassion. Though their rage was not yet glutted, they wished to get me to their country alive, and so they tenderly picked me up and carried me all bleeding to the stage they had prepared. When I came to, they brought me down and began to offer me a thousand and one insults, making me the sport and the target of their reviling. They started beating me once again: On my head, on my neck, and all over my body another storm of blows rained down. I lack space to set down in writing the full extent of my sufferings. They burned one of my fingers and crushed another with their teeth, they squeezed and twisted those that were already torn with a demonic rage, they scratched at my wounds with their nails, and, when strength failed me, they applied fire to my arm and thighs.

"My companions were treated about the same as I was. One of those barbarians advanced with a large knife in his right hand, took my nose in his left hand, as if to cut it off, but then stopped suddenly, as if surprised, and went away without doing anything to me. He returned a quarter of an hour later, as if angry with himself for his cowardice, and grasped me again in the same place. You know, my God, what I said to you at that moment, in the depth of my heart. In the end, I know not what invisible force repulsed him a second time. My life was finished if he had proceeded, for they are not accustomed to leave long on the earth those who have been severely mutilated. Among the Hurons, the worst treated was that worthy and valiant Christian, Eustache. After making him suffer like the others, they cut off the thumbs of both his hands and then thrust a pointed stick into the incisions, right up to the elbow. Seeing this extreme torment, [I] could not contain [my] tears. Eustache perceived this, and fearing lest the Iroquois should regard [me] as effeminate, said to them: 'Do not suppose that those tears proceed from weakness; it is the love and affection that he feels for me, and not a lack of courage, that brings them to his eyes. He has never wept in his own torments; his face has always appeared dry and always cheerful. Your rage, and my pains, and his love are the occasion and the cause of his tears.'

"'It is true,' [I] answered, 'that I feel your pain more keenly than my own, and though I am covered with blood and with wounds, my body feels its tortures less as my heart is afflicted with your sufferings. But take courage, my dear brother, and remember that there is another life than this; remember, too, that there is a God who sees everything and who will reward the anguish that we suffer on his account.'

"'I remember very well,' replied that good neophyte. 'I will remain firm even 'til death.' And, indeed, his constancy was ever admirable and ever Christian.

"After they had made a sacrifice of our blood, those warriors went their way and we went ours. The tenth day after our capture, we arrived at a place where we had to leave the water and proceed by land. The path, about four days long, was extremely painful for us. The man who was guarding me was unable to carry all his booty, and so he put part of it on my torn back. In three days, we ate only a few wild fruits, which we gathered along the way. Greatly weakened by our wounds and by the intensity of the sun during this hottest part of the summer, we fell behind the others. Seeing ourselves considerably separated from them and night falling, I told poor René that he should escape. Indeed, we could have done so, though for myself, I would rather suffer any sort of torture than abandon to their death those whom I could in any way console, and upon whom I could confer the blood of my Savior through the sacraments of His church. This good young man, seeing that I wished to follow my little flock, would never leave me: 'I will die with you,' said he. 'I could never forsake you.'

"I had always thought that the day on which the whole church rejoices in the glory of the Blessed Virgin — her glorious and triumphant Assumption — would be for us a day of pain. I gave thanks to my Savior, Jesus Christ, because, on that day of gladness and joy, he was making us share his suffering and admitting us to participation in his crosses. We arrived on the eve of that sacred day at a little river, distant from the first village of the Iroquois about a quarter of a league. There, on both banks, were many men and youths armed with sticks, which they let loose upon us with their accustomed rage. By then, I had only two fingernails left, and those barbarians tore them from me with their teeth, rending the flesh from beneath and cutting it clean to the bone with their nails, which they grow very long. A Huron, to whom they had given his liberty in that country, exclaimed, 'You are dead, Frenchmen, you are dead; there is no liberty for you. Think no more of life; you will be burned; prepare yourselves for death.' This fine reception did not afflict us to the degree that our enemies believed it would. My guard, seeing me all covered with blood and touched with some sort of compassion, told me that I was in a pitiable state, and, in order to make me more recognizable in the eyes of his people, he wiped my face.

"After they had glutted their cruelty, they led us in triumph into that first village. All the youth were outside the gates, arranged in lines and armed with sticks. Some even had iron rods, which they procure easily from the Dutch nearby. Casting our eyes upon these weapons of the Passion, we remembered the words of Saint Augustine: Those who turn aside from the scourges of God turn aside from the number of his children. Accordingly, we offered ourselves with all our hearts to his paternal goodness, ready at His convenience to be sacrificial victims to His loving anger, all for the salvation of these nations.

"Here is the order that was followed in that stately and funereal entry: One Frenchman was placed at the head of the line, another in the middle of the Hurons, and me the very last. We followed one another at an equal distance, and, to ensure that our executioners had ample time to beat us at their ease, some Iroquois thrust themselves into our ranks in order to prevent us from running and from avoiding any blows. As the procession began to enter this narrow road to paradise, a din was heard on all sides. It was then that I could say with my Lord and master, 'The wicked have wrought upon my back.'[2] I was naked to my shirt, like a poor criminal, and the others were completely naked, except poor René Goupil, to whom they allowed the same favor as to me. The more slowly the procession marched along this long road, the more blows we received. I received one above the loins, with the pommel of a knife or with an iron knob the size of a fist, which shook my whole body and took away my breath. Such was our entrance into that Babylon. We could hardly make it as far as the scaffold which had been prepared for us in the middle of the village, so beaten were we; our bodies were all livid and our faces all bloody. But René Goupil was more disfigured than the rest, so that nothing white appeared in his face except his eyes. I found him all the more beautiful in his resemblance to Him [Jesus], who bore a face which was viewed with delight by the angels, though he appeared to us, in the midst of his anguish, like a leper.

"When I ascended that scaffold, I exclaimed in my heart: 'For we are made a spectacle unto the world and to angels, and to men. . . for Christ's sake.'[3] We found some rest in that place of triumph and of glory. The Iroquois no longer persecuted us except with their tongues, filling the air and our ears with their insults, which did us no great hurt, but this calm did not last long. A captain exclaimed that the Frenchmen ought to be caressed. No sooner said than done, a wretch jumped up on the stage and dealt three heavy blows with a club to each Frenchman, without touching the Hurons. Meanwhile, others drew their knives and approached: They treated me as a captain, that is to say, with more fury than the rest. The deference of the French, and the respect that the Hurons showed me, were the cause of this advantage. An old man took my left hand and commanded a captive Algonquin woman to cut off one of my fingers, but she turned away three or four times, unable to force herself to carry out this cruelty. Finally, she had to obey, and she cut the thumb from my left hand. The same caresses were extended to the other prisoners. When this poor woman had thrown my thumb down on the

---

[2] Ps. 129:3; Latin in original.
[3] I Cor. 4:9–10; Latin in original.

stage, I picked it up and offered it to you, O my God! Remembering the sacrifices that I had presented to you for seven years past, upon the altars of your church, I accepted this torture as a loving vengeance for the want of love and respect that I had shown your holy body. You heard the cries of my soul. One of my two French companions, having perceived me, told me that if those barbarians saw me keep my thumb, they would make me eat it and swallow it raw; therefore, I should throw it away. I obeyed him instantly. They used an oyster shell to cut off the right thumb of the other Frenchman, so as to cause him more pain. The blood flowed from our wounds in such abundance that we were about to faint, when an Iroquois, tearing off a little end of my shirt, which alone had been left to me, bound them up for us, and that was all the dressing or medical treatment applied to them.

"In the evening, they took us down and led us into the cabins to be the playthings of the children. For food they gave us a little boiled corn, then they made us lie down on pieces of bark, binding us by the arms and the feet to four stakes fastened in the ground in the shape of a Saint Andrew's cross. The children, in order to learn the cruelty of their parents, threw coals and burning cinders on our stomachs, taking pleasure in watching us broil and roast. Oh, my God, what nights! To remain always in an extremely constrained position; to be unable to stir or to turn; to be under the attack of countless vermin that assailed us on all sides; to be covered with wounds, some recent and others all putrid; not to have half the food needed to sustain life: In truth, these torments are great, but God is infinite. At sunrise, they led us back upon our scaffold, where we spent three days and three nights in the sufferings that I have described.

"At the end of those three days, they paraded us into two other villages, where we made our entrance as into the first. They give us the same salutes of beatings, but to enhance the cruelty they beat us severely on the bones, either at random or on the shin of the legs, a place very sensitive to pain. As we were leaving the first village, a wretch took away my shirt and gave me an old rag to cover what ought to be concealed. This nakedness was very painful to me, and I could not abstain from reproaching one of those who had had the largest part of our spoils, saying: 'Are you not ashamed to see me in this nakedness, you who have had so great a share of my baggage?' These words shamed him somewhat, and he took a piece of coarse cloth, with which a bundle had been wrapped, and tossed it to me. I put it on my back to defend myself from the burning sun, which heated and corrupted my wounds, but this cloth mingled with my lesions and became stuck like glue, and so I was constrained to tear it off, in spite of the pain, and to abandon myself to the mercy of the air. My skin was detaching itself from my body in several places. So that I might say that I had passed 'through fire and water,' through cold and heat, for the love of my God, I stood on the scaffold under a cold rain for three days, which greatly renewed the pain of my wounds. One of those barbarians, noticing that Guillaume Couture, although he had his hands all torn, had not yet lost any of his fingers, seized his hand and tried to cut off his forefinger with a dull old knife. Since he could not manage that way, he twisted it, and in tearing it off, he pulled a sinew out of the arm, the length of a palm. His poor arm swelled, and I felt the pain to the bottom of my heart.

"We left that second village and were dragged to the third, these villages being situated several leagues from one another. In addition to the salute and the caresses, as well as the reception that was given us at the two preceding ones, we received a new torture here. The young men thrust thorns or pointed sticks into our wounds and scratched the ends of our fingers (the nails missing) and tore them down to the quick flesh. In order to honor me above the others, they bound me to pieces of wood fastened crosswise. Because my feet were not supported, the weight of my body inflicted such hellish torture upon me that, after suffering this torment about a quarter of an hour, I felt that I was about to faint, which made me beseech those barbarians to loosen my bonds a little. They came running at my call, but instead of loosening them, they tightened them, in order to cause me more pain. An Indian from a more distant country, touched with compassion, broke through the crowd, drew a knife and boldly cut all the cords with which I was bound. This charity was afterward rewarded a hundredfold, as we shall see.[4]

"That act was not without providence: For at the same time that I was unbound, word arrived that some warriors, or hunters of men, were bringing some recently captured Hurons. I made my way there as best I could. I consoled those poor captives, and having sufficiently instructed them, I conferred upon them holy baptism. As a reward, I was told that I must die with them. I was told of the sentence decreed in the council: The following night would be — so they said — the end of my torments and of my life.

"My soul was well pleased with these words, but God was not yet ready; instead he willed to prolong my martyrdom. Those barbarians reconsidered the matter and then announced that the Frenchmen should

[4] Months later, while still a prisoner among the Mohawks, Jogues came upon this man. He was sick and dying, and, according to the missionary's account, Jogues gave him instruction in Christian doctrine and then baptized him. "Shortly after, he took his flight to heaven" (*JR* 31:91).

be given life, or, more exactly, their death should be postponed. They hoped to find more moderation at our forts on this account. They accordingly sent Guillaume Couture to the largest village, while René Goupil and I were lodged together in another one. Life being granted us, they did us no more harm. But alas! It was then that we had time to feel the effects of the torments that had been inflicted on us. They gave us for beds the bark of trees laid upon the ground; and for refreshment they gave us a little cornmeal, with sometimes a bit of half-cooked squash. Since our hands and fingers were all broken, they had to feed us like children. Patience was our physician. Some women, more merciful than the rest, regarded us with much charity and were unable to look at our sores without compassion."

God Preserves Father Isaac Jogues after the Murder of His Companion; He Instructs Him in a Very Remarkable Manner

When those poor captives had recovered a little of their strength, the principal men of the country talked of conducting them back to Three Rivers in order to restore them to the French, and arrangements went ahead so that it seemed certain. But the Iroquois were unable to agree among themselves, and so the father and his companions once more died a thousand deaths. Those barbarians are accustomed to give prisoners whom they do not select for execution to families who have lost relatives in war. These prisoners take the place of the deceased and are incorporated into that family, which alone has the right to kill them or to let them live. No one else would dare to offend them. But when they retain some public prisoner, such as the father, without giving him to any individual, this poor man spends every day within a hairbreadth of death. If some rascal were to knock his brains out, no one would do anything about it. If he drags out his poor life, it is by the grace of some individuals who have love for him. In such condition was the father, as well as one of the Frenchmen, for the other had been given to take the place of an Iroquois killed in war.

The young Frenchman [René Goupil] who was the father's companion was in the habit of playing with the little children and teaching them to make the sign of the cross. On one occasion, an old man noticed him making this sacred sign upon the forehead of his grandson and taking the child's hand to show him how to do it himself. He said to a nephew of his: "Kill that dog. The Dutch tell us that what he is doing is not good; it will cause some harm to my grandson." The nephew rushed to obey.

An opportunity to commit this murder outside the village presented itself in the following way: Father Jogues was coming to warn his poor companion that the plan to release the French prisoners had been abandoned and that consequently some young men had come looking for him at his cabin, in order to torture him and treat him as a victim destined to death. Wishing to prepare René for this fate, he led him to a grove near the village and told him of the danger in which they stood. Both of them prayed, and then they recited the rosary of the Blessed Virgin. In sum, they cheerfully prepared to die, drawing strength from him who never fails those who seek and love him. While they were returning toward their village, conversing on the blessings of the afterlife, the old man's nephew, along with another Indian, stood watching for an opportunity, their hatchets in hand. As they approached, one of these men said to the father, "Keep walking ahead." In an instant, he had smashed the head of poor René Goupil. As he fell to the ground, his last breath pronounced the holy name of Jesus. The father, seeing him prostrate, fell upon him and embraced him, but those barbarians pulled him off and dealt two final blows to that blessed body.

"Give me a moment's time," the father said to them, assuming that they would accord him the same favor as his companion. Accordingly, he fell to his knees, offering himself in sacrifice to the deity. He turned toward those barbarians, saying, "Do as you wish; I fear not death."

"Get up," they replied. "You will not die this time."

They dragged the corpse through the streets of the village and later cast it away in some out-of-the-way place. The father, wishing to pay him the last honors, searched everywhere for him until at last some children showed him where the body lay in a stream. He covered it with large stones to protect it from the claws and beaks of the birds, until he might come to bury it. But it rained all the following night, and this torrent became so violent and so deep that he could not find that blessed body. This death occurred on the twenty-ninth of September in the year 1642....

After that young man, or that blessed martyr, had been thus slain, the father returned to his cabin. His people put their hands to his breast to see whether his heart was agitated with fear. Finding it steady, they said to him: "From now on, do not go outside the village unless you are accompanied by one of us. There are plans to kill you, so be careful." ...
This good father then spent every day like a bird on the branch, his life hanging by a thread, and it seemed to him at any moment it would be cut. But He who held the end of it, was not willing to let it go so soon.

Sometime after the death of his companion, God communicated to him in his sleep, as he did long ago to the ancient patriarchs, what I am about to relate. He [Father Jogues] himself has set it down in writing with his own hand: He wrote in the Latin language, but it is here translated into French [and now into English].

"After the death of my dearest companion, of happy memory, when my death was being plotted every day, and when my soul was filled with anguish, what I am about to tell happened to me in my sleep.

"I had gone forth from our village, as was my habit, in order to groan more freely before you, O my God, in order to offer to you my prayer and, in your presence, to open the floodgates of my anguish. On my return, I found everything altered. The tall posts surrounding our village appeared changed into towers, ramparts, and walls of an illustrious beauty, and yet nothing seemed to be newly built; rather it was a city of venerable antiquity. I could not believe that it was our village, until I saw some Iroquois whom I knew very well coming out, and they seemed to assure me that it was indeed. Filled with astonishment, I approached the city and passed through the first gate; then I saw engraved in large letters upon the right column of the second gate the two letters 'L. N.' Next I came upon a little lamb which had been slaughtered. I was surprised, for I could not understand how barbarians with no knowledge of our alphabet could have engraved those characters. As I was searching my mind for an explanation, I saw a scroll overhead, and on it were written three words: *'Laudent nomen ejus'* [Let them praise his name]. At the same time, I received a great inner illumination that told me those who truly praise the name of the Lamb are those who, in their distress and tribulation, strive to imitate the gentleness of Him who, like a lamb, said not a word to those who robbed him of his fleece and led him to his death. . . ."

[Father Jogues's dream continued: He entered the city, only to be arrested and taken before a stern judge who proceeded to beat him with an instrument resembling a Roman fasces, producing a pain like that of the beatings he had been subjected to by the Iroquois. Finally, the judge (God) stopped the punishment and, admiring the Jesuit's patience, embraced and consoled him. At this point, Jogues awoke.]

"Having returned to myself, I could not doubt that God had wrought wonders in my soul, not only because of the connections which these things had among themselves, but especially because of the great fire of love which my judge had kindled in the depth of my heart, the mere remembrance of which, several months later, drew from me tears of the sweetest consolation.

"The conviction also that my death was delayed was several times impressed upon me in my sleep. It was my belief that I was following my dear companion who had been received into blessedness, running after him over a winding path so that I could never catch sight of him. Sometimes, while pursuing him, I came to gorgeous temples and went inside, attracted by their beauty. While I was offering prayers, charmed by the sweetness of the voices that I heard in those great buildings, I would become reconciled to his absence. But as soon as I left those delights, I once again felt the desire to follow him."

All this was taken, almost word for word, from the memoirs of that good father. At the time, he did not realize that the blows delivered to him by his judge betokened his return into that country, where he was to find entry into holy Zion by a hatchet blow destined to send him to live forever with his dear companion René Goupil.

A NATIVE SAINT

What follows is a religious life story concerning a native woman. Following the pattern set by hundreds of European narratives of female saintliness, this one concentrates on themes of inner spirituality, heroic struggles to avoid the entanglements of sex and marriage, and extreme ascetic practices. The fact that this account focuses on a native woman sets it apart from others of the genre, for European missionaries of the early modern era were not in the habit of recognizing "mere Indians" as paragons of Christian holiness.

Catherine Tegahkouita (or Kateri Tekakwitha, as she is usually called today) was a Mohawk who lived the last four years of her short life at the Jesuit mission of Sault St. Louis/Kahnawake, near Montreal. She was a central figure in the group of native women who in the 1670s pursued a life of Christian perfection as described in chapter 6 (see pages 146–154). Years after her death, the Jesuits published her life story in France, and it quickly achieved immense popularity, with Spanish, English, German, and Dutch translations following in rapid succession. The text reproduced here is taken not from the Jesuit Relations, *but from the* History and General Description of New France, *originally published in 1744, long after the* Relations *had been discontinued, by Father Pierre François Xavier Charle-*

*voix, a French Jesuit who spent many years in Canada in the early eigh-
teenth century. Charlevoix's chapter is actually an abridged version of a biography written by Pierre Cholenec, Catherine's Jesuit confessor.*

P. F. X. DE CHARLEVOIX

Catherine Tegahkouita:
An Iroquois Virgin

1744

New France has had her apostles and martyrs, and has given the church
saints in all conditions, and I do not hesitate to say that they would have
done honor to the primitive ages of Christianity. Several I have made
known so far as the course of this history permitted me. The lives of
some have been published, but God—who exalted his glory during
their lifetime by the great things that he effected through them; by the
luster which their sanctity has diffused over this vast continent; by the
courage which he inspired in them to found with untold toil a new Chris-
tendom amid the most fearful barbarism, and to cement it with their
blood—chose none of these to have all the riches of his power and
mercy displayed on their tombs. Instead he conferred this honor on a
young neophyte, almost unknown to the whole country during her life.
For more than sixty years she has been regarded as the protectress of
Canada, and it has been impossible to oppose a kind of cult publicly rendered to her.

This holy virgin, so celebrated under the name of Catherine Tegahkouita, was born in 1656 at Gandaouagué, a town in the Mohawk canton,
of a heathen Iroquois father and a Christian Algonquin mother. She lost
her mother at the age of four and was still quite young when her father
died, leaving her to the care of one of her aunts and under the control
of an uncle who had the chief authority in his village. The smallpox
which she had in her infancy having weakened her sight, she was long
compelled as it were to remain in the corner of a cabin, her eyes being

P. F. X. de Charlevoix, *History and General Description of New France* (New York: Francis
P. Harper, 1900), 4:283–96. For the original French version, see P. F. X. de Charlevoix, *His-
toire et description générale de la Nouvelle France* (Paris: Nyon Fils, 1744), 1:572–87. As
with the *Jesuit Relations,* the text presented here is an edited and corrected version of the
published English translation.

CATHERINE TEGAHKOUITA IROQUOISE
Morte en odeur de Sainteté dans le Canada.

Gravé par N. Ransonnette Graveur O.re de Monsieur.

Catherine [Kateri] Tegahkouita

A Mohawk convert who died "in odor of sanctity" at Sault St. Louis/Kahnawake in 1680.

Courtesy of the Newberry Library, Chicago.

unable to stand the light, and this retirement was the first source of her happiness. What she did at first out of necessity, she continued to do by choice, thereby avoiding whatever could cause her to lose that moral purity so difficult to preserve amid idolatrous and then very dissolute youth.

As soon as she saw herself of age to act, she took on herself almost all the toil of the household, and this shielded her from two dangers fatal to most Indian girls — that is, private conversations and idleness. Her relatives, however, wished her to use the decorations common to young persons of her sex, and although she yielded from simple compliance with their wishes, and with all possible repugnance, it was a matter of much scruple to her when, favored by the light of faith, she learned how dangerous it is to seek to please men.

The first knowledge that she acquired of Christianity was imparted by some missionaries sent to the Iroquois after Monsieur de Tracy's expedition. On their way they passed through the town where she lived and were received at her cabin. She was appointed to take care of them and waited on them in a manner that surprised them. She had herself, on beholding them, been moved by an impulse that excited sentiments in her heart, regarded subsequently by her as the first sparks of the heavenly fire which later inflamed her so completely. The fervor and recollection of those religious in their devotions inspired her with the desire of praying with them, and she informed them of it. They understood much more than she expressed. They instructed her in the Christian truth, as far as the short stay that they made in that town permitted them, and left her with a regret that she heartily reciprocated. Sometime after, a match [marriage] was proposed to her, but as she showed strong opposition, her relatives did not press it. However, they soon returned to the charge, and to save themselves the trouble of overcoming her resistance, they, without mentioning it to her, betrothed her to a young man, who at once went to her cabin and sat down beside her. To ratify the marriage, it only required that she should remain near the husband selected for her, such being the way of these tribes, but she abruptly left the cabin and protested that she would not return till he withdrew. This conduct brought her much ill treatment, which she endured with unalterable patience. She was more sensitive to the reproach made that she lacked affection for her kindred, that she hated her nation and gave all her attachment to that to which her mother belonged. But nothing could overcome her repugnance for the state of life in which they sought to involve her.

Meanwhile Father Jacques de Lamberville arrived at Gandaouagué, with orders to found a mission there. Tegahkouita then felt her former desires to become a Christian revive, but she was still for some time without mentioning it, either out of respect for her uncle, who did not relish our religion, or from pure timidity. At last an opportunity came for avowing her conviction, and she was not wanting. A wound in the foot kept her in the cabin, while all the other women were busy harvesting the Indian corn. Father de Lamberville, compelled to suspend his public instructions, which no one would attend, took this time to visit the cabins and instruct those who were confined there by age or infirmity. One day he entered the cabin of Tegahkouita.

Unable to dissemble the joy that this visit caused her, she did not hesitate to open her mind to the missionary in the presence of two or three women, who were in company with her, on her design of embracing Christianity. She added that she would have great obstacles to overcome but that nothing appalled her. The energy with which she spoke, the courage she displayed, and a certain modest yet resolute air that lighted up her countenance at once told the missionary that his new proselyte would not be an ordinary Christian. Accordingly, he carefully taught her many things that he did not explain to all preparing for baptism. God doubtless infuses into hearts of which he has especially reserved possession a sort of purely spiritual sympathy, forming even in this life the sacred bond which will unite them hereafter in the abode of glory. Father de Lamberville, whom I knew well, was one of the most holy missionaries of New France. He died at Sault St. Louis, spent with toil and austerity, and, if I may use the expression, in the arms of Charity. He often declared that in his first interview with Tegahkouita, he thought he could discern that God had great designs as to that virgin, yet he would not exercise any haste in conferring baptism on her. He adopted in her case all the precautions that experience had shown to be necessary to make sure [of the sincerity and commitment] of the Indians before administering the sacrament of regeneration.

The whole winter was spent in these trials, and on her side the young catechumen employed this precious time in rendering herself worthy of a grace, whose importance she fully comprehended. Before granting it to adults, the missionaries take great pains to inquire privately into their conduct and morality. Father de Lamberville asked all who knew Tegahkouita and was greatly surprised to find that there was not one, even among those who had given her most to suffer, who did not sound her praises. This was all the more glorious for her, as Indians are much given to slander and naturally inclined to put an evil interpretation on the most innocent actions. The missionary accordingly no longer hesitated to grant her what she solicited with such earnestness. She was baptized on Easter Sunday, 1676, and received the name of Catherine.

The grace of the sacrament, received into a heart which her uprightness and innocence had so well prepared, produced wondrous effects. Whatever impression the missionary already had of the young Iroquois maiden, he was astonished to find in her, immediately after baptism, not a neophyte needing to be confirmed in the faith, but a soul filled with the most precious gifts of Heaven who had to be guided in the most sublime spiritual ways. At the outset her virtue excited the admiration even of the people who were least inclined to imitate her. Those on whom she depended allowed her to follow every impulse of her zeal, though this freedom did not last long. The innocence of her life, the precautions which she took to avoid all that could in the least affect it, and especially her extreme reserve as to whatever could in the slightest degree offend purity, appeared to the young men of her village as a reproach toward the dissolute life they led, and many laid snares for her with the sole view of dimming a virtue which dazzled them.

On the other hand, although she had relaxed nothing in her domestic occupations and was ever found ready to give her services to all, her relatives were displeased to see her devote all her free time to prayer. In order to prevent her from suspending on Sundays and holidays the work which the church forbids on those days consecrated to the Lord, they made her pass them without food. Seeing, however, that they gained nothing by this course, they had recourse to still more violent means. They often mistreated her shamefully: When she went to the chapel, they sent young men after her to jeer and pelt her with stones, and men who were drunk, or who pretended to be drunk, rushed upon her as though they intended to take her life. But, undismayed by these artifices and acts of violence, she continued her devotions as though she enjoyed the most perfect liberty.

One day when she was in her cabin, a young man entered abruptly, with flashing eyes, brandishing his hatchet as if intending to tomahawk her. At this sight she displayed no emotion and bowed down her head to receive the blow; but the madman, seized at this instant by a panic fear, fled as precipitately as though pursued by a war party. These first storms were succeeded by a still more dangerous persecution. Catherine's aunt was a woman of morose disposition who was displeased with all that her niece did to satisfy her, for the simple reason that she could find nothing to reprove. One day the virtuous neophyte happened to call the husband of this woman by his own name, instead of calling him Father, as usual. Her aunt imagined, or pretended to believe, that this familiar mode of speaking showed an improper connection between the uncle and niece, and she hastened on the spot to Father de Lamberville to assert that she had surprised Catherine soliciting her husband to sin. The father promised to examine the case, and when he learned on what this atrocious accusation rested, he gave the slanderer a rebuke that covered her with confusion; reactions against the priest's reproaches only resulted in further vexation for the innocent girl.

Had all this involved merely suffering, she would never have thought of changing her abode, for nothing was more to her liking than suffering. But she feared that she could not always hold firm against the seduction of bad example, or escape being overcome gradually by human respect, so powerful in the Indian mind. She accordingly began to look for an asylum, where her innocence and her religion would be shielded from danger. La Prairie de la Magdeleine,[1] where several Iroquois Christians began to settle, seemed to her well suited to this purpose, and she felt an ardent desire to go there, but this was not easily done.

Her uncle beheld with great displeasure the depopulation of his canton, and he declared himself the avowed enemy of all who contributed to it. It was therefore apparently impossible to obtain his consent, and it was not easy for Catherine to leave him without it. But God, who had destined her to be the example and ornament of this transplanted Christian colony, facilitated what had at first seemed impossible. She had an adopted sister, a neophyte like herself, who had married a Christian filled with zeal for the conversion of his countrymen. This man had already taken up his abode at La Prairie de la Magdeleine, and he was one of those who, under various pretexts, traversed the Iroquois towns in order to make proselytes. He knew that the greatest favor he could do Catherine would be to take her to his home. He spoke of the matter to his wife, who confirmed him in his design and earnestly exhorted him to give her sister this consolation.

He resolved on the project, and to effect it more surely, he pretended to go hunting with one of his friends in the direction of New York, and set out, after warning Tegahkouita to hold herself in readiness at a fixed time. Fortunately for her, her uncle was away, though not far distant, and he was almost at once informed of his niece's departure. Without losing

---

[1] La Prairie, near Montreal, was the original site of the Jesuit-sponsored Iroquois community. Not long after Tegahkouita's arrival, the village moved a short distance upstream to the spot the French called Sault St. Louis and the Iroquois called Kahnawake.

a moment, he set out in pursuit, bent on bringing her back dead or alive
and on tomahawking the first who resisted him. He soon overtook the
two hunters, but not finding his niece with them, because, whenever
they halted, they took the precaution to conceal her in the woods, he
thought that he had been misinformed. Accordingly, without avowing
his purpose, he conversed for a time on indifferent topics and left them,
convinced that Catherine had taken some other route with other guides.

Rescued from this peril, the saintly girl gaily pursued her journey
and at last reached the destination which had been the object of her
prayers. This was in the month of October 1677. Her sister had not yet a
cabin to herself and dwelt with her husband in that of a fervent Christian
woman named Anastasia, whose sole employment it was to prepare persons of her own sex for baptism. A hostess of this character and dedicated to such duties was most pleasing to Catherine. She was, moreover,
enchanted with all that was happening in the village. She was constantly
amazed at the power of divine grace to transform wolves into lambs, as
she bore witness to the mercies of the Lord, seeing men now dwelling in
the purity of gospel morality whose debauchery had so often filled her
with horror.

Animated by new fervor at this sight, she gave herself unreservedly
to God, renouncing in future the least thought of self, and began to run
with giant steps along the paths of holiness. Prayers, toil, and spiritual
conversation were henceforward her sole occupation, and, following the
example of Saint Anthony, she made it a duty to imitate every edifying
trait that she perceived in those who composed this new church. She
spent all her spare time at the foot of the altar, she lived solely by her own
labor, and though she appeared outwardly busy and active, her heart
was ever in constant communion with God.

She had not yet made her first Communion when she arrived in the
colony, and it is not usual in these missions to grant this favor to neophytes until after long trials. Catherine was fearful that she would be
subjected to this rule, but her virtue, far more than her repeated entreaties, soon induced her director to make an exception in her favor, nor
had he any reason to repent. The frequent Communions which she was
permitted to receive did not diminish in the least her fervor in preparing
for them. It was enough to see her in her most ordinary actions for others to be roused to devotion, but when she partook of the divine mysteries, it was impossible to be near her without being filled with the most
tender love for God.

When she was obliged to go with the others on their hunting expeditions, she did not let the dissipation that always accompanied that ac-

tivity disturb her interior life. She built herself an oratory and spent all her time there. She avoided company as much as possible, and when she could not, she was more apt to communicate her spirit of meditation to others than to join in their amusements. Yet there was nothing constrained in her manners, and her devotion was neither forbidding nor troublesome. She was even wonderfully dexterous in concealing from the public her private practices of piety and her austerities, which were great. One of her most common pious acts was to mingle earth with all she ate, and very few perceived it.

Besides her director, without whose permission she did nothing of this kind, she also concealed nothing from two women of great virtue, who helped one another to rise to an eminent degree of sanctity. One was Anastasia, who had welcomed her on her reaching the colony, and the other was a young widow named Teresa, who after living some time in utter forgetfulness of her baptismal promises, returned to her duty when threatened by a great danger, from which she was convinced God had miraculously delivered her. Yet even after this she led quite an indifferent life, deferring from one day to the next the execution of the design she had conceived to atone by penance for past disorders.

A conversation with Catherine completed her conversion. She was one day attentively looking at the church, then under construction at Sault St. Louis, where the Iroquois town had been relocated from La Prairie de la Magdeleine. Catherine noticed her and felt inspired to address her, although she had never yet spoken to her. To open the conversation, she asked her which part of the new church was intended for the women, and Teresa pointed it out to her. "Alas!" replied Catherine. "It is not in these material temples that God takes most pleasure; our heart is the sanctuary most agreeable to Him. But how often have I, wretch that I am, driven Him from that heart where He wishes to reign alone? Do I not richly deserve that He should, for my ingratitude, close forever on me the door of this sanctuary that is being built to His glory?"

These words touched Teresa to the quick; she reproached herself with her tepid faith and felt strongly urged to fulfill at last what she had so frequently promised the Almighty. She at once revealed all to Catherine and found in that saintly girl an open heart which induced her to withhold nothing that was passing in her own and which completely gained her to Christ. Her [Catherine's] penitence was such as to raise up the greatest sinners, almost without intermediate steps, and, something even more difficult, to bring the most cowardly souls to heroic perfection. She [Teresa] became attached to Catherine by bonds that divine love drew still more closely, and henceforward these two chosen souls concealed from each other nothing bearing on their interior life. They consoled each other — gave counsel in doubts and strength in the assaults which Hell and the world more than once made on them.

About this time Catherine had to contend with a severe assault, one which came from the very person from whom she least expected something of this sort. The adopted sister who had urged her to come and live with her there took it into her head to marry her off, and she went to great lengths to overcome Catherine's resistance. She began by telling her that though she and her husband deemed it a pleasure to meet all her wants, still it might well be that, burdened with a large family, they might not always be in a position to continue supplying her with necessaries and that, moreover, in case of their death, she would be left without support.

This virtuous girl was particularly afflicted by these words because she was not her sister's dependent. She nevertheless thanked her for her attention and promised to reflect upon what she had just said. She immediately went to her confessor and expressed her grief that a sister who until then had given her so many marks of sincere friendship now wished to hamper her in the only thing in which she wished to be free. The father, after listening calmly to her, told her that, in fact, her sister was not so far wrong in speaking as she had done, that she should thank her for the precautions which she wished her to take in order to assure a decent subsistence, and that the matter deserved calm consideration. "This is no longer the time for deliberation," replied Catherine. "I am no longer my own, I have given myself unreservedly to Jesus Christ,"

"But," rejoined the missionary, "who will feed you and assist you in your infirmities, should God remove your sister?"

"That is my least anxiety," replied the generous neophyte. "He who feeds the birds of the air will not let me lack the little I need to live."

The father gave no appearance of yielding; instead he dismissed his penitent, bidding her to again consult the Lord on this question, for it was not yet clear what His will was. She went away very sad.

That same day her sister again pressed the matter, and finding her inflexible, Anastasia, whose age and virtue caused both to regard her as a mother, was induced to speak to her on this point. Anastasia at first agreed with the sister's views because it was unheard-of among the Iroquois for a girl to remain celibate, the missionaries having so far deemed it inexpedient to give these Indians the counsel which Saint Paul gave the primitive Christians.[2] Anastasia accordingly undertook to persuade

---

[2]"There is a difference also between a wife and a virgin. The unmarried woman careth for the things of the Lord, that she may be holy both in body and spirit; but she

Catherine to conform to her sister's wishes. She gained nothing and seemed somewhat nettled. This she showed Catherine by reproaches and threats of interposing the authority of their common director.

The saintly girl anticipated her, and after assuring her spiritual father that she could no longer doubt the will of God, she begged him to consent, in order to put an end to this persecution, that she should take a vow of virginity. The missionary replied that an engagement of that kind should not be taken lightly, that he gave her three days to think it over, and that during that time he permitted her to redouble her prayers and austerities to discover from the Almighty what He desired of her. Catherine left him promising obedience, but a quarter of an hour later she returned and, approaching him with an air that was not natural to her, exclaimed: "Father, I have considered it fully, and I will never have any spouse but Jesus Christ." Her action and the tone in which she spoke touched the director. He saw clearly that it would be vain to oppose a movement that had every mark of divine inspiration. He consoled his penitent by giving her hope of his consent to what she desired, exhorted her then to think of nothing but gaining the heart of the heavenly spouse whom she had chosen, and promised her to stop all further importunity on the part of her sister or her friends.

She had scarcely gone when Anastasia entered the missionary's abode with loud complaints of Catherine's stubbornness. After hearing her out, the missionary rebuked her mildly for her precipitation in blaming what she did not know and for the slight esteem which she seemed to entertain for a state which raises mortal creatures to the condition of angels. Anastasia received this correction with humility, and Catherine ever after found in her a truly Christian friend, disposed to second her in her pious designs and attentive to relieve her in her wants and afflictions. For her part, Catherine believed herself bound by the resolution she had taken to live more than ever in seclusion, practicing humility, charity, and penance. She was seen to advance visibly in virtue. Already naught was spoken of in the country except her eminent sanctity. The people were never weary admiring the secret spring of divine goodness, which, amid a nation the most hostile to the establishment of Christianity, had drawn forth a young girl to serve as the perfect model of all the Christian virtues.

There then reigned in the mission of Sault St.Louis a spirit of mortification that went to great lengths. These neophytes had just been declared by all the Iroquois cantons the enemies of their country, and they

---

that is married careth for the things of the world, how she may please her husband" (I Cor. 7:34).

confidently expected that after this outburst, all who fell into the hands of their idolatrous brethren would be given over without mercy to the most fearful tortures. Hence they thought only of preparing for martyrdom by all the means that austerity can suggest for chastising the flesh. Men, women, and even children proceeded to excesses that the missionaries never would have permitted had they been fully informed of them.

Catherine, more fully possessed by the interior spirit than all the others, was also the most unsparing to herself. She was guided only by her own fervor, believing herself under no obligation to consult her spiritual director as she had done in the past, for she thought that he must be aware of the involvement of the entire village in this behavior and that his silence amounted to consent. She was soon reduced to a state of languor and suffering, from which she never recovered. Some time later she paid a visit to Montreal, where the sight of the hospital nuns, whom she had never even heard mentioned, increased her desire to consecrate herself to God by the vow of chastity. She renewed her entreaties to her confessor, who judged it his duty no longer to withhold his consent. She accordingly took the long-desired vow, with a joy that seemed to revive all her strength, and she was the first of her tribe who took upon herself such an engagement with Heaven.

The heavenly spouse of chaste souls was not slow in giving her manifest proofs that he had accepted her sacrifice and in treating her as his well-beloved spouse. She, in turn, did her best to respond with perfect fidelity and unreserved love to his caresses and to the intimate communications with which he favored her. But her strength could not long sustain its ardor, and the flesh soon gave way beneath the efforts of the spirit. She fell dangerously ill and was able then to lead only a lingering existence subject to constant pain. In this state she united herself more and more with Jesus by meditating on His death and suffering and by attending Mass. She could no longer endure human conversation; Anastasia and Teresa were the only two persons with whom she retained any kind of intimacy, because they spoke to her only of God.

She felt well only at the foot of the altar, where, buried in profound contemplation and shedding torrents of tears, whose inexhaustible fountain was His love and the wound it had inflicted on her heart, she often so forgot the wants of her body as not even to feel the cold which benumbed her whole frame. She always came from this contemplation with a renewed love of suffering, and it is difficult to conceive how ingenious her mind was in inventing means to crucify her flesh. Sometimes she walked barefoot on the ice and snow until she lost all feeling. Sometimes she covered her bed with thorns. She rolled for three days in succession on branches of thorns, which pierced deeply into her flesh, causing inexpressible pain. Another time she burned her feet, as war captives are burned, wishing thus to brand herself as a slave of Christ. But the solidity of her virtue is best seen in the unalterable gentleness, patience, joy even, that she manifested in the sufferings she experienced in her last days.

It would seem that no sacrifice should be difficult for those who carry mortification as far as this saintly girl did. Yet this is rarely the case. Men are often astonished to behold those who practice the greatest austerities — more sensitive than others to any annoying or humiliating event that happens — simply because there is nothing of their own choice in it. Self-will is always the last victim and is often found missing from the holocaust. Catherine understood the superiority of the crosses presented by the hand of the Lord over those which are self-imposed, and suffering in which her will had least share was always dearest to her heart.

She was at last attacked by this malady, which was at once deemed mortal. It struck at a time when everyone was busy with labors in the field, so that she could scarcely expect care from anyone. She remained alone whole days with a platter of Indian corn and a little water beside her bed. Delighted to behold herself thus forsaken of men, she communed constantly with her God and found the days only too short. On Tuesday in Holy Week, 1678 [*sic:* actually 1680], she grew worse and received holy viaticum.[3] The missionary wished also to administer extreme unction[4] at once, but she assured him that it could be deferred until the next day. She spent all the ensuing night in a loving colloquy with her divine Savior and with His holy mother, whom she had always singularly honored, regarding herself as a spouse of Christ, attached to the retinue of the queen of virgins.

On Wednesday morning she received the sacred anointing, and about three o'clock in the afternoon she expired after a gentle agony of half an hour, retaining complete consciousness and sound judgment until her last sigh. Thus lived, and thus in her twenty-fifth [*sic* actually her twenty-fourth] year died, Catherine Tegahkouita. The example of her most holy life had produced a very great fervor among the Iroquois of Sault St. Louis. The wonders that God soon began to work in favor of those who had recourse to her intercession are still at this day, for these neophytes

[3] One of the last rites.
[4] One of the last rites.

and indeed for all of New France, a powerful motive to serve in spirit and in truth so liberal a Master, who, without respect of persons, lavishes his most precious gifts on those who abandon themselves to Him without reserve.

Her countenance, extremely attenuated by austerity and by her last illness, suddenly changed as soon as she ceased to live. It was seen assuming a rosy tint that she had never had, nor were her features the same. Nothing could be more beautiful but with that beauty which inspires the love of virtue. The people were never weary gazing on her, and each left with his heart full of the desire to become a saint. As a distinction, her body was placed in a coffin, and her tomb soon became famous for the crowds of the faithful who flocked from all parts of Canada, and for the miracles wrought there. Especially notable are the juridical attestations of two persons, whose character leaves no doubt as to the truth of their depositions. One is the Abbé de La Colombière, grand archdeacon, vicar general of Quebec, and clerical councilor in the Superior Council of New France. The other is Monsieur Du Luth, captain of an infantry company, one of the bravest officers the king has had in the colony. . . .

The former declares in a signed statement that having been sick from the month of January to that of June 1695 — with a slow fever that had baffled all remedies and a dysentery that nothing could check — he was advised to take a vow that if it pleased God to restore his health, he would proceed to the Mission of St. Francis Xavier at Sault St. Louis to pray at the tomb of Catherine Tegahkouita; that he followed this advice and the fever left him that very day, while the dysentery diminished considerably; that having set out some days after to fulfill his vow, he was entirely cured before he had proceeded more than a league.

The second certifies juridically that having been tortured with the gout for twenty-five years, accompanied by excessive pain that sometimes lasted for three months without respite, he invoked Catherine Tegahkouita, the Iroquois virgin who died at Sault St. Louis in the odor of sanctity, and promised to visit her tomb if, through her intercession, God delivered him from this cruel disease; that at the end of a novena that he performed in her honor, he was perfectly cured; and that for the last fifteen months he had felt no symptoms of gout.

Every year on the anniversary of the death of the Good Catherine (this being the name under which, out of respect for the Holy See, this saintly girl is honored in Canada), several parishes in the neighborhood come to chant in the church of Sault St. Louis a solemn Mass of the holy Trinity. Monsieur Remy, parish priest at Lachine, a village on the island of Montreal, who had recently arrived from France, on being informed by his parishioners of this custom, replied that he deemed it a duty not to sanction by his presence a public cult which was not yet permitted by the church. On hearing him speak thus, most people could not refrain from saying that he would soon be punished for his refusal, and in fact he fell dangerously ill the same day. He at once understood the cause of this unexpected attack. He bound himself by a vow to follow the example of his predecessors and was instantly cured.

Thus New France, like the capital of Old France, beheld the glory of a poor Indian girl and of a shepherdess [Ste. Genevieve] shining above that of so many apostolic men who were martyrs and other saints of all conditions of life, God doubtless wishing for our instruction and the consolation of the humble to glorify His saints in proportion to their smallness and obscurity on earth.

8

Exploring the Mississippi

Jesuits were occasionally involved in French voyages of exploration, serving as chaplains as they scouted potential new mission fields. The most famous of these missionary-explorers was Jacques Marquette, who, in the summer of 1673, helped to open the route from Canada, via the Great Lakes, to the Mississippi River. The party was actually led by Louis Jolliet, a French Canadian fur trader with Jesuit connections. (He would later become professor of hydrography at the Jesuit College of Quebec.) But Marquette acquired more fame than Jolliet, due in part to his writings, which form the bulk of historians' source material.

The Mississippi was well-known to the missionaries, fur traders, and officials of New France long before any Frenchman had set eyes on the river. The Illinois and other Indians visiting the French outposts on Lake Superior and Lake Michigan had informed the French of the great river that ran generally southward into a distant sea. At that time, it was not clear to the colonial government whether the sinuous Mississippi flowed into the Pacific Ocean or the Gulf of Mexico, but they decided to send out a party to establish a French presence in the area before the Spanish laid claim to it.

Setting off from Michilimackinac at the top of Lake Michigan, Marquette and Jolliet traveled to Green Bay, then up the Fox River and, by a series of smaller streams and portages, to the Wisconsin River. The Wisconsin conducted them to the Mississippi, and the explorers followed that stream south to about the point where the states of Arkansas and Louisiana now meet. By that time, they knew they were near the Gulf of Mexico, and fearing the hostility of natives downriver, as well as the Spanish (they did not realize that they were still quite far from the military outposts of Florida), they decided to turn back.

Marquette made the acquaintance of several Indian nations in the course of his travels, some of whom had never before encountered Europeans. He speaks of the "Wild Rice People," or Menominees, of Green Bay, as well as their neighbors, the Maskoutens. However, his most

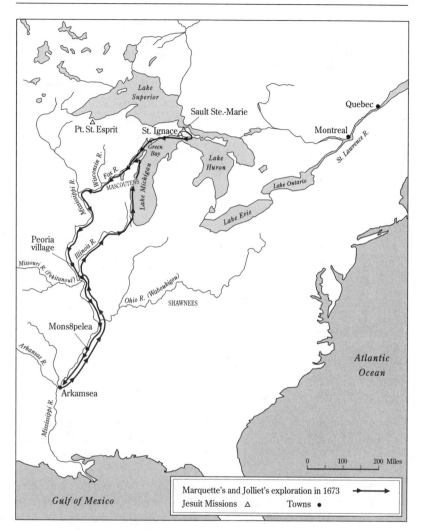

Map of Father Jacques Marquette's Route
[1]The Jesuits used *8* to denote the English *w* sound, which doesn't exist in French.

interesting and complete ethnographic material concerns the Peoria nation of the Illinois confederacy. These Algonquian peoples, much more populous than the Montagnais and Algonquins of the North, drew their subsistence both from agriculture and by hunting the bison, or "wild cattle" as Marquette calls them, in the area. Soon after his initial visit, the Jesuits established regular missions among the Illinois, who worked to establish closer relations with the French through trade, religious conversion, and assistance in wartime. In the 1680s, these peoples suffered greatly from the combined effects of epidemic diseases and Iroquois attacks.

The text that follows is the journal Marquette wrote during the winter following the expedition. It is preceded by an introduction written by the Jesuit superior, Claude Dablon. This text would have formed part of the *Relation of 1673–74,* but it arrived in France just after publication of the *Jesuit Relations* ceased. The manuscript was preserved in Europe and published only in the nineteenth century.

JACQUES MARQUETTE

On the First Voyage by Father Marquette toward New Mexico and How the Idea Was Conceived

1674

The Father had long premeditated this undertaking, influenced by a most ardent desire to extend the kingdom of Jesus Christ and to make him known and adored by all the peoples of that country. He saw himself, as it were, at the door of these new nations when, in the year 1670, he was laboring in the Mission of Point St. Esprit,[1] at the extremity of Lake Superior, among the Ottawas. Occasionally, he even saw various persons belonging to these new peoples and got to know them as well as he could. This induced him to make several efforts to begin this undertaking, but always in vain, and just when he had given up all hope of success, God presented him with an opportunity.

In the year 1673, Monsieur Count Frontenac, our governor, and Monsieur Talon, then our intendant, were aware of the importance of such exploration, either to discover a passage from here to the Sea of China [Pacific Ocean], by the river that discharges into the Vermilion, or California, Sea, or to verify reports of two kingdoms, Theguaio and Quiuira, which supposedly border on Canada and where there are said to be numerous gold mines. These gentlemen, as I say, then appointed for this

[1] The Mission of Point St. Esprit was on Chequamegon Bay, Wisconsin, on the south shore of Lake Superior.

JR 59:86–161, Jacques Marquette, "Le premier Voyage qu'a fait le P. Marquette vers le nouveau Mexique," manuscript written in 1674.

undertaking Sieur Jolliet, whom they considered very fit for so great an enterprise, and they were pleased to include Father Marquette in the party.

They were not mistaken in the choice that they made of Sieur Jolliet, for he is a young man, born in this country, who possesses all the qualifications that could be desired for such an undertaking. He has experience and knows the languages spoken in the country of the Ottawas, where he has passed several years already. He possesses tact and prudence, which are the chief qualities necessary for the success of such a difficult and dangerous voyage. Finally, he has the courage to dread nothing where everything is to be feared. Consequently, he has fulfilled all the expectations entertained of him, and if, after having passed through a thousand dangers, he had not unfortunately been shipwrecked on returning to port (his canoe capsized below Sault St. Louis, near Montreal, where he lost both his men and his papers, and whence he escaped only by a sort of miracle), his voyage would have been deemed a complete success.

I. Departure of Father Jacques Marquette for the Discovery of the Great River Called by the Indians Mississippi, Which Leads to New Mexico.

The Feast of the Immaculate Conception of the Blessed Virgin — whom I have always invoked since I have been in this country of the Ottawas, to obtain from God the grace of being able to visit the nations who dwell along the Mississippi River — was precisely the day on which Monsieur Jolliet arrived with orders from Count Frontenac, our governor, and Monsieur Talon, our intendant, to accomplish this discovery with me. I was all the more delighted at this good news, since I saw that my plans were about to be accomplished, and since I found myself in the blessed necessity of exposing my life for the salvation of all these peoples, and especially for the Illinois, who had very urgently entreated me, when I was at Point St. Esprit, to carry the word of God to their country.

We were not long in assembling our crew and equipment, even though we were about to begin a voyage of unknown duration. Indian corn, with some smoked meat, constituted all our provisions. With these we embarked — Monsieur Jolliet and myself, with five men — in two bark canoes, fully resolved to accept any hardships for such a glorious expedition.

Accordingly, on the seventeenth day of May, 1673, we started from the Mission of St. Ignace at Michilimackinac, where I was at the time.

The joy that we felt at being selected for this expedition raised our spirits and rendered the labor of paddling from morning to night agreeable to us. And because we were going to seek unknown countries, we took every precaution in our power, so that even if our undertaking was hazardous, it should not be foolhardy. To that end, we obtained all the information that we could from the Indians who had frequented those regions, and we even traced out from their reports a map of the whole of that new country. On this map we indicated the rivers which we were to navigate, the names of the peoples and of the places through which we were to pass, the course of the great river, and the direction we were to follow when we reached it.

Above all, I placed our voyage under the protection of the Blessed Virgin Immaculate, promising her that if she granted us the favor of discovering the great river, I would give it the name of La Conception and that the first mission that I should establish among those new peoples would bear the same name. This I have actually done, among the Illinois.

II. The Father Visits, in Passing, the Wild Rice People. What That Wild Rice Is. He Enters Green Bay; Some Particulars about That Bay. He Arrives among the Fire Nation.

With all these precautions, we joyfully plied our paddles on a portion of Lake Huron, on the Lake of the Illinois [Lake Michigan], and on Green Bay.

The first nation that we came to was that of the Wild Rice [Menominees]. I entered their river, to go and visit these peoples to whom we have preached the gospel for several years, and consequently there are several good Christians among them.

The wild rice, whose name these people bear because it is found in their country, is a sort of grass that grows naturally in the small rivers with muddy bottoms and in swampy places. It greatly resembles the wild rice that grows amid our wheat. The ears grow upon hollow stems, jointed at intervals. They emerge from the water about the month of June and continue growing until they rise about two feet above it. The grain is not thicker than that of our oats, but it is twice as long, and it produces more abundant meal. The Indians gather and prepare it for food as follows. In the month of September, which is the proper time for the harvest, they go in canoes through these fields of wild rice and shake its ears into the canoe, on both sides, as they pass through. If it is ripe, the grain falls out easily, and they obtain their supply in a short time. In order to clean off the straw and remove the husk in which it is enclosed, they dry it in the smoke upon a wooden grating, under which they maintain a slow fire for some days. When the oats are thoroughly dry, they put them in a skin formed into a pouch, thrust it into a hole dug in the ground for this purpose, and tread it with their feet, so long and so vigorously that the grain separates from the straw and is easily winnowed. After this, they pound it to reduce it to flour, or, leaving it unground, they boil it in water and season it with fat. Cooked in this fashion, the wild rice has almost as delicate a taste as real rice has when no better seasoning is added.

I told these Wild Rice People of my design to go and discover remote nations in order to teach them the mysteries of our holy religion. They were greatly surprised and did their best to dissuade me. They told me that I would meet nations who never show mercy to strangers, but break their heads for no reason, and that war was raging among various peoples who dwelt upon our route, which exposed us to the further manifest danger of being killed by the bands of warriors in their campaigns. They also said that the great river was very dangerous when one does not know the difficult passages, that it was full of horrible monsters who devoured men and canoes together, that there was even a demon who was heard from a great distance and who barred the way, swallowing up all who ventured to approach him, and finally that the heat was so excessive in those countries that it would inevitably cause our death.

I thanked them for the good advice they gave me but told them that I could not follow it because the salvation of souls was at stake, for which I would be delighted to give my life; that I scoffed at the alleged demon; that we would easily defend ourselves against those sea monsters; and, moreover, that we would be on our guard to avoid the other dangers with which they threatened us. After leading them in a prayer to God and giving them some instruction, I separated from them. Embarking then in our canoes, we arrived shortly afterward at the bottom of Green Bay, where our fathers have been laboring with success for the conversion of these peoples, over two thousand of whom they have baptized since they arrived there. . . .

The bay is about thirty leagues in depth and eight in width at its mouth. It narrows gradually to the bottom, where it is easy to observe a tide which has its regular ebb and flow, almost like that of the sea. This is not the place to inquire whether these are real tides, whether they are due to the wind or to some other cause; nor whether any winds might precede or follow the moon, and consequently agitate the lake and give it an apparent ebb and flow whenever the moon ascends above the horizon. What I can positively state is that when the water is very calm, it can easily be observed to rise and fall with the motions of the moon. However, I do not deny that this movement may be caused by very remote winds, which, pressing on the middle of the lake, cause the edges to rise and fall in the manner which is visible to our eyes.

We left this bay to enter the river [the Fox] that discharges into it. It is very beautiful at its mouth and flows gently. It is full of bustards, ducks, teal, and other birds who are attracted by the wild rice, of which they are very fond. But after one ascends the river a short distance, it becomes a very difficult passage, on account of both the currents and the sharp rocks which cut the canoes, as well as the feet of those who are obliged to drag them, especially when the waters are low. Nevertheless, we successfully passed those rapids, and, as we neared the Maskoutens (or the Fire Nation), I grew curious to drink the mineral waters of the river that is not far from that village. I also took the time to look for a medicinal plant that an Indian who knows its secret showed to Father Allouez[2] with many ceremonies. Its root is used to counteract snakebites, God having been pleased to provide this antidote against a poison that is very common in these countries. It is very pungent and tastes like powder when crushed with the teeth; it must be masticated and placed upon the snakebite. The reptile has so great a horror of it that it even flees from a person who has rubbed himself with it. The plant bears several stalks, a foot high, with rather long leaves and a white flower, which greatly resembles the wallflower. I put some in my canoe, in order to examine it at leisure while we continued to advance toward Maskoutens, where we arrived on the seventh of June.

III. Description of the Village of Maskoutens; What Passed There between the Father and the Indians. The French Begin to Enter a New and Unknown Country and Arrive at Mississippi.

Here we are at Maskoutens. This word in Algonquin may mean "the Fire Nation," which, indeed, is the name given to this people. This is the limit of the discoveries the French have made, for they have not yet gone any farther.

This town consists of three nations who have gathered there: Miamis, Maskoutens, and Kickapoos. The former are the most civil, the most liberal, and the best-looking. They wear two long locks over their ears, which give them a pleasing appearance. They are regarded as warriors

---

[2] Claude Allouez (1622–1689), a Jesuit missionary who had preceded Marquette in the Great Lakes region. See the selection on pages 91–93.

and rarely undertake expeditions without being successful. They are very docile and listen quietly to what is said to them; and they appeared so eager to hear Father Allouez when he instructed them that they gave him little rest, even during the night. The Maskoutens and Kickapoos are ruder and seem to be mere peasants compared with the others. As bark for making cabins is scarce in this country, they use rushes for walls and roofs, though these do not afford them much protection against the winds and still less against the rains when they fall abundantly. The advantage of cabins of this kind is that they can be bound up and transported easily wherever the people wish during the hunting season.

When I visited them, I was greatly consoled by the sight of a handsome cross erected in the middle of the town and adorned with many white skins, red belts, and bows and arrows which these good people had offered to the great Manitou (this is the name which they give to God). They did this to thank him for having pity on them during the winter and for giving them an abundance of game when they most dreaded famine.

I took pleasure in observing the situation of this village. It is truly pleasing, standing upon an eminence from which one beholds prairies, extending on every side as far as the eye can see, with scattered groves and lofty forests. The soil is very fertile and yields much Indian corn. The Indians gather quantities of plums and grapes, with which much wine could be made, if desired.

No sooner had we arrived than Monsieur Jolliet and I assembled the elders together and he told them that he was sent by Monsieur the governor to discover new countries, while I was sent by God to illuminate them with the light of the holy gospel. He told them that the sovereign master of our lives wished to be known by all the nations; and that in obeying His will, I fearlessly exposed myself to death in perilous voyages. He informed them that we needed two guides to show us the way, and we gave them a present as we asked them to grant us the guides. To this they very civilly consented; and they also spoke to us by means of a present, consisting of a mat to serve us as a bed on our voyage.

On the following day, the tenth of June, two Miamis who were given to us as guides embarked with us, in the sight of a great crowd. Those gathered could not sufficiently express their astonishment at the sight of seven Frenchmen, alone in two canoes, daring to undertake so extraordinary and so hazardous an expedition.

We knew that there was a river three leagues from Maskoutens that discharged into the Mississippi. We also knew that the direction we were to follow in order to reach it was west-southwesterly. But the route is broken by so many swamps and small lakes that it is easy to lose one's way, especially as the river is so full of wild rice that it is difficult to find the channel. For this reason we had great need of our two guides, who conducted us safely to a portage of twenty-seven hundred paces and helped us to transport our canoes to enter that river. Afterward, they returned home, leaving us alone in this unknown country, in the hands of Providence.

Thus we left the waters which flow to Quebec, four hundred to five hundred leagues from here, and took those that would thenceforward lead us into strange lands. Before setting out, we all began a new devotion to the Blessed Virgin Immaculate, which we practiced daily, addressing to her special prayers to place under her protection both our persons and the success of our voyage; and, after encouraging one another, we entered our canoes.

The river on which we embarked is called Meskousing [the Wisconsin]. It is very wide and has a sandy bottom that forms various shoals that make navigation very difficult. It is full of islands covered with vines. On the banks one sees fertile land, with woods, prairies, and hills succeeding one another. There are oak, walnut, and basswood trees; and another kind, whose branches are armed with long thorns. We saw there neither feathered game nor fish, but many deer and a large number of cattle [bison]. Our route lay to the southwest, and after traveling about thirty leagues, we came to a place with all the appearances of an iron deposit. In fact, one of our party who has seen such mines assures us that the one which we found is very good and very rich. It is covered with three feet of good soil and is quite near a chain of rocks, the base of which is covered by very fine trees. After proceeding forty leagues on this route, we arrived at the mouth of our river, and at forty-two and a half degrees of latitude, we safely entered the Mississippi on the seventeenth of June, with a joy that I cannot express.

IV. Of the Great River Called Mississippi; Its Most Notable Features; of Various Animals, and Especially the Pisikious, or Wild Cattle, Their Shape and Nature; Of the First Villages of the Illinois, Where the French Arrived.

We are here, then, on this famous river, all of whose peculiar features I have endeavored to note carefully. The Mississippi River has its source in various lakes in the country of the northern nations. It is narrow at the place where the Meskousing empties into it. The current, which flows southward, is slow and gentle. To the right, a great range of high mountains is seen, while on the left are beautiful lands. In various places, the stream is divided by islands. On sounding, we found ten fathoms of water. Its breadth is very uneven: Sometimes it is three-quarters of a league, and sometimes it narrows to three *arpents*.[3] We slowly followed its course, which runs toward the south and southeast, as far as the forty-second degree of latitude. Here we saw plainly that it had changed completely. There are hardly any woods or mountains, and the islands are more beautiful and are covered with finer trees. We saw only deer and cattle, bustards, and swans without wings because they drop their plumage in this country. From time to time, we came upon monstrous fish, one of which struck our canoe with such violence that I thought that it was a great tree, about to break the canoe to pieces. On another occasion, we saw on the water a monster with a head of a tiger, a sharp nose like that of a skunk, with whiskers and straight, erect ears; the head was gray and the neck quite black. We saw no more creatures of this sort. When we cast our nets into the water, we caught sturgeons, and a very extraordinary kind of fish. It resembles the trout, but its mouth is larger and near its nose — which is smaller, as are its eyes; it is a large thing shaped like a woman's bust, three fingers wide and a cubit long, at the end of which is a disk as wide as one's hand. This frequently causes it to fall backward when it leaps out of the water. When we reached the parallel of 41 degrees, 28 minutes, following the same direction, we found that the main game fowl was the wild turkey, while the main game animal was the *pisikious,* or wild cattle.

We call them wild cattle because they are very similar to our domestic cattle. They are not longer, but are nearly twice as wide and more corpulent. When our people killed one, three persons had much difficulty in moving it. The head is very large; the forehead is flat and a foot and a half wide between the horns, which are exactly like those of our oxen, though black and much larger. Under the neck they have a sort of large dewlap, which hangs down, and on the back is a rather high hump. The whole of the head, the neck, and a portion of the shoulders are covered with a thick mane like that of a horse. This mane forms a crest a foot long that makes them hideous, and because it falls over their eyes, it prevents them from seeing what is before them. The remainder of the body is covered with a heavy coat of curly hair, almost like that of our sheep but much stronger and thicker. It falls off in summer, and the skin becomes as soft as velvet. During that season, the Indians use the hides for

---

[3]Approximately five hundred feet. An arpent was a French unit of measurement.

making fine robes, which they paint in various colors. The flesh and the fat of the *pisikious* are excellent and constitute the best dish at feasts. Moreover, they are very fierce, and not a year passes without their killing some Indians. When attacked, they catch a man on their horns, if they can, toss him in the air, and then throw him on the ground, after which they trample him underfoot and kill him. If a person fires at them from a distance, with either a bow or a gun, he must, immediately after the shot, throw himself down and hide in the grass; for if they perceive the one who fired, they will run at him and attack him. As their legs are thick and rather short, they do not generally run very fast, except when angry. They are scattered across the prairie in herds; I saw one band numbering four hundred.

We continued to advance, but as we knew not where we were going — for we had proceeded over one hundred leagues without discovering anything except animals and birds — we remained on our guard. Thus, we would make only a small fire on land to prepare our evening meal, and after supper we would remove ourselves as far from it as possible and pass the night in our canoes that we anchored in the river at some distance from the shore. Even so, we always posted one of the party as a sentinel, for fear of a surprise. Proceeding still in a southerly and south-southwesterly direction, we found ourselves at the parallel of forty-one degrees. . . without having discovered anything.

Finally, on the 25th of June, we perceived at the water's edge some human tracks and a narrow and somewhat beaten path leading to a fine meadow. We stopped to examine it, and thinking that it was a trail that led to some village of Indians, we resolved to go and reconnoiter it. We left our two canoes under the guard of our people, strictly charging them not to allow themselves to be taken by surprise, and then Monsieur Joliet and I set off on a rather dangerous mission for two men who exposed themselves, alone, to the mercy of a barbarous and unknown people. We silently followed the narrow path, and after walking about two leagues, we discovered a village on the bank of a river and two others on a hill distant about half a league from the first. At this point, we heartily commended ourselves to God, and after imploring his aid, we went on, but no one noticed us. We approached so near that we could even hear the Indians talking. We therefore decided that it was time to reveal ourselves. Stopping and advancing no further, we began to yell as loudly as we could. On hearing the shout, the Indians quickly issued from their cabins, and having probably recognized us as Frenchmen, especially when they saw a black robe — or, at least, having no cause for distrust, as we were only two men and had given them notice of our arrival — they appointed four old men to come and speak to us. Two of these bore tobacco pipes, finely ornamented and adorned with various feathers. They walked slowly and raised their pipes toward the sun, seemingly offering them to it to be smoked by the sun, though they never spoke a word. It took them rather a long time to make their way to us from their village. Finally, when they had drawn near, they stopped to look at us attentively. I was reassured when I observed these ceremonies, which they perform only among friends, and much more so when I saw them clad in cloth, for I judged thereby that they were our allies. I therefore spoke to them first, asking them who they were. They replied that they were Illinois, and as a token of peace, they offered us their pipes to smoke. Afterward, they invited us to enter their village, where all the people impatiently awaited us. These pipes for smoking tobacco are called calumets in this country. This word has come so much into use that, in order to be understood, I shall be obliged to use it, for I shall often have to speak of these pipes.

V. How the Illinois Received the Father in Their Village.

At the door of the cabin where we would be received stood an old man who awaited us in a rather surprising posture, which constitutes a part of the ceremony that they observe when they receive strangers. This man was standing stark naked, with his hands extended and lifted toward the sun as if he wished to protect himself from its rays, which nevertheless shone upon his face through his fingers. When we came near him, he paid us this compliment: "How beautiful the sun is, O Frenchmen, when you come to visit us! All our village awaits you, and you shall enter all our cabins in peace." Having said this, he brought us into his own cabin, where there was a crowd of people who devoured us with their eyes, though they observed a profound silence. However, we could hear these words, which were addressed to us from time to time in a low voice: "How good it is, my brothers, that you should visit us."

After we had taken our places, the usual civility of the country was paid to us, which consisted in offering us the calumet. This must not be refused, unless one wishes to be considered an enemy, or at least impolite, though it is enough to make even a pretense of smoking. After we had smoked, the assembly honored us by smoking in their turn. While they were passing the calumet, we received an invitation on behalf of the great captain of all the Illinois to proceed to his village, where he wished to hold a council with us. We went there with a large escort, for all these people, who had never seen any Frenchman among them, could

Captain of the Illinois Nation. He is carrying his pipe and his spear.
A pen-and-ink drawing attributed to the Jesuit Louis Nicolas and dating from about 1700.
Courtesy of the Newberry Library, Chicago.

not cease looking at us. They lay on the grass beside the trail; they went ahead of us and then retraced their steps to come and see us again. All this was done noiselessly and with marks of great respect for us.

When we reached the village, we saw the great captain at the entrance of his cabin standing between two old men, all three naked and holding their calumet turned toward the sun. He harangued us in a few words, congratulating us upon our arrival. Afterward, he offered us his calumet and invited us to smoke as we entered his cabin, where we received all their usual kind attentions.

Seeing all assembled and silent, I spoke to them by four presents that I gave them. By the first, I told them that we were journeying peacefully to visit the nations dwelling along the river as far as the sea. By the second, I announced to them that God, who had created them, had taken pity on them, inasmuch as after they had so long been ignorant of him, he wished to make himself known to all the peoples. I was sent by Him for that purpose, and it was up to them to acknowledge and obey Him. By the third, I said that the great captain of the French wished to inform them that it was he who established peace everywhere and that it was he who had subdued the Iroquois. Finally, by the fourth, we begged them to give us all the information that they had about the sea and about the nations we must pass to reach it.

When I had finished my speech, the captain arose, and resting his hand upon the head of a little slave whom he wished to give us, he spoke thus: "I thank you, Black Robe and you, O Frenchman," addressing Monsieur Jolliet, "for having taken so much trouble to come to visit us. Never has the earth been so beautiful or the sun so bright as today. Never has our river been so calm or so clear of rocks, which your canoes have removed as they traveled. Never has our tobacco tasted so good or our corn appeared so fine as we now see them. Here is my son, whom I give you so that you will know my heart. I beg you to have pity on me and on all of my nation. It is you who know the Great Spirit who has made us all. It is you who speak to Him and who hear his words. Beg Him to give me life and health and to come and dwell with us, in order to make us know him." Having said this, he placed the little slave beside us and gave us a second present, in the form of a very mysterious calumet, upon which they place more value than upon a slave. By this gift, he expressed to us the esteem that he had for Monsieur the governor, based on what we had told him of the latter. By a third, he begged us on behalf of all his nation not to go farther, on account of the great dangers to which we would expose ourselves.

I replied that I feared not death and that I believed there was no greater happiness than that of losing my life for the glory of Him who has made all. This is what these poor people cannot understand.

The council was followed by a great feast consisting of four dishes, each of which had to be eaten in its special way. The first course was a great wooden platter full of *sagamité,* that is to say, Indian cornmeal boiled in water and seasoned with fat. The master of ceremonies filled a spoon with *sagamité* three or four times and put it into my mouth as if I were a little child. He did the same to Monsieur Jolliet. As a second course, he caused a second platter to be brought, on which there were three fish. He took some pieces of them, removed the bones, and after blowing upon them to cool them, put them in our mouths as one would give food to a bird. For the third course, they brought a large dog that had just been killed, but when they learned that we did not eat this meat, they removed it from before us. Finally, the fourth course was a piece of wild ox, the fattest morsels of which were placed in our mouths.

After this feast, we had to go to visit the whole village, which consists of three hundred cabins. While we walked through the streets, an orator was continually announcing that people must not annoy us when they came to see us. Everywhere we were presented with belts, garters, and other articles made of the hair of bears and cattle dyed red, yellow, and gray. These are all the rarities they possess. As they are of no great value, we did not burden ourselves with them.

We slept in the captain's cabin, and on the following day we took leave of him, promising to revisit his town in four moons. He conducted us to our canoes, together with nearly six hundred persons who watched us set off, giving every possible manifestation of the joy that our visit had caused them. For my own part, I promised, on bidding them adieu, that I would come the following year and reside with them to instruct them. But before quitting the Illinois country, it is proper that I should relate what I observed of their customs and usages.

VI. Of the Character of the Illinois; Of Their Habits and Customs; And of the Esteem That They Have for the Calumet, or Tobacco Pipe, and of the Dance They Perform in Its Honor.

When one speaks the word *Illinois,* it is as if one said in their language, "the men," as if the other Indians were merely animals. It must also be admitted that they have an air of humanity that we have not observed in the other nations that we have seen upon our route. The shortness of my stay among them did not allow me to secure all the information that I would have desired, but among all their customs, the following is what I have observed.

They are divided into many villages, some of which are quite distant from that of which we speak, which is called Peoria. This causes some difference in their language, which, on the whole, resembles Algonquin, so that we easily understood each other. They are of a gentle and tractable disposition, as we discovered by the reception that they gave us.

They have several wives, of whom they are extremely jealous. They watch them very closely and cut off their noses or ears when they misbehave. I saw several women who bore the marks of their misconduct.

Their bodies are well made; they are active and very skillful with bows and arrows. They also use guns, which they buy from our Indian allies who trade with our French. They use them especially to terrify their enemies with the noise and smoke, as these adversaries do not use guns and have never seen any, since they live too far to the west. They are warlike and make themselves dreaded by the distant tribes to the south and west where they go to procure slaves. These they barter, selling them at a high price to other nations in exchange for other wares. Those very distant Indians against whom they wage war have no knowledge of Europeans, nor do they know anything of iron or of copper, and they have only stone knives.

When the Illinois go to war, the whole village must be notified by a loud shout, which is uttered at the doors of the cabins the night and the morning before their departure. The captains are distinguished from the soldiers by wearing red sashes. These are made, with considerable skill, from the hair of bears and wild cattle. They paint their faces with red ocher, great quantities of which are found at a distance of some days' journey from the town.

They live by hunting, game being plentiful in that country, and on corn, of which they always have a good crop. Consequently, they have never suffered from famine. They also sow excellent beans and melons, especially those that have red seeds. Their squashes are not of the best; they dry them in the sun and eat them in winter and spring. Their cabins are very large and are roofed and floored with mats made of rushes. Their dishes are made of wood, and their ladles from the skulls of cattle, skillfully shaped to make a spoon for eating *sagamité.*

They are liberal in cases of illness and think that the effect of the medicines administered to them is in proportion to the presents given to the physician. Their garments consist only of skins. The women are always clad very modestly and very becomingly, while the men do not take the trouble to cover themselves.

I know not through what superstition some [male] Illinois (the Sioux have a similar custom), while still young, assume the garb of women and retain it throughout their lives. There is some mystery in this, for they never marry and glory in demeaning themselves to do everything that the women do. They go to war, however, but can use only clubs, and not bows and arrows, which are the weapons proper to men. They are present at all the rituals and at the solemn dances in honor of the calumet; at these they sing but must not dance. They are summoned to the councils, and nothing can be decided without their advice. Finally, through their profession of leading an extraordinary life, they pass for manitous, that is to say, for spirits or persons of consequence.

There remains no more, except to speak of the calumet. There is nothing more mysterious or more respected among them. Less honor is paid to the crowns and scepters of kings than the Indians bestow upon this object. It seems to be the god of peace and of war, the arbiter of life and of death. It has but to be carried upon one's person and displayed to enable one to walk safely through the midst of enemies, who, in the heat of battle, will lay down their arms when it is shown. For that reason, the Illinois gave me one, to serve as a safeguard among all the nations through whom I had to pass during my voyage. There is one calumet for peace and one for war, which are distinguished solely by the color of the feathers with which they are adorned: Red is a sign of war. They also use it to put an end to their disputes, to strengthen their alliances, and to speak to strangers. It is fashioned from a red stone, polished like marble, and bored in such a manner that one end serves as a receptacle for the tobacco, while the other fits into the stem. The stem is a piece of wood two feet long, as thick as an ordinary cane, and bored through the middle. It is ornamented with the heads and necks of various birds of gorgeous plumage, and all along its length are attached long red, green, and other colors. They have a great regard for it, because they look upon it as the calumet of the sun, and, in fact, they offer it to the latter to smoke when they wish to obtain a calm, or rain, or fine weather. They refrain from bathing and from eating fresh fruit at the beginning of summer until after they have performed a dance in its honor. This is how it is done.

The calumet dance, which is very famous among these peoples, is performed only on important occasions, sometimes to strengthen peace or to unite themselves for some great war, or at other times for public rejoicing. Sometimes they do honor to a nation who are invited to be present, sometimes it is danced to welcome some important personage, as if they wished to give him the diversion of a ball or a play. In winter the ceremony takes place in a cabin, but in summer it is held in the open fields. When the spot is selected, it is completely surrounded by trees, so that all may sit in the shade afforded by their leaves, in order to be protected from the heat of the sun. A large mat of rushes, painted in various colors, is spread in the middle of the place and serves as a carpet and a place of honor for the god of the person who is to give the dance, for each of them has his own god, which they call their manitou. This is a serpent, a bird, or other similar thing, of which they have dreamed while sleeping and in which they place all their confidence for the success of their war, their fishing, and their hunting. Just to the right of this manitou is placed the calumet, in honor of which the feast is given, and all around it a sort of trophy is formed displaying the weapons used by the warriors of those nations: clubs, war hatchets, bows, quivers, and arrows.

Everything being thus arranged, and the hour of the dance drawing near, those appointed to sing take the most honorable place under the branches. These are the men and women with the best voices, and they sing together in perfect harmony. Afterward, everyone comes to take their seats in a circle under the branches, but each one, upon arriving, must salute the manitou. This he does by inhaling smoke and blowing it from his mouth upon the manitou, as if he were offering to it incense. Everyone, at the outset, takes the calumet in a respectful manner and, supporting it with both hands, causes it to dance in cadence, keeping time with the songs. He makes it execute many different figures; sometimes he shows it to the whole assembly, turning himself from side to side. After that, the person who is to begin the dance appears in the middle of the assembly and at once continues this. Sometimes he offers it to the sun, as if he wished the latter to smoke it; sometimes he inclines it toward the earth; other times he makes it spread its wings as if about to fly; then he brings it to the mouths of those present, that they may smoke. The whole dance is done to a rhythm. It resembles the first scene of a ballet.

The second [scene] consists of a battle carried on to the sound of a kind of drum, which succeeds the songs, or even unites with them, harmonizing very well with them. The dancer makes a sign to some warrior to come take the weapons which lie upon the mat and invites him to fight to the sound of the drums. The latter approaches, takes up the bow and arrows and the war hatchet, and begins the duel with the other, whose sole defense is the calumet. This spectacle is very pleasing, especially as all is done in rhythm. As one dancer attacks, the other defends himself; as one strikes blows, the other parries them; as one takes to flight, the other pursues, and then he who was fleeing faces about and forces his adversary to flee. This is done so well, with slow and measured steps and to the rhythmic sound of the voices and drums, that it might pass for a very fine opening of a ballet in France.

The third scene consists of a lofty discourse, delivered by the man who holds the calumet. The combat having concluded without bloodshed, he recounts the battles at which he has been present, the victories that he has won, the names of the defeated nations, their locations, and the captives he took. And to reward this man, he who presides at the dance makes him a present of a fine robe of beaver skins or some other article. Having received it, he then hands the calumet to another, the latter to a third, and so on until everyone has done his duty. Then the chairman presents the calumet itself to the nation that has been invited to the ceremony, as a token of the everlasting peace that is to exist between the two peoples.

Here is one of the songs that they are in the habit of singing. They give it a certain tone which cannot be sufficiently expressed on paper but which nevertheless constitutes all its grace:

"Ninahani, ninahani, ninahani, nani ongo."

VII. Departure of the Father from the Illinois; Of the Painted Monsters Which He Saw upon the Great River Mississippi; Of the River Pekitanouï. . . .

We took leave of our Illinois at the end of June, about three o'clock in the afternoon. We embarked with all the people watching, admiring our little canoes, for they have never seen any like them.

We descended, following the current of a river called Pekitanouï [the Missouri], which discharges into the Mississippi from the northwest. I shall have something important to say about that after I have related all that I observed along this river.

Passing close to the rocky cliffs that line the river, I noticed an herb that seemed to me quite extraordinary. The root looks like small turnips fastened together by little filaments and it has a taste like carrots. From this root springs a leaf as wide as one's hand and half a finger thick, with spots in the middle; from this leaf grow other leaves resembling the sconces used for candles in our halls. Each leaf bears five or six yellow flowers shaped like little bells.

We found quantities of blackberries as large as those of France, as well as a small fruit that we first took for an olive but that tasted like an orange. There was another fruit as large as a hen's egg, which we cut in half; inside were two divisions, in each of which eight or ten fruits were encased; these are shaped like almonds and are very good when ripe. However, the tree that bears them has a very bad odor; its leaves resemble those of the walnut tree. In the meadows there is also a fruit similar to the hazelnut but more delicate. The leaves are very large and grow from a stalk, at the end of which is a head similar to that of a sunflower, in which all the nuts are regularly arranged. These are very good, both cooked and raw.

While skirting some frightfully huge rocks, we saw upon one of them two monsters painted there that startled us at first. Even the boldest Indians dare not rest their eyes on them for long. They are as large as a calf, with horns on their heads like those of deer, a horrible look, red eyes, a beard like a tiger's, a face somewhat like a man's, a body covered with scales, and a long tail that encircles the body, passing above the head and going back between the legs, ending in a fish's tail. Green, red, and black are the three colors composing the picture. These two monsters were so well painted that we could not believe that they were executed by a savage. The best artists of France could not have done better, especially if they had to paint on such high and inaccessible rocks. . . .

As we were gliding along peacefully through the clear, calm water, conversing among ourselves about these monsters, we heard the noise of a rapid, into which we were about to run. I have never seen anything so dreadful. An amalgam of large trees, branches, and floating islands was issuing from the mouth of the river Pekitanouï with such force that we could not risk passing through. So much mud was churned up that the water could not recover its clarity.

Pekitanouï is a large river coming a great distance from the northwest before emptying into the Mississippi. There are many villages of Indians along this river. I hope to follow it in order to discover the Vermilion, or California, Sea.

Judging from the direction of the course of the Mississippi, we think that if it continues the same way, it must discharge into the Gulf of Mexico. It would be a great advantage to find the river leading to the South Sea [Pacific Ocean] in the vicinity of California, and, as I said, I hope to do just that by following Pekitanouï. According to what the Indians told me, one travels five or six days up this river until one reaches a beautiful prairie extending twenty to thirty leagues. Crossing the plain in a northwesterly direction, one ends up at another small river, where one may set off by water once again (for it is not difficult to transport canoes over that fine, level prairie). This second river flows to the southwest for ten to fifteen leagues, then enters a small and deep lake, the source of another deep river which flows toward the west and into the sea.[4] I have little doubt but that this is the Vermilion Sea, and I do not despair of discovering it someday, if God grant me the grace and the health to do so, in order that I may preach the gospel to all the peoples of this new world who have wallowed so long in the darkness of infidelity.

[4] "This supposition of Marquette's has been confirmed by later explorations, which show that the headwaters of the Platte, tributary to the Missouri, closely approach those of the Colorado, which falls into the Gulf of California" (*JR* 59:312 n. 34).

Let us resume our route, after escaping as best we could from the dangerous rapid caused by the obstruction which I have mentioned.

VIII. Of the New Countries Discovered by the Father. Various Particulars. Meeting with Some Indians. First News of the Sea and of Europeans. Great Danger Avoided by Means of the Calumet.

After proceeding about twenty leagues to the south and a little less than that to the southeast, we found ourselves at a river called Waboukigou [the Ohio], the mouth of which is at thirty-six degrees latitude. Before reaching it, we passed by a place much dreaded by the Indians on account of the manitou — that is to say, demon — that lurks there and devours passing travelers. The Indians, wishing to divert us from our undertaking, warned us against it. Here is what this demon amounts to: There is a small cove, surrounded by rocks twenty feet high, into which the whole current of the river rushes and is deflected back against the waters following it. Because of a nearby island, the water must pass through a narrow channel. This is not done without a violent clash of all these waters, and a great din ensues, inspiring terror in the Indians, who fear everything. But this did not prevent us from passing through and arriving at Waboukigou. This river flows from the lands of the east, where dwell the people called the Chaouanons [Shawnees] in great numbers — in one district there are as many as twenty-three villages, and fifteen in another nearby. They are not at all warlike, and yet the Iroquois travel great distances to wage war against them for no reason. Because these poor people cannot defend themselves, they allow themselves to be captured and taken like flocks of sheep. Innocent though they are, they nevertheless experience the barbarity of the Iroquois, who cruelly burn them.

A short distance above this river [the Ohio] are cliffs where our Frenchmen noticed an iron deposit that they consider very rich. There are several veins of ore, one of them a foot thick, and one sees large lumps of it, studded with small stones. A clayey soil is found there of various colors: purple, violet, and red. When washed, this earth turns the water the color of blood. There is also a very heavy red sand. I placed some on a paddle, and it was stained so deeply that the color remained after fifteen days of paddling.

Soon we began to see canes, or large reeds, growing along the riverbank. They are of a very pleasing green color, and every joint in the stem sprouts a crown of long, narrow, pointed leaves. The reeds grow so high and so thick along the shore that the wild cattle have some difficulty forcing their way through.

Up to this point, we had not been bothered greatly by mosquitoes, but here we found ourselves entering into their chosen domain. The Indians of this region take measures to protect themselves from the mosquitoes. They erect scaffolding with a floor made only of poles, with space for the air to pass through. They build a fire underneath so that the smoke comes up and drives away those tiny creatures, for they cannot endure it. The Indians sleep upon the poles under a canopy of bark that protects them from the rain. These platforms also serve as protection against the intense and unbearable heat of this country, for the roof provides shade to the floor below, and thus they are protected against the sun's rays, but they can enjoy the cooling breeze that wafts through the porous structure. With the same object, we were compelled to erect a sort of cabin on the water, with our sails as a protection against the mosquitoes and the sun.

Drifting with the current, we perceived some Indians armed with guns and waiting for us on the shore.[5] I at once presented my plumed calumet, while our Frenchmen prepared to defend themselves. They held their fire, waiting to see whether the Indians would fire first. I spoke to the latter in Huron, but they answered me by a word that seemed to me a declaration of war. However, they were as frightened as we were, and what we had taken for a signal for battle was actually an invitation to approach nearer so that they might give us food. We therefore landed, and upon our entering their cabins, they offered us wild cattle meat and bear's grease with white plums, which are very good. They have guns, hatchets, hoes, knives, beads, and flasks of double glass, in which they put their powder. They wear their hair long and tattoo their bodies after the Iroquois fashion. The women wear headdresses and garments like those of the Huron women. They assured us that we were no more than ten days' journey from the sea, that they bought cloth and all other goods from the Europeans who lived to the east, that these Europeans had rosaries and pictures, that they played upon instruments, that some of them looked like me, and that they had been well received by these Europeans. Nevertheless, I saw none who seemed to have received any instruction in the faith, and so I gave them as much as I could, together with some medals.

[5] These natives, labeled "Mons8pelea" (the Jesuits used *8* for a sound comparable to the English *w* sound, which doesn't exist in French) on Marquette's map, have never been identified. He encountered them somewhere near the future site of Memphis, Tennessee. Their report of visiting "Europeans" suggests that they were in contact with the Spanish settlements and missions of Florida.

This news [that we were close to the sea] raised our spirits, and we took up our paddles with renewed energy. And so we advanced, no longer passing through prairies but past tall trees which lined the river. The cottonwood, elm, and basswood grow wondrously high and thick there. Yet we could hear great numbers of wild cattle bellowing, which led us to conclude that the prairies were nearby. We also saw quail at the water's edge. We killed a little parrot, which had a head that was half red, while the other half of the head and the neck were yellow; the body was entirely green.

We descended, almost always in a southerly direction, until we reached thirty-three degrees latitude, where we perceived a village at the water's edge called Mitchigamea.[6] We had recourse to our patroness and guide, the Blessed Virgin Immaculate, whose assistance we certainly needed, for in the distance we could hear the Indians shouting continually to prepare themselves for combat. Armed with bows, arrows, hatchets, clubs, and shields, they made ready to attack us on both land and water. Some of them embarked in great wooden canoes, one party going upriver, the other downriver, in order to intercept us and surround us on all sides. Those who were on land went back and forth, as if to open the attack. In fact, some young men plunged into the water to come and seize my canoe, but the current forced them to return to land. One of them hurled his club, which passed over our heads without striking us. In vain I showed the calumet and made them signs that we were not coming to make war. The alarm continued, and they were already preparing to pierce us with arrows from all sides when God suddenly touched the hearts of the old men who were standing at the water's edge. No doubt this event came about through the sight of our calumet; they had not recognized it from a distance, but as I continued to display it, it finally had an effect, and they checked the ardor of their young men. Two of these elders even entered the canoe, after first throwing down their bows and quivers at our feet in order to reassure us, and got us to move toward the shore. There we landed, though not without fear. At first, we had to speak by signs, because none of them understood the six languages which I spoke. At last, we found an old man who could speak a little Illinois.

We informed them, by our presents, that we were going to the sea. They understood us very well, but I know not whether they comprehended what I told them about God and about matters pertaining to their salvation. This is a seed cast onto the ground which will bear fruit in its

---

[6] The Mitchigamea people have been identified as a branch of the Illinois confederacy.

time. We obtained no other answer than that we would learn all that we desired at another large village, called Akamsea,[7] which was only eight to ten leagues farther down. They offered us *sagamité* and fish, and we passed the night among them in some anxiety.

IX. Reception Given to the French in the Last Village Which They Saw. The Manners and Customs of Those Indians. Reasons for Not Going Farther.

We embarked early the following day with our interpreter. A canoe containing ten Indians went a short distance ahead of us. When we arrived within half a league of Akamsea, we saw two canoes coming to meet us. The man in command was standing upright, holding in his hand the calumet, with which he made various signs, according to the custom of the country. He joined us, singing very agreeably, and gave us tobacco to smoke. After that, he offered us *sagamité* and bread made of Indian corn, of which we ate a little. After signaling us to follow him slowly, he went on ahead of us. A place had been prepared for us under the platform of the chief of the warriors. It was clean and carpeted with fine rush mats. Upon these we were told to sit, with the elders around us. Beyond them were the warriors and, finally, all the common people in a crowd. There we luckily found a young man who understood Illinois much better than did the interpreter whom we had brought from Mitchigamea. Through him, I was at last able to address the whole assembly, using the usual presents. They were amazed at what I told them about God and the mysteries of our holy faith, and they manifested a great desire to keep me among them, so that I might instruct them.

Afterward, we asked them what they knew about the sea. They replied that we were only ten days' journey from it, though we could cover the distance in five days. They were not acquainted with the nations who dwelt there because their enemies prevented them from trading with those Europeans. The hatchets, knives, and beads that we saw were sold to them partly by nations from the east and partly by an Illinois village situated four days' journey to the west. They also told us that the Indians with guns whom we had met were their enemies, and these barred their way to the sea, preventing them from becoming acquainted with the Europeans and from carrying on any trade with them. They added that we would expose ourselves to great dangers in going farther, on account of the constant raids of their enemies along the river. Since these people

[7]A village of the Arkansa, or Quapaw, people.

had guns and were very warlike, we could not without manifest danger proceed down the river, which they constantly occupy.

During this conversation, food was continually brought to us in large wooden platters: *sagamité,* whole corn, and a piece of dog's flesh. The entire day was spent in feasting. These people are very obliging and liberal with what they have, but they are miserably short of food, for they dare not go and hunt wild cattle, on account of their enemies. It is true that they have an abundance of Indian corn, which they sow at all seasons. We saw some ripe corn, some that had just sprouted, and still other corn that was milky; this indicates that they sow three times a year. They cook it in great earthen jars, which are very well made. They also have pottery dishes that they use for various purposes. The men go naked and wear their hair short; their noses are pierced and hung with beads, likewise their ears. The women are clad in wretched skins. They tie their hair in two tresses that they throw behind their ears, and they have no ornaments with which to adorn themselves. Their feasts are given without any ceremony. Guests are presented with large dishes, from which everyone eats as much as they wish, then they offer one another the bits that remain. Their language is exceedingly difficult, and I could succeed in pronouncing only a few words in spite of all my efforts. Their cabins are long and wide and made of bark. They sleep at the two ends that are raised two feet above the ground. They store their corn in large baskets made of reeds or in gourds as large as kegs. They have no idea what a beaver is. Their wealth consists in the skins of wild cattle. They never see snow in their country, and winter is signaled only by the rains, which fall more frequently then than in summer. We ate no fruit other than watermelons. If they knew how to till their soil, they would have fruits of all kinds.

In the evening, the elders held a secret council, since some of them planned to smash our heads and rob us, but the chief put a stop to all these plots. After sending for us, he danced the calumet before us, in the manner I have already described, and to relieve us of all fear, he made me a present of it.

Monsieur Jolliet and I held our own council to deliberate upon what we should do — whether we should push on or remain content with the discovery which we had made. After careful consideration, we decided that we were not far from the Gulf of Mexico, the basin of which is at the latitude of 31 degrees, 60 minutes, while we were at 33 degrees, 40 minutes. We judged that we could not be more than two or three days' journey from it and that, beyond a doubt, the Mississippi River discharges in Florida or the Gulf of Mexico, and not to the east in Virginia, where the seacoast is at 34 degrees latitude, which we had passed without reaching the sea, nor does it discharge to the west in California, because in that case our route would have been to the west or the west-southwest, whereas we had always continued southward. We further considered that we risked losing the results of this voyage, of which we could give no information if we proceeded to fling ourselves into the hands of the Spaniards, who, without a doubt, would at the least have detained us as captives. Moreover, we saw very plainly that we were not in a condition to resist Indians allied to the Europeans, who were numerous and expert in firing guns, and who continually infested the lower part of the river. Finally, we had obtained all the information that could be desired in regard to this discovery. All these reasons induced us to decide upon returning; this we announced to the Indians, and after a day's rest, we made our preparations for the voyage.

Chronology of Events
Related to the *Jesuit Relations*
(1534–1773)

1534   Society of Jesus (Jesuits) is founded.

1604   French settlement in Acadia is established.

1608   Quebec is founded as the capital of a new French colony, Canada (New France).

1611–13   First Jesuit mission is established in Acadia.

1625–29   Jesuit mission begins in Canada.

1627–63   Canada is owned and administered by the Company of New France.

1629–32   English occupy Canada. Jesuits expelled.

1632   Jesuits, led by Paul Le Jeune, return to Quebec.

1634   After earlier attempts, the Jesuits establish a regular mission among the Hurons.

1634–39   Series of epidemics of European origin devastate the Indians of New France.

1639   Fortified post of Ste. Marie is established as the headquarters of the Jesuit mission among the Hurons.

ca. 1640   Long-standing hostilities intensify, as the Iroquois step up attacks on the Hurons, Montagnais, Algonquins, and French.

1645   Negotiations at Three Rivers establish a short-lived truce.

1649   Iroquois destroy Huron settlements.

1663   Louis XIV imposes direct royal rule on New France.

1667   After the French invasion of their territory, the Iroquois make peace and allow the Jesuits to enter their villages.

1673   *Jesuit Relations* are discontinued.
        Jacques Marquette and Louis Jolliet explore the Mississippi River.

1676 Mohawk migration to the Jesuit mission of Sault St. Louis, near Montreal, reaches its peak.

1760 Canada is surrendered to the British.
Jesuits are forbidden to recruit new members.

1773 Society of Jesus is dissolved by the pope. (It was reconstituted in the early nineteenth century.)

Questions for Consideration

1. How did the Montagnais hunters observed by Paul Le Jeune manage to survive in the inhospitable environment of Quebec?
2. Imagine that you are Mestigoit. What do you think of Paul Le Jeune as a traveling companion and as an observer of Montagnais ways?
3. In what important ways did Huron society as described by Jean de Brébeuf differ from that of the Montagnais?
4. What parts of Huron culture does Brébeuf praise? What parts does he criticize? How do you explain his divergent reactions?
5. What do the *Jesuit Relations* reveal about the different approaches of Hurons and Europeans to issues concerning health, illness, and curing?
6. How did different Indian nations, with their diverse languages and in the absence of writing, manage to communicate, negotiate, and record their agreements?
7. What was the meaning and purpose of war in Iroquoian societies of the seventeenth century?
8. What are the main differences in the way the French and the natives viewed the environment and the natural world?
9. Why did so many Mohawks, once enemies of the French, convert to Christianity after 1667?
10. What did conversion mean to the Indians of this period? Did they become culturally European upon accepting Catholic baptism?
11. What motivated Jesuits such as Isaac Jogues to take on the risks and hardships of the missionary's life?
12. Was Jacques Marquette a perceptive observer of the Mississippi Valley?
13. Why were the Jesuits so interested in Indian beliefs and rituals that resembled those of Christianity?

Selected Bibliography

Anderson, Karen. *Chain Her by One Foot: The Subjugation of Women in Seventeenth-Century New France.* London: Routledge, 1991.

Axtell, James. *The Invasion Within: The Contest of Cultures in Colonial North America.* New York: Oxford University Press, 1985.

———. *After Columbus: Essays in the Ethnohistory of Colonial North America.* New York: Oxford University Press, 1988.

Bailey, Alfred G. *The Conflict of European and Eastern Algonkian Cultures, 1504–1700.* St. John: New Brunswick Museum, 1937.

Blanchard, David. ". . . To the Other Side of the Sky: Catholicism at Kahnawake, 1667–1700," *Anthropologica* 24 (1982): 77–102.

Bossy, John. *Christianity in the West, 1400–1700.* Oxford: Oxford University Press, 1985.

Campeau, Lucien, ed. *Monumenta Novae Franciae.* 7 vols. Quebec: Presses de l'Université Laval, 1967–87, and Montreal: Editions Bellarmin, 1989.

Delâge, Denys. *Bitter Feast: Amerindians and Europeans in Northeast North America, 1600–64.* Vancouver: University of British Columbia Press, 1993.

Delumeau, Jean. *Catholicism between Luther and Voltaire: A New View of the Catholic Reform.* London: Burns & Oates, 1977.

Dickason, Olive P. *The Myth of the Savage and the Beginnings of French Colonialism in the Americas.* Edmonton: University of Alberta Press, 1984.

Donnelly, Joseph P. *Jacques Marquette, S.J., 1637–1675.* Chicago: Loyola University Press, 1968.

Goddard, Peter. "The Devil in New France: Jesuit Demonology, 1611–50," *Canadian Historical Review* 78 (March 1997): 40–62.

Grant, John Webster. *Moon of Wintertime: Missionaries and the Indians of Canada in Encounter since 1534.* Toronto: University of Toronto Press, 1984.

Greer, Allan. "Colonial Saints: Gender, Race, and Hagiography in New France," *William and Mary Quarterly* (forthcoming, 2000).

Hall, Robert L. *An Archaeology of the Soul: North American Indian Belief and Ritual.* Urbana and Chicago: University of Illinois Press, 1997.

Harris, Cole, ed. *Historical Atlas of Canada.* Vol. 1: *From the Beginning to 1800.* Toronto: University of Toronto Press, 1987.

Jaenen, Cornelius J. *Friend and Foe: Aspects of French-Amerindian Cultural Contact in the Sixteenth and Seventeenth Centuries.* Toronto: McClelland & Stewart, 1976.

Jennings, Francis. *The Ambiguous Iroquois Empire: The Covenant Chain Confederation of Indian Tribes with English Colonies from Its Beginnings to the Lancaster Treaty of 1744.* New York: Norton, 1984.

Kennedy, J. H. *Jesuit and Savage in New France.* New Haven, Conn.: Yale University Press, 1950.

Koppedrayer, K. I. "The Making of the First Iroquois Virgin: Early Jesuit Biographies of the Blessed Kateri Tekakwitha." *Ethnohistory* 40, no. 2 (Spring 1993): 277–306.

Leahey, Margaret J. "'Comment peut un muet prescher l'évangile?' Jesuit Missionaries and the Native Languages of New France," *French Historical Studies* 19 (Spring 1995): 105–31.

Le Clercq, Chrestien. *First Establishment of the Faith in New France.* 2 vols. Translated by John Gilmary Shea. New York: John G. Shea, 1881.

Pagden, Anthony. *The Fall of Natural Man.* Cambridge: Cambridge University Press, 1982.

Parkman, Francis. *The Jesuits in North America in the Seventeenth Century.* Boston: Little, Brown, 1867.

Richter, Daniel K. "Iroquois versus Iroquois: Jesuit Mission and Christianity in Village Politics, 1642–1686," *Ethnohistory* 32 (1985): 1–16.

———. *The Ordeal of the Longhouse: The Peoples of the Iroquois League in the Era of European Colonization.* Chapel Hill: University of North Carolina Press, 1992.

Ronda, James P. "'We Are Well as We Are': An Indian Critique of Seventeenth-Century Christian Mission," *William and Mary Quarterly,* 3rd ser., 34 (1977): 66–82.

———. "The Sillery Experiment: A Jesuit-Indian Village in New France, 1637–1663," *American Indian Culture and Research Journal* 3 (1979): 1–18.

Salisbury, Neal. "Religious Encounters in a Colonial Context: New England and New France in the Seventeenth Century," *American Indian Quarterly* 16 (1992): 501–9.

Sayre, Gordon M. *Les Sauvages Américaines: Representations of Native Americans in French and English Colonial Literature.* Chapel Hill: University of North Carolina Press, 1997.

Sioui, Georges. *Les Wendats: une civilisation méconnue.* Quebec: Presses de l'Université Laval, 1994.

Snow, Dean R. *The Iroquois.* Oxford: Blackwell, 1994.

Steckley, John. "The Warrior and the Lineage: Jesuit Use of Iroquoian Images to Communicate Christianity," *Ethnohistory* 39 (Fall 1992): 478–509.

Thwaites, Reuben G., ed. *The Jesuit Relations and Allied Documents.* 73 vol. Cleveland: Burrows Brothers, 1896–1900.

Tooker, Elisabeth, ed. *Native North American Spirituality of the Eastern Woodlands: Sacred Myths, Dreams, Visions, Speeches, Healing Formulas, Rituals and Ceremonials.* New York: Paulist Press, 1979.

Trigger, Bruce G. *The Children of Aataentsic: A History of the Huron People to 1660.* Kingston and Montreal: McGill-Queen's University Press, 1976.

———. *Natives and Newcomers: Canada's 'Heroic Age' Reconsidered.* Kingston and Montreal: McGill-Queen's University Press, 1985.

———. *Handbook of North American Indians,* Vol. 15: *Northeast.* Washington, D.C.: Smithsonian Institute, 1978.

Trigger, Bruce G., and Wilcomb E. Washburn, eds. *Cambridge History of the Native Peoples of the Americas.* Vol. 1: *North America.* Cambridge: Cambridge University Press, 1996.

Trudel, Marcel. *Introduction to New France.* Toronto: Holt, Rinehart & Winston, 1968.

Wright, A. D. *The Counter-Reformation: Catholic Europe and the Non-Christian World.* New York: St. Martin's Press, 1982.

Index